Catching the Impossible

Martin Bowler Hugh Miles

First Published in November 2008

© Text - Martin Bowler and Hugh Miles
© Pictures - Martin Bowler, Hugh Miles
and contributors
© Artwork - Rodger McPhail
© Design - Mpress (Media) Ltd

ISBN Number: 978-0-9555917-9-2

Other titles by author Hugh Miles:

The Track of the Wild Otter - 1984
Kingdom of the Ice Bear with Mike Salisbury - 1985
The Great Wood of Caledon with Brian Jackman - 1991
A Passion for Angling with Chris Yates and Bob James - 1993

designed and published by m press (Media) LTD.
Unit Four, Ashton Gate, Harold Hill, Romford, RM3 8UF

This book is dedicated to our wives, Jo and Sue,
whose love and support has made it possible
to complete this 'impossible' journey through angling.

Acknowledgements

It is a tradition for authors to thank every man and his dog but in the case of 'Catching the Impossible' it would be absolutely true to say that without so much generous help and kindness from so many, this project would not have even been able to make a first cast.

There's not enough space to mention them in person but so many landowners and fisheries allowed us the privilege of access to their waters that we were able to paint a portrait showing the great beauty and variety of the freshwater world, while catching some of Britain's biggest fish along the way, so we can't thank you all enough.

Numerous bailiffs made huge efforts to help us succeed, becoming good friends in the process and as for our fishing pals, well they not only provided us with great company and lots of laughs but some wonderful fish as well. We've listed those who performed for the cameras separately and to you all, our grateful thanks.

One of them, 'Uncle' John Wilson was tireless in his help and encouragement and kindly provided a foreword for the book. Also we think you'll agree that Cliff at MPress and above all our designer Paul Moulder have created a lovely book. Friend and computer whizz Matt Donovan kindly designed the front cover and the websites too, so thank you Matt.

Steve Partner had the tough task of editing our text but if some of the writing is a tad 'sketchy', that is purely our fault. As for the mountain of words that needed typing and collating, then changing and correcting ....and so on....we've got Jo Motto and Margaret Clarke to thank for scaling the heights and surviving the avalanche of paper to the end. So a big thank you to you all for your patience and perseverance.

We have provided a separate credits list for our friends who took the wildlife photographs and what a wonderful contribution you've made. So to Laurie Campbell, Neil McIntyre, Mike Read, Mike Richards, Mick Rouse and Richard Bowler, our grateful thanks. And to Rodger McPhail, who so generously provided the artistic embellishments that make this book a bit special, thank you for the lovely illustrations.

As for the films which lie at the heart of this book, we really couldn't have finished them properly without our computer guru Chris Wild and the team of ace technicians in Bristol, so thank you to you all for your skill and friendship.

To Bernard, who stood by us for so many years and made the long journey enjoyable, a big thank you. Finally, to our friends and most of all our families, thank you for standing by us through thick and thin, the long days and sleepless nights, and our apologies for our absence all these years.

We won't do it again .... until the next time.

The Team

Bernard Cribbins

A true 'entertainer', famous actor and comedian who needs little introduction. Played leading roles in many films including The Railway Children, Two Way Stretch and the 'Carry On' series with co-stars like Peter Sellers, David Niven and Alfred Hitchcock. Also played theatre, music hall and T.V. including The Wombles, Jackanory and more recently, Coronation Street and Dr. Who. He first met Hugh when writing and narrating the RSPB/BBC award winning film 'Round Robin'. A keen angler since childhood, he fishes every week, often for charity and he narrated the classic BBC2 series 'A Passion for Angling'.

Martin Bowler

One of Britain's leading anglers with a list of monster fish that few can match. A professional angler and photo-journalist, with a weekly feature in the biggest selling angling magazine 'The Angling Times'. Also sponsored by leading tackle manufacturers. Has fished since childhood and is a true all-rounder, with knowledge of all species and his exceptional skill has led to the capture of two British record fish.

Hugh Miles

Freelance wildlife film-maker for all the major broadcasters. Has filmed and produced nearly sixty films and many have won multiple awards including three British Academy Awards, several Emmy's and ten 'green oscars' at Wildscreen, including the Lifetime Achievement Award. Also filmed and produced BBC2's much acclaimed 'A Passion for Angling', said to be the best fishing series ever made. Even today, fifteen years after first transmission, it is still showing in the UK and around the world.

Rodger McPhail

Famous as a wildlife artist, Rodger has also illustrated over twenty books, including 'A Passion for Angling', and has worked on one with Hugh about Pumas in the Andes. He also paints portraits, cartoons, and stage sets. One of the many perks of Rodger's job is that it enables him to indulge in some of the finest fishing both in Britain and abroad. As he also gets paid for doing this, he considers himself a very lucky man.

Contents

Foreword 01

Introduction 02

Chapter 01: The Journey Begins 06

Chapter 02: Rainbow's End 18

Chapter 03: Friends Reunited 28

Chapter 04: Missing Monsters 44

Chapter 05: Heads You Win - Tails You Loose 60

Chapter 06: Make or Break 70

Chapter 07: Spring Struggles 86

Chapter 08: Tinca, Tinca 100

Chapter 09: Searching For Gold 114

Chapter 10: Bernard's Carp 124

Chapter 11: Going Against the Flow 140

Chapter 12: Myth Becomes Reality 152

Chapter 13: Impossible Becomes Incredible 164

Chapter 14: A River Record 180

Chapter 15: Echoes of Walker 200

Chapter 16: Catfish Capers 216

Chapter 17: Capturing the Imagination 224

Chapter 18: Nights From Hell 240

Chapter 19: Autumn Colours 248

Chapter 20: Floods and Frost 266

Chapter 21: Tying Loose Ends 280

Chapter 22: North of the Border 292

Chapter 23: Long Journeys 310

Chapter 24: Keeping Bernard Busy 326

Chapter 25: Light in the Tunnel 336

Chapter 26: Last Casts 348

Foreword

I felt immensely proud when asked by its authors, my good friends Hugh and Martin to pen this foreword of what is not only a wonderfully illustrated and compiled work of true dedication, but one inextricably tied to a unique television series of the same name. In my opinion, the finest freshwater angling series ever filmed. I am even prompted to say to you the reader that if you are not truly captivated by such a lavish selection of colour plates and not totally mesmerised and enthralled from sharing in the lows and joys of two angling greats by what you are about to read, who together spent a staggering 1000 plus days in research, filming and in post production of the programmes and this book during a love affair with natural history lasting over four years, (now that is dedication) you'd better take up table tennis or skate boarding.

Frankly I don't really know whether I personally could have stayed the course, having always been involved with producing angling programmes where mere months have elapsed between filming on the first shoot, to actually appreciating my work and the entire series on the small screen. And I know by the lengthy, late night phone calls from Martin seeking guidance when he felt down, that there were times when light at the end of the tunnel seemed to this lone angler, who's success on camera and thus the series depended on him subsequently landing an array of whoppers come rain or shine, seemed a million miles away. But Hugh, being the consummate professional wildlife photographer with a lifetime's portfolio of experiences and patience to call upon, managed to pull him through, resulting in a series of eight one hour

programmes, each as evocative as they are inspiring, with this lovely book documenting exactly how they achieved such enviable results, plus the trials, tribulations, and of course the drama.

I particularly like the use of this book's mini photos in film strip, which incidentally have been pulled directly from the live video footage of the programmes (I have not seen this in any angling volume previously) and the wealth of artistic paintings from artist Rodger McPhail, help thread the strand of natural history from the first, through to the very last page. I also love the way either a mini perch (Martin) or a roach (Hugh) depict the change in story line from one author to the other. A really nice touch this.

Moreover, I think the continual use of stunning underwater footage seen throughout the programmes (I have never seen such close range and detailed footage before) much of it showing the actual fish that were caught, is what helps separate these iconic angling programmes from all others before them. Even Hugh's first monumental series 'A Passion for Angling'.

So please, find a comfortable chair, fill your glass with an easy drinking red wine, (or whatever your tipple) and be enthused, entertained and liberated by the most productive and successful freshwater angler in the British Isles and one of natures most dedicated cameramen and film makers. You'll have trouble putting it down.

John Wilson
Great Witchingham.

Introduction

 EMBARKING on a major angling series for television could be likened to rowing across the Atlantic. You know there will be lots of ups and downs, you know you will be fighting against the weather, you know it will be hard work and, above all, you know it will take an awful long time. There will, of course, be plenty of exciting and enjoyable moments on the way too and a huge sense of fulfilment and relief if – and when - you reach your destination. And all of this means that careful consideration should be given to such an idea before setting out.

Angling enthusiasts will know that I'd already set out on a similar journey nearly twenty years ago and after an inspiring and gruelling four-and-a-half years, finally made it to the finish line. That series was called 'A Passion for Angling', – six one hour films made for BBC 2 with Chris Yates and Bob James. We set out to capture the magic of angling in its truest sense and the investment in time and money was our way of attempting to put something back into a hobby that had given us so much enjoyment during our lives. It took us

Being a wildlife film-maker, I'm constantly searching for new stories and new challenges, and it struck me that not much had ever been shown on television of freshwater fish and their natural behaviour in a truly wild, underwater environment. There has always been a large audience for British wildlife, so what better than to show them something they'd never seen? As a keen angler, I knew that living undiscovered below the surface of some of Britain's loveliest rivers and lakes lurked monster fish so large and beautiful that they

The "Passion" crew.

twelve years to recover the financial investment and the small profits we now receive are far outweighed in value by the sense of fulfilment we are still enjoying as a result of its critical acclaim. In fact, despite a lifetime making wildlife films around the world, I've never made a programme that has touched the audience so deeply or for so long as 'A Passion for Angling.'

The series was first shown in 1993 and it strikes me as remarkable that despite all the changes in television since then it is still being transmitted in the UK and around the world. I guess it just serves to prove what an enduring appeal angling has for so many people. The trouble is, the continuing enthusiasm for 'A Passion for Angling' finally got to me and I started to think about embarking on the same crazy journey once again. But how could we make a new series different - and perhaps even better?

would astonish every wildlife enthusiast in the land. All we had to do was find them, film them, then maybe catch them. But who could catch – for the camera I might add - the biggest freshwater fish in Britain?

Fortunately, angling is blessed by an abundance of skilful and suitably eccentric characters who, if they'd agree to contribute their time, would surely prove entertaining to

I have loved fishing all my life and it's given me so much enjoyment I was keen that, like 'A Passion for Angling,' the new project would try to repay this debt of gratitude by benefiting angling as a whole. One way of achieving this was to ensure it appealed to a wide audience, but this meant getting a showing on television. We both knew if that was going to happen we had to come up with a storyline that might appeal to a TV executive.

Happy days.

an audience jaundiced by 'Big Brother' and the like. What I needed was a 'leading man,' someone who could catch the fish I required to make the film. I didn't need to look any further than a young friend of mine, Martin Bowler. I'd first met him several years before while stalking big tench at the Cotswold Water Park. I'd since filmed him with Chris Yates as they tried to catch barbel and perch – a sort of screen test, if you like - and his enthusiasm and professionalism were infectious. The fact he happened to be arguably the UK's finest young angler with not just one, but two record fish to his name was also a factor. Even more importantly, he came with an excellent reputation in the fishing community, so I was convinced he would bring a deal of goodwill to the project – something that was essential if we were to succeed. Fortunately, a short phone call and a long meeting later, he agreed to join me in what would no doubt prove to be a long and arduous four year struggle. The plan was to make six one hour films of the highest quality. All we had to do was decide on the content of the stories and what we hoped to achieve.

'A Passion for Angling' captured audiences of up to 6.3 million but television has changed a lot in the last fourteen years, with reality shows now dominating the schedules. So could we find an attractive formula?

If you stand and watch walkers crossing a bridge over water you can almost guarantee that they will stop and lean over the parapet to gaze down and see if they can spot any fish. The habit is one we get into as kids when armed with net and jam-jar and, in my experience, the

The 'Impossible' pair.

fascination with water lasts a lifetime. It's often suppressed by adult life and 'responsibilities' but the interest still lingers and I felt sure that by showing the underwater world we could reawaken those childhood memories. Mind you, knowing how shy fish can be, filming their behaviour in the wild would no doubt be difficult. However, like Martin, I love a good challenge, so we weren't going to let a few obstacles stand in our way. And if we could also capture some lovely images of wildlife above the surface and the beauty of the British countryside in all its glorious profusion, then surely we were on to a winner.

We would need a story-teller of course, and were delighted when Bernard Cribbins agreed to breathe magic over the pictures, while adding his own humour to proceedings too. It was Bernard's distinctive narration that was one of the most popular aspects of 'Passion' but the difference this time was that Bernard would get to fish. He's been a mad keen angler since childhood so when he had the time, he'd come along, have a cast and maybe even show Martin how it should be done. Whatever the outcome, having Bernard with us would be fun.

This story was very much a shared experience, so Martin and I have shared the story-telling too. And to help you understand which of us is the author of each section, we have identifying symbols.

Martin's is his favourite fish, a perch and mine is the fish that most inspired me in childhood, a roach.

As for the story itself, I devised a challenge for Martin and his friends. There is in the angling world a widely accepted 'specimen' weight for each species to which all of us keen anglers aspire. These creatures are often described as 'fish of a lifetime,' like a 2lb roach or a 20lb pike, and it struck me as a potentially entertaining idea if our anglers had Impossible target weights for each species. This challenge would surely keep Martin and his friends amused, and if they found them too easy, then I'd just raise the target - just to keep them interested of course! We felt sure that anglers would find this combination of seriously big fish and underwater action inspiring, and hoped that non-anglers would be amazed at the size of the monsters they caught. We also hoped the title we chose – 'Catching the Impossible' - would prove suitably prophetic.

The Journey Begins

 IT'S often said that there's more to fishing than catching fish, and though true, it also serves as one of the many excuses used when an angler returns home empty-handed. And having set ourselves impossible targets to achieve, we would no doubt need every excuse in the book! But despite the inevitable failures, it was important we didn't lose sight of the true spirit of angling. We just had to show how enjoyable a day by a river or lake can be - with or without fish.

Our plan therefore was to film our quarry underwater, along with the other wildlife and the varied British countryside with the same care and devotion as we applied to catching our *'Impossibles'*. So decisions on where and when to film each sequence weren't simply based on what we'd catch. Life is never that straightforward, however much we'd like it to be. Martin hoped we'd be able to hit all our targets within two years - but I think we both knew that given the size of the challenge and the erratic British weather it might be nearer four. We'd almost certainly need three summers and three winters and our first summer was already passing us by. We hadn't even decided what all our *'Impossible'* targets would be, though one thing was certain, we'd require a big summer barbel. We had reached July already, so we needed to get our barbel hats on pronto.

Pound for pound, barbel are probably our most powerful freshwater fish. They are beautiful too - golden bars of muscle that love fast-flowing rivers. It sometimes seems bizarre that fishermen insist on weighing such magnificent wild creatures but because all passionate anglers invariably want to catch a bigger one, we have to put numbers on them to quantify our 'achievements.'

Perhaps even more odd to the non-angling public is our penchant for giving fish names – characterising those individuals that are recognisable due to fin shapes and marks on their scales. These fish tend to be big, and subsequently old too. A barbel might live for more than thirty years and most will have stories to tell about surviving attacks from pike, herons, otters and cormorants - and maybe they even dine out on these tales about how they've fallen to a variety of famous anglers! Getting caught several times is a fact of life for most fish and though sceptics may believe that angling is cruel, the fact is that fish seem largely oblivious to the experience. I once caught the same large trout four times in the space of an hour and I warned it that if it took my fly once more I'd fry it in a pan! More sensible fish treat anglers like any other natural danger and try to avoid our cunning ploys.

Contrary to what you might expect, fish grow bigger and older despite being caught. Indeed, it is usually due to all the food provided by angler's bait that they thrive. What's more, anglers play a huge role in protecting them from pollution - and self interest will ensure that no fisherman will knowingly harm a creature he enjoys catching. So giving individual barbel names simply confirms an affection and respect for what is widely regarded as one of Europe's most beautiful fish.

Due to their popularity, it is no surprise that barbel are honoured by having specialist clubs dedicated to their survival and capture. Perhaps this is due in part to the lovely places they live - fast flowing rivers with well-oxygenated water curling through lovely landscapes. And barbel are perfectly designed for their river habitat, slim, streamlined and muscular. They also have four barbels, two at the tip of their nose and two at the sides of their mouth which are sensitive to both taste and smell, vital in helping them to find food hidden in the gravel. Tough lips are well supplied with sensory buds and by digging into

Asking for another favour.

the river's bed they can crunch crustaceans and larvae off the stones. A big, old barbel will have travelled widely and know its section of river like the proverbial back of its fins.

An old fish is not just a big fish but also a wise fish, so anyone who catches a barbel of 10lb has a specimen to be proud of. A twelve-pounder is exceptional and when I started fishing as a boy more than 50 years ago, the largest ever caught in Britain weighed 14lb 6 oz. This target has since been raised several times and Martin himself held the record for a while. Most of these history-making barbel have been caught on the upper reaches of the Great Ouse in Bedfordshire, so we felt it was important to celebrate this historic waterway with a sequence in our series.

So at dawn on the 22nd July, 2004, I walked down into the misty valley to join Martin by the river. He had arrived the day before to prepare himself mentally and physically for the first *'Impossible'* challenge - a barbel of more than 15lb. Despite our optimism, I was in no doubt that if Martin actually caught one of that size, it would be a considerable achievement.

 The 21st of July 2004 is when the journey commenced. I had no idea at the time where this voyage through the angling world would take me but I knew that I simply could not refuse the opportunity to portray my beloved sport through the lens of top wildlife cameraman Hugh Miles. So the epic began.

Once again I was asking a river which had already been generous enough to give me many huge perch and even a British record barbel, the Great Ouse, to come up trumps and produce the first of many *'Impossibles'* required – a barbel of over 15lb. Arriving at the famous Kickles Farm stretch I eagerly wandered down over the rolling meadows, avoiding the thistle beds which blocked a path. In the distance I could see the shimmering blue ribbon draped across fields that is home to the monsters of the barbel world.

For me the jaunts to the Bedfordshire countryside had diminished somewhat following a move to Wiltshire. With so much new fishing to explore locally I had ignored this old friend and I just hoped that she hadn't taken umbrage. Richard, my older brother, had remained local and a few days earlier had spotted a

shoal of large barbel on the stretch in question. This was a good sign, as the fish tend to wander between the water directly above Adam's Mill and Kickles itself. Richard had kindly left the fish unmolested in readiness, hopefully, to be caught on camera.

By following his instructions I was soon standing directly opposite a huge willow that gave cover and shade to a quarter of the river's width; it was a classic barbel haunt. Fortunately the swim was vacant and I could feel my heartbeat quickening with excitement. Quite why fish do this to me I'm really not sure, but the thought of doing battle with a giant is something I never tire of.

The famous Adam's Mill.

Donning the polaroid glasses I spent a while studying the riverbed. Unlike many rivers the Ouse is capable of running clear with little flow and this gives you an amazing opportunity to study the barbel's behaviour closely. While the majority of the bottom was coated in a fine silkweed one area stood out, or should I say shone out. Polished gravel tight to the far bank raft appeared to be the fish's underwater dining table, unsurprising really as the nearby shade would be to their liking on bright summer days. My plan was to feed the barbel and

hope they would be drawn from the shadows to give me an idea of my target. Once I had made the assessment and felt sure an 'Impossible' was present I would make a 'phone call to Hugh and arrange a dawn rendezvous the following morning.

Instead of introducing my feed via a catapult I decided to be far more accurate with the use of a 13 metre pole. By connecting a cup to the end I could ensure that my bait was positioned on the gravel under the tree with pin-point precision. A combination of 3mm and 6mm marine halibut pellets provided the attraction, topped off with some corn steep liquor. This heavy, pungent additive fell through the water, clouding up on its way, hopefully giving the barbel a little more confidence. With the area baited there was no more I could do but sit and wait for silhouettes to begin ghosting over the gravel, heralding the barbel's arrival. I knew it could take some time. It's in situations like this that non-anglers would perhaps start to question my sanity. To me, though, I am the luckiest man alive in having the British countryside as my 'office'.

So why did I choose to become an angler? I certainly wasn't the quietest or most patient of children, a characteristic most people who don't fish would feel necessary for such a pursuit. The honest answer? I don't know, I was just drawn to water by a magnetic pull and couldn't pass a ditch, stream or pond without dipping in a net. A minnow was a fine catch but a stickleback, well, that really was a Red Letter Day.

From there I managed to cobble some tackle together and accompany my elder brother on the long bike ride to the Grand Union Canal. To this day I can still remember that first bite. My 2BB onion

Holidays at Uncle John's.

float, which had sat motionless for what seemed like an eternity under the rod tip, sunk away as if caught in slow motion and this wide-eyed boy looked on in amazement and wonder. Frozen in anticipation, I finally lifted the rod and felt it jerk into life as the culprit fought back and moments later my palm became wet with a handful of shimmering scales. I had now entered a whole new magical world.

From 'tiny acorns' as they say, my spare time was soon filled with all things fishy. The bedroom walls became covered in centre page images from Angling Times and Christmas and birthdays were filled with gifts of a fishing nature. Now I thought I was the king of the canal as I stood there holding my first carbon rod, hands grasping the 'full duplon handle.'

Big fish though, always had a pull for me and what child wouldn't dream of rod-busting, line-breaking monsters. I simply wanted to know what lived in that world I couldn't enter. Trips to Uncle John's (the famous TV angler John Wilson) lakes cemented this fascination still further.

With teenage years came the obvious distraction of girls but still angling burned deep within. Of course I had quiet periods where I would not wet a line for a few months but a world outside of angling gives balance – and provides you with a yearning and desire to return to the bankside. It was a book,

Early memories.

Blinkered by carp.

Elstow - rudd heaven.

though, that really fired my imagination. Reading Rod Hutchinson's 'Carp Strikes Back' became a seminal moment and after I had followed his marvellous journey I was fired with an enthusiasm to not just catch any carp but catch BIG carp.

While working part-time in Tesco's I met a like-minded friend, Gary Archer, who was, in fairness, a far better angler than I. As well as having superior tackle, he possessed one thing that made his acquaintance absolutely invaluable – a car. Through his kindness I was able to join him on adventures to a little-known Bedfordshire gravel pit, Elstow, and little did we know what was in store for us both on that lake. As our ability grew, so did the size of the fish until this pit in Southern England was spoken about in hushed tones throughout the country.

On June 16th 1987 I set up in a swim called the Ramp and tempted a 17-pounder with a prawn cocktail flavoured boilie. Dressed head to toe in an army camouflage (which believe me was fashionable then!) I really felt I had arrived. Within a few months I had somehow managed to take the lake record at 27lb and for the next few years my angling life revolved around Elstow. But while the carp continued to grow, so did the number of anglers and the seriousness of it all. Was I there because I wanted to be or was I desperate to add another notch to my carp rod? The defining moment came when 'our' peaceful club lake became gobbled up by the world of modern carping. The words 'syndicate', 'rotas' and 'draws' reared their ugly heads and Elstow changed forever. A season of this was enough and I had little enthusiasm or stomach for such a battle. In hindsight the change was a blessing in disguise as it forced me to face new horizons....or quit.

Unmolested by the carp-crazed anglers the venue's rudd had now grown to Goliath proportions and as I've always been a sucker for bites, I had, over the years, often been tempted by these magnificent creatures. In fact, I have a picture with a net-full when they 'only' touched 2lb. Disillusioned with carp fishing and with the rudd having now reached 3lb, I just had to try to catch them again, and when I succeeded an 'all-rounder' was born and no longer would carp hold such a grip on my life. As luck would have it my local river, the Great Ouse, was also coming out of the doldrums and producing massive barbel and perch – a trend which continues to this day.

My dreams came true on January 21st 1999 when I caught a British record barbel of 16lb 13oz. Not only did it mean I would enter angling's history books, but it also gave me a shot at publicity. During my carp days it was in-vogue to be secretive but I did not see the point now. Partly because of my ego and partly because I wanted to share my success, I began my apprenticeship in the public eye with catch reports, slide shows and monthly columns. Along the way I was fortunate enough to be blessed with more than my fair share of Red Letter Days - including another British record with a crucian carp of 4lb 9oz 9drm.

At last I had reached my aim – I became a professional angler, working as a consultant within the industry. For me though the highlight was, and still is, my weekly Angling Times column. How could the boy who had pinned such stories on his bedroom wall have ended up writing them? But I would like to add that although I do get paid to promote angling, I make no assumptions about my ability and have met many better anglers who choose to shun publicity.

I do, however, enjoy trying to bring an adventure to life in words and pictures, hopefully sparking its reader into wetting a line in the process. I still remember a school teacher chucking my angling magazine in the bin, insisting that revising for 'A Levels' was more important and telling me not to waste my time. How wrong could he be? I have always insisted that a person touched by angling is luckier than most will ever know.

Almost everyone I meet seems to have been enthralled by the TV series 'A Passion for Angling.' Yes, Chris Yates and Bob James were the presenters

A golden giant.

and stars but the true genius was the cameraman / director, Hugh Miles. To have the whole angling world agreeing on the film's brilliance is a rare trick indeed. Hugh and I crossed paths a decade later after the first transmission of 'Passion' and somehow the end result was us embarking on this mission called 'Catching The Impossible.' I feel that angling may never have a better opportunity again to showcase itself via the skill of a wildlife cameraman respected the world over. All I hoped was that I could do the series justice.

My mind was quickly dragged back from these thoughts to the present time when, an hour after introducing the feed, a barbel swept in over the bait. It certainly wasn't a monster – but at about 11lb it was a good start and I knew that once I had encouraged one to feed the rest would soon follow. Sure enough, with another hour gone, five barbel were swimming in front of me, gorging on the pellet. Alongside the 11-pounder sat a specimen of similar proportions while the remaining three were far bigger. My guess was that two weighed 15lb and the other looked every inch a 16-pounder. The odds were looking remarkably good for our first '*Impossible*' target – it was just down to me to catch one.

The promised 'phone call to Hugh was made and then all I could do was wait for his arrival the following morning. Sleep didn't come easily that night - in fact I don't think I slept at all. Eventually the sun began to

rise again and the first day of filming could begin.

Prior to Hugh's arrival I re-baited the swim and prepared my tackle A 1lb 4oz test curve rod was combined with a small fixed spool reel to provide the basics. Clear monofilament line of 10lb would hopefully take the strain. The terminal tackle comprised a 0.5oz backlead placed 6ft up the line (this would ensure my mainline was pinned along the bottom and didn't spook the fish), then a 1.5oz flat lead was trapped between two float stops and with a 6 inch hooklength following this. Before I connected the hook a PVA mesh bag of 3mm and 6mm pellets was threaded on. By doing this not only would I have a tight gathering of pellets by my hookbait but the hooklength would be disguised. Finally I connected the hook, a very strong model in a size 14. Now you would expect most rigs to be finished off with a pellet hookbait attached via a hair, this being a standard approach for anglers. But it doesn't take long for the barbel to wise up.

Over the last few years I have become convinced the fish are looking for the hook so rather than being a plus, the hair-rig can actually be a hindrance. Therefore my hookbait - a 6mm marine halibut pellet - was banded onto the shank. As a finishing touch a 6mm artificial and buoyant pellet was then nicked on. This not only counterbalances the hook's weight but causes it to flip and be hidden under the two pellets. Now when any barbel approached they would surely be fooled into making a mistake.

With Hugh's arrival came my first experience of the filming journey ahead. Believe me, however much I was told to 'just enjoy it' I couldn't help but feel nervous. I knew if I didn't mess it up a big fish could be on the cards and recorded on film. Although he arrived at 6am it wasn't until 10am that I felt the swim was suitably primed. If at all possible, never be in too much of a rush to cast out when barbelling, as your patience will almost always be rewarded. So it was that during mid-morning I dropped the rig into the feeding area, but again for maximum accuracy and minimum disturbance, I did it via the pole. Even with very little noise these cunning creatures retreated back under the overhanging tree and there was little else we could do now but play the waiting game. For the first hour nothing reappeared and I was starting to become concerned. Surely I hadn't been sitting here this long for them to disappear?

Eventually the first set of whiskers nudged back out, followed by her companions to once again begin feeding. At this point my nerves were jangling – anyone who believes fishing is a sedate pastime really should experience this kind of nervous excitement! Perhaps it's something primeval associated with being a hunter again but the tension was truly exhilarating.

From my sitting position I was suddenly grabbing hold of my rod as a force on the other end tried to reach the sanctuary of the tree roots. Plunging the rod tip beneath the surface to protect the line I refused to yield. Thirty seconds of stalemate followed before I began to gain the upper hand. Immediately I knew I had lured one of the smaller fish, as no monster would allow me to win that easily and sure enough as my prize headed net-bound it became apparent that it wasn't the target.

At 11lb 6oz it wasn't a bad way to break our duck but I knew from the outset that 'good' just wouldn't be enough. Something special had to be produced.

After all the commotion it came as no surprise to find the remaining shoal had fled. Now began the long, arduous task of gaining their confidence once again. Four cupfuls of pellets were sprinkled over the area before I decided the best thing to do was leave the swim alone. I would not introduce my hookbait again until the fish were feeding so instead of twiddling our thumbs we made the hundred yard or so walk to the irrigation pond situated behind us. Over years of floods, carp had made their way into the venue from pits further up the river's course. If we were really lucky, a stalked carp could be filmed as an added bonus. Unfortunately the fish had other plans. They may have waved their tails in a feeding motion over my bait but I could not raise a single bite - it's not always the angler who has the last laugh!

What a start!

By 4pm I remained fish-less but a more pressing situation had arisen – the four remaining barbel were once again enjoying the delights of my pellets. Carefully I lowered my rig into the swim and sat rather nervously in anticipation of what might follow. The odds now were clearly stacked in our favour.

Within half-an-hour I got my next chance. Again the rod was plunged beneath the surface and the carbon rod creaked with the strain. I tried desperately to prevent line being taken, knowing that if the barbel reached the sanctuary of the tree roots our quest would be over. For what seemed an eternity neither angler nor fish budged until eventually I cranked the reel handle and somehow the size 14 hook hung in there. My heart was pounding and I was shaking with nerves as I desperately tried to get it into open water. With another turn of the handle I saw my copper-flanked opponent for the first time. This was no ordinary barbel....it was a leviathan.

Having reached open water I watched as she buried her head directly into the weed and sent up clouds of silt. I still needed to keep my concentration because to lose her now, when I could almost touch her, would have been too hard to bear. But the battle wasn't over yet. Again

and again she surged towards the tree branches until eventually, with a final crash of the tail she submitted to the inevitable and I gently pushed out the landing net and scooped her up. Physically and emotionally exhausted, I collapsed on the bank knowing that we had caught what we came for. When the scales read 15lb 7oz there were smiles all round and I cradled her gently in my arms for the camera. Wildlife in Great Britain struggles to match the beauty of our freshwater fish and I felt privileged to be admiring such a creature. Carefully I slipped her back into the water, ensuring she had fully recovered. With one final push, the enormous rudder-like tail propelled her back into her world.

An *'Impossible'* on our first day of filming – we certainly had every reason to be happy. What's more, the scale of our success didn't truly come to light until a few days later when on inspection of the photographs we recognised her as a barbel known by the local anglers as 'Liner.' She just happens to be the third biggest inhabitant of the record-breaking stretch of the Ouse and in future years a fish that could make history.

 What a start! To catch such a rare and beautiful creature on our first days filming suggested that angling's patron saint, Isaac Walton, was smiling down on our endeavours, and though he'd be reluctant to admit it the catch also served to prove what a skilful angler Martin is. What is more, his 'performance' in front of the camera proved he was a 'natural', so any worries I might have had on that count just vanished. The future for our long journey certainly looked bright.

On returning home to look at the film on the computer, the scale of the battle the barbel had fought with Martin became clear. From bite and hooking until the tug of war went in Martin's favour and the fish appeared from under the tree was a rod-wrenching 2 minutes 24 seconds. What's more, the clear water allowed the camera to see every violent twist and turn as the barbel tried to muscle its way back to the sanctuary of the tree roots. I've filmed polar bears and tigers hunting but this was just as tense.

My admiration for the power of barbel grew by the minute, for Martin was pulling with all his strength and yet the fish only succumbed to the landing net after 6 minutes and 40 seconds. No wonder Martin flopped backwards on to the grass in sheer relief. Why his tackle hadn't been smashed I'll never know.

As the barbel lay resting in the net I looked in awe at this magnificent creature that had started life as a tiny egg in the gravels of this famous river as much as thirty years ago. She had survived any number of attempts on her life, from kingfishers and grebes, otters, herons, and pike to grow into this much loved fish called 'Liner'.

It was warm handshakes of delight all round. Then with eager anticipation we discussed the next challenge in our exciting journey.

Rainbow's End

 THERE is one ancient fish that anglers have great affection for but which has become increasingly rare in recent years - the crucian carp. A lover of small, muddy farm ponds, they also thrive in all sorts of lowland waters, especially silty lakes and gravel pits where they root around in the mud for small invertebrates.

Crucians don't grow big like other carp, weighing an average of a pound or so, but what they lack in size they make up for in looks. A creature of summer, they seem to reflect the sun with their lovely, buttery golden colour and are almost as deep bodied as they are long. They are natives of south-east England and have lived in Britain since our islands became separated from the mainland of Europe by rising sea levels. Since then they have been moved around the country, but hybridization with common carp and the destruction of farm ponds by the relentless march of intensive farming has led to pure crucians becoming rare. It's a story that anglers find particularly sad because they are a much-loved species, not just for their aesthetic beauty but also for the peaceful places in which they live. They can also be tricky to catch and all fishermen love a challenge. Crucians are notoriously delicate, cautious feeders and even the most sensitive float can fail to register a bite... and even if it does, the fish is often missed on the strike - exasperating but fun!

I was once lucky enough to know of a water not far from home that supported a small population of ancient crucians, wise to the cunning ways of anglers. They lived in a large gravel pit containing big carp and tench, together with hordes of roach, rudd and bream, so finding them and avoiding the other species was the first challenge. However, early one morning, fishing 'roach style' with fine line, small hooks and with casters for bait I was fortunate to catch six crucians over 2lb, four of which were over the magical 3lb barrier. Sad to say, like in so many other lakes, this population of crucians has died out and all that those who fished for them can do is dream of those glorious dawns and dusks and cherish the memories of missed bites and rare successes.

Size-wise, a 2lb crucian is a good specimen but Martin holds the British record with an absolute monster of 4lb 9oz 9drms. We set our 'Impossible' target at 3lb and with their increasing rarity perhaps Martin's greatest challenge was to find a water containing crucians. Fortunately, he knows a

thing or two about catching this elusive species and the best places to try.

 Over the last few years a weedy twenty acre lake in the Blackwater Valley has dominated the crucian carp scene. With the gene pool of these magnificent creatures having become increasingly diluted by other strains of carp elsewhere, this population come with the best possible guarantee – they have been authenticated by the late Alwyne Wheeler, scientific advisor to the British Record Fish Committee, so these fish are the real deal.

The business end.

As I pushed my barrow down the overgrown path I knew exactly where I was heading before even looking at the water. The crucian carp's Achilles heel is in their predictability. Unlike most other species they seem to have clearly defined homes, normally moving between only one or two swims. Angling pressure or weather conditions do little to alter this pattern and that gives the angler a tremendous advantage. A return to the record swim was the plan in the hope that lightening could strike twice. Excitedly I reached the scene of my success and noted that little had changed in the intervening year. It was certainly good to be back in a place that had given me a very special moment in my life.

My initial approach was to leger using 1lb 4oz test curve rods with 6lb mainline. A 1.5oz lead supplied the 'bolt' in the bolt rig, followed by a tiny 3ins braided hooklength and a size 12 hook. Off this sat a hair with a small grain of maize combined with a piece of yellow rig foam to balance everything out, creating a slow-sinking hookbait. Crucians are shy biters and I hoped this semi buoyant bait would waft up into a feeding fish's mouth more easily.

The venue's record potential was first exploited by a friend of mine, Adrian Eves, when he tempted two fish over the magic 4lb barrier in 1998 and 1999. The best went a whopping 4lb 5oz. Luckily for me I gained an invitation to fish the venue, which is controlled by CEMEX Angling, and during that trip in May 2003 I caught a British record fish of 4lb 9oz 9drms. Although my love affair with the lake had been short, it was certainly sweet and I felt no need to revisit the water – I suppose it was a case of 'what more could I do?' Happy with my lot, I headed off to pastures new - that was until I teamed up with Hugh to make 'Catching the Impossible' and he requested the need to capture a monster crucian on film. Well, I knew the place to go, but first we had to secure permission to return to the home of my record. Fortunately this was granted and dates were booked. All I could do was keep my fingers crossed and hope that Lady Luck would smile down on me once again.

For a finishing touch I intended to use a method that I came up with on my previous visit. Prior to this, the standard approach for anglers on the lake had been to fill a cage feeder with liquidised bread.

Clearing the hot spot.

Although effective, it looked somewhat crude and I knew it could be improved upon. By adapting a dynamite stick method (basically a water soluble stocking mesh containing free food) I filled it with liquidised bread, crushed hemp, 3mm marine halibut pellets and corn steep liquor powder. A quick marginal test showed the advantage over the feeder with the hookbait sitting smack, bang in the centre of the free offerings as the PVA mesh dissolved.

These tiny changes can make all the difference when it comes to the very biggest of our coarse fish. Indeed

must seem over the top, but it's just this precision that is vital if you are to be consistently successful. Luck can, and does, play a part in angling but it's amazing how the harder you try the luckier you become.

With the rigs now ready it was time to assess the margin where I intended to place my hookbaits. Unlike the previous year, the gravel slope a rod length out had become covered in Canadian pond weed. Now, although I felt sure that the crucians would still feed here my presentation could be severely impaired. Hugh, fortunately, had the answer

Searching for gold.

such was the success of this particular edge that directly after I caught my record crucian it became the 'in' technique and had, by the time I returned with Hugh, accounted for the vast majority of captures at the venue by other anglers.

Because of this I decided to darken off the mix with a little meaty marine groundbait to prevent any fish spooking over the light coloured crumb - a common problem with bread-based feeds. To anyone but the most dedicated of anglers this attention to detail

in his camper van – a weed rake, made up of two garden rake heads strapped back to back and connected to a length of strong rope. This contraption is then thrown out into the lake and drawn back across the bottom with the aim being to cut a narrow channel through the weed, giving a clear area on which to present the bait.

Perhaps the sight of a rake crashing down on the surface seems crazy to the uninitiated, but believe me it is highly effective. Not only does it provide a clear surface to fish on but it also stirs up any bloodworm, shrimps and snails that may be present, providing easy pickings for the fish. I also strongly concur with the train of thought that says the commotion plays on the inquisitive nature of fish.

Half an hour later and with a little sweat expelled I could now feel the rake 'tapping' across a clean gravel slope. For a finishing touch I sprinkled in a few handfuls of halibut pellets and hemp before lowering down my two leads. Satisfyingly, both landed with a resounding 'donk' which indicated a perfect presentation

It was time to be proactive. Two crucians rolling in the swim at dawn had given me hope but just to be safe I prepared another spot 50 yards to my left in slightly shallower water. The plan was to (if no action was forthcoming) fish my last night in the current swim and then move to the second spot at dawn. Anyone who tells you that angling is a lazy pursuit doesn't know what they are talking about. Once again I went through the baiting ritual at dusk, the only difference being that I introduced six dynamite sticks as free offerings. I wondered if the fish were spooked because the only stick in the

A dawn brace.

on clean gravel. Crucians are margin-loving creatures so to catch them it was vital that my baits did not sit too far out into the lake. It was now a question of waiting to see if all the effort would be worthwhile.

A gentle breeze pushed in against the bank as I settled back with Hugh to await events. Unfortunately we settled back for rather a long time – until the following day! (to be exact). Fish have an uncanny habit of failing to read the script, especially when a camera is waiting for them.

swim contained a hookbait, especially as this method had been used regularly on the lake over the past year. I hoped the 'safe sticks' would help build up their confidence.

Sleep that night was hard to come by as my mind raced with the thought of failure. It was unlikely that we would be able to gain permission to return so this was our big chance to film a monster crucian and it looked like I was going to blow it. Factor in the sheer rarity of these creatures and that there

Waiting and worrying.

herald the end of this feeding spell. Should I reel in and change the rig, or keep my confidence in a method that had produced a record fish for me?

With a huge 'crack' my dilemma had been resolved when my right hand bobbin hit the butt and I grabbed the rod. The jag, jag sensation with the line going round and round in circles convinced me that a crucian was the culprit. They are not the fiercest of opponents but knowing how important this fish could be to the film I took the affair very seriously. A gorgeous golden back broke the surface and, holding my breath, I drew her into the net.

"Yes!," I shouted. The mission had been accomplished - or so I thought. At 3lb 11oz she was a big crucian but Hugh decided that to make it really special a 'four' was needed. At this point I pondered on how easily I could fall out with the cameraman!

Joking aside, the standard required for the films was incredibly high and as a fair percentage of the catching would fall on my shoulders, the road ahead certainly wasn't going to be a smooth one. For the first time in my fishing career I needed to achieve someone else's ambitions as well as my own.

was no Plan B venue, then you can see why I was a worried man. A mild wind rippled the surface and I questioned why we hadn't received any action. However experienced you become there are always situations that you read wrongly. Would I want to change these days when it's such a struggle? Not really. Success in all walks of life – angling included – is so much sweeter if you have to suffer a degree of frustration. It's an essential part of the joy of angling.

By dawn my confidence was at rock bottom... until my alarm beeped and the bobbin shook. Not a bite but a 'liner', so at last something was feeding in the baited area. Over the next couple of hours the bobbins skipped and jumped along with my heart as the liners continued. I could imagine three or four crucians busily scoffing my grub whilst wagging their tails like small dogs and bumping into the line.

But why hadn't I hooked one? Time was running out. I knew that full daylight would, in all probability,

Placing the rod back in position I hardly had time to put it in the rests before it was away again. This time it was a slightly smaller specimen of 3lb 6oz. Amazing. Like buses you wait an age and then two come along at once! With the sun slowly beginning to rise it was decision time – stay, or move to the second swim. My gut instinct said we had to move if a 'four' was to be tempted as surely a larger crucian would have been the greediest and fallen foul of my rig by now.

Time for crucians.

A nice suprise.

still pushing for a 'four.' Did he not realise how difficult that aim was? I love a challenge though, and was determined not to be beaten.

When the next bite came I was taken a little by surprise. The power of the fish was so much stronger and if it was a crucian, then it had to be massive. Alas, the buttery scales were substituted with an olive green

I grabbed the 17ft float rod that I'd combined with a centrepin and headed off to my pre-baited spot. If the truth be known I have never really thought that catching crucians on bolt rigs was playing cricket anyway and I hoped my float could put that right. For me, crucian fishing conjures up an image of a surface fizzing like a witch's cauldron, a sight created by fish busily sifting through silt and debris for their breakfast. In my imagination I could see a float placed inside this maelstrom beginning to sway from side to side as the line is nudged in the feeding frenzy. On the bank, angler's nerve endings begin to fray as he is teased to the point of madness.

Although I was using a rod and reel for this swim I opted instead for a pole float to give added sensitivity for these shy-biting fish. I gently lowered the two casters, which were impaled on a size 18 barbless hook and began to stare intently at the fluorescent orange tip. A while later it gently slid away and I struck firmly, connecting with a solid resistance. At last I had a big crucian on a float. After a wonderful fight a gold bar weighing 3lb 6oz was lying in the bottom of the net. This was crazy – a hat-trick of 'threes' in a few hours yet Hugh was complexion and a red eye – it was a tench. I love catching tench but I couldn't help but feel a little disappointed, especially as the average size is low on the water. Still unconvinced of its proportions I nonchalantly scooped her up and it was only then that I realised my mistake. A huge gravid stomach accompanied her and ensured that a sizeable chunk was added to the weight. So as not to stress her I quickly got on with the weighing – 9lb 2oz is a big tench from anywhere. My day was just getting better and better.

The float went back out, followed by a little free 3mm pellet. The occasional bubble popped on the surface and I raised my concentration. Once again the tip buried and I knew this was the one - it was now make or break. A colossal golden back broke the surface and my silence spoke a thousand words. I had to concentrate. I'm not a religious man but I couldn't help but ask for assistance from a higher level. Prayers were sent up to the fish gods. Although as one of the UK's smaller species many may think their proportions uninspiring, on a percentage basis against the current record I was doubtful if we would hook a bigger fish during the filming of the entire series. I needed to land this crucian.

Whether it had been down to avoiding walking under a ladder or seeing two magpies, I don't know, but Lady Luck shone on us. There, in the folds of my net, lay a true monster of a crucian carp at 4lb 4oz of gold. I fell into my chair with the release of pressure. I couldn't have done any more and, in all fairness, probably wouldn't have achieved so much without Hugh's drive.

We had found what was at the end of the rainbow.

Rainbows end.

Friends Reunited

 THE Gods were smiling on us. Our long journey was only a month old and Martin had already caught two *'Impossible'* fish. We had also captured two memorable sequences on film - surely we weren't going to find all the challenges so easy?

Whatever the outcome, there was much more we wanted to say about angling and the great outdoors and one of these was the joy of sharing our adventures with friends. I had tried to capture this camaraderie in 'A Passion for Angling' and its success proved to Martin and I the appeal of the idea, especially after sharing a couple of days with Chris Yates while shooting stills for Martin's weekly column in Angling Times. Chris and I were also working on the series 'Caught in Time', an illustrated fishing diary of Chris's angling adventures, so this filming was going to serve as a sort of 'screen test' for Martin and our epic challenge, 'Catching the Impossible'.

The first of our February days followed an invitation by Martin to fish his local stretch of the Bristol Avon. Barbel were the target and conditions seemed perfect, though after several hours of skilful angling it was clear the barbel didn't think so. It became a chub match instead, with honours even at the end of a laughter-filled day of tea, cake and tangles in trees.

On the second of our winter days we were joined by old friend Mick Rouse, chief photographer at Angling Times. He was there to record our adventures on the Great Ouse and the large fish we were going to catch but with the water temperature at 34F, ice-covered margins and a wind straight from the Arctic, it seemed more likely that we'd catch polar bears!

On such a cold day the only way to start was with a mug of hot tea, particularly after Martin got a wet foot testing the depth of the ice. Unfortunately he didn't enjoy the joke as much as we did! By late afternoon we were frozen and fishless but then Martin pulled a couple of beautiful frame-filling perch out of the hat for Mick's cameras, both topping three pounds. Job done and film in the can, but then, just as darkness fell, Chris caught a lovely fish of well over 2lb. By now I was desperate for a cast and as it was too dark to film I put the camera down, cast out into the tail of Chris's swim and promptly poached a perch of 4lb 7oz. It was the first perch I'd ever seen over 4lb and this creature was truly memorable - perch this size really are BIG. As we walked back home across the dark fields Martin reminded me that we'd have to repeat the trick for the series, but with me behind the camera. No problem we thought.

We'd had such enjoyable days with Chris and Mick that it was obvious we had to include 'guests' in our new series, especially as we might need help with some of

Madness.

A winter warmer.

Mist swirled around the lake's surface while small rudd pimpled and whirly gig beetles buzzed about their business. Occasionally a large black back rose from the water before a sheet of bubbles erupted – the bream were feeding. With little finesse my spod-full of pellets, casters and maggots crashed down some 50 yards out as I prepared a royal feast that I hoped would tempt the bream away from their natural diet and onto mine.

For our first try at an *'Impossible'* bream we had come to a Wokingham and District Council water called Dinton Pastures. Famed for its massive carp, we also hoped that the bream grew to similar specimen proportions. Our host, Countryside Officer Simon Bartlam, assured us that monsters were regularly tempted by carpers, huge fish that were chucked back unweighed and treated as a nuisance by this

our *'Impossible'* fish. Such an idea would also enable us to share our adventures with some of the great characters in the fishing world, an idea that would surely appeal to a wide audience.

One of our film stories would feature the Hampshire Avon, following it from source to sea and for this we needed a 10lb barbel. No film on the Avon would be complete without Pete Reading, the Head of Science at Ringwood School, and a teacher who prefers outwitting fish to trying to outwit cunning pupils! During the school's summer holidays Pete had already caught several large barbel so it was going to be a simple task to wander up with Martin in mid-August and film the pair of them landing another one. But the pressure created by being filmed makes it a funny old business.

Suddenly, all Pete caught were carp, even if they were lovely 14lb commons. And after three days of trying in swims where barbel could be clearly seen, our target eluded us. As soon as we went filming elsewhere, Pete started catching big barbel again, all of which served to indicate just how difficult some of our challenges were going to be. Our next *'Impossible'* was a 14lb bream, which just over twenty years ago would have beaten the British record!

Anticipation.

single-minded group. Simon himself had tempted fish to over 18lb and with pictures to prove it, Dintons certainly appeared to have the potential to supply us with what we wanted. On arrival we found the lake unruffled by wind, with the sky blue and brittle – in fact it was typical of a fine September day. The conditions were hardly ideal for bream and with a full moon predicted I was unsure of what lay ahead. But delaying the trip was not an option, for Hugh was due to have a hip replacement the following week. This session would be our last for some six to eight weeks.

I felt sure that bream were present though, as the occasional fizz popped to the surface over the baited area. My swim selection had been made by previous experience of large shoals of big bronze slabs - being a communal fish they have a strong desire to group together. Weed-choked water prevents this so large, open spaces are sought. Both ends of Dintons were solid with Canadian pond weed, therefore I felt these areas could be ignored. The middle of the lake gave the only open water so, unsurprisingly, this was where I set up.

I was certain that the bream were now feeding so my groundbait certainly appeared to be working but we had yet to receive a take. For a few hours it played on my mind that something was wrong. Carefully I ran through my tactics to check for a weak link. The problem, I surmised, had to be with the terminal tackle - somehow it was causing the fish concern and preventing a pick up. It was a Method feeder that sat at the business end and this had been combined with a short, carp-style sheathed hooklength material tied to a size 8 hook. Bait was two meaty-flavoured 10mm boilies. Perhaps it was a little too crude. After all, this was a set-up not too dissimilar to those the carp anglers used and which had been responsible for the vast majority of the bream accidentally caught on the venue. Maybe they had grown cautious of this approach and I wondered if a change was needed?

Reeling in, I took off the hooklength and dropped down the hook size to a 10. Most importantly, the coated braid was swapped to a pre-stretched 10lb monofilament - something I felt sure would make the difference. As before I squeezed my Method mix around the feeder, hoping the combination of scalded marine halibut pellets, a good glug of corn steep liquor, tinned flaked tuna and a sprinkling of casters would work its magic. I pressed my double boilie hookbait into the side of the groundbait ball just to make sure it would all land on the lake bed in a nice, neat pile.

Deadly method.

Splosh! The feeder hit the water, sending ripples across the calm, glass-like surface. Accuracy is vital in all forms of bream fishing and I knew it was over the baited area by the pole elastic marker tied around my mainline. Slowly it fell the 9ft to the bottom, landing with a 'donk' that indicated a clean, solid lake bed. I clipped up the indicator and slowly pulled it down as I took up the slack. With line still between my fingers I felt a tug and looked out at the water fully expecting a bird to be the culprit. But there wasn't a sign. My first reaction was one of puzzlement - perhaps I had imagined it. Waiting five seconds, it to happened again - only harder this time. Lifting the rod I swept it back, not sure whether the strike would evaporate into thin air but the tip cranked over and began tapping. I had a fish on! Line was gained easily over the

First cast.

deeper body of the lake, only becoming tricky when I drew the fish into the margins where it began pulling a little harder as it tried its best to reach cover. But bream aren't blessed with much power and a big, bronze flank soon popped to the surface before surrendering.

When I lifted up the fish in the landing net I was surprised by the bulk and hoped the scales would bring me a double. At 11lb 2oz it was much more than that – Dinton had provided me with a wonderful specimen at the same time as teaching me a valuable lesson too. By scaling down my tackle I had saved a blank – it was that simple. The more I fish the more I realise how small the percentage is between success and failure. To my mind the wealth of knowledge freely available allows everyone to operate at 90 per cent, but it's that final 10 per cent that makes all the difference. And that could be as small as changing a hooklength or a bait.

Catching a double-figure bream from a new water is more than enough to call it a good day in my book but

I couldn't rest on my laurels. Even though the sun shone high in the sky with a blue backdrop, the bream continued to feed in earnest. The angling text books would have told me that I was wasting my time but fortunately fish don't read an awful lot. Within a few minutes I was holding another bronze dustbin lid weighing in at exactly 12lb and by dusk another nine doubles and ten other fish over 8lb had fallen to my rods. Was Dinton an incredible bream water or had we been lucky enough to visit it on a red letter day? Perhaps I would find out the following morning, as we still had until lunchtime before the camera needed to be packed away. With a glass of red wine, both Hugh and I watched as the full moon rose and mulled over what dawn would bring.

The day was young and the sky still a deep crimson when two Method balls sailed out into the lake and once again the bream's breakfast gong was sounded. It didn't take long for the indicator to slowly rise and for line to begin ticking from the reel. Silhouetted against the sky, 12 feet of carbon arced over and 50 yards out a huge flank twisted and turned in alarm. His companions though, seemed unfazed and continued grazing. Only a few yards away from the unfolding drama another bream rose sharply upwards, it too agitated by a hook taking hold. To have two fish on at once is a moment of good fortune to cherish for any angler and it wasn't lost on me. The rest of the morning followed a similar pattern to the day before and by the time we hit the finishing line I had caught a lifetime's worth of big bream. I packed away a shell-shocked and weary man.

The final statistics read thirty bream over 8lb with seventeen doubles, four of these pulling the scales down to 12lb. The best went 12lb 10oz. Even though we hadn't hit the 14lb target it was clear that with such a catch our '*Impossible*' had been achieved.

Beautiful bream.

 After Martin's epic catch there was time for some mature reflection and I became aware that he'd caught so many bream I had not had time to include the abundant wildlife on the lake. So next week I returned with my big camera and filmed the swans, grebes and tufted ducks. On my last morning there was a spectacular red dawn - which required the camera of course - but this heralded rain and the end of work for the day. Luckily I'd packed a rod and a bit of bait - funny I should do that! - and as I'd always wanted to catch a double figure bream and only ever managed one of 8lb 15oz (from a river mind) I fancied a cast or two.

Having spodded out some bait to Martin's hotspot it wasn't long before I had a large bream in the net but it only weighed 8lb 12oz so I needed another cast. The next fish pulled harder and as it neared the net I could see it was bigger - a lot bigger. At 12lb 4oz. It was mission accomplished. So it was a happy angler who lay on the slab in the hospital three days later and, with sweet dreams, succumbed to the anaesthetic.

Thirty years of wildlife film-making, including chasing elusive critters up mountains with heavy cameras had destroyed my hips. I woke up with one of the two arthritic hips replaced and after three days of pain I was feeling well enough to chat up the nurses; it was time to go home! Walking out of the hospital with only a stick shows what a miracle cure it really is and though I was 'grounded' for six weeks there was not much pain. However I wasn't allowed to drive and this prevented any filming. I did, however, have to supervise the editing of a film at the BBC about the Inuit culture, (Eskimos to you and I) and their relationship with polar bears and other wildlife which we'd been filming for two years. So it was off to Bristol every week with my wife Sue driving.

But as soon as my six-week 'grounding' was over I was out of the door like a shot. The Royalty Fishery on the Hampshire Avon called. I had a date with Martin and Ray Walton, the rolling meat maestro and even if climbing fences with my new hip was a bit painful, we needed a 10lb barbel.

Hip replacement country.

Ask any angler to name a famous barbel fisherman and the name Ray Walton would probably be at the top of their list. Ray's angling CV is as good as anyone's but it's his character that makes him stand out from the crowd. Being vertically challenged certainly doesn't dampen his persona and if you find a group of barbelers, smack bang in the centre will be Ray Walton holding court. His style has seen him clash with more than one person and no matter what, there's always something to protest about – he's the original barbel anarchist! That said, he has a passion for promoting and protecting the species that few can match.

missed out on the recent big barbel boom. Pellets have hit town, with bag after bag being chucked in during the summer months and such an oil-rich diet, originally designed for stew pond trout, is also very agreeable to most coarse fish - including barbel. This in turn has seen the fish stacking on weight, culminating in a new Royalty record of over 16lb. Not bad for a day-ticket fishery. So how could I resist? A day with Ray is always good fun and with the prospect of a fish or two just made it all the more appealing. With Hugh just about mobile again after his hip replacement, he decided it would be worth joining us for the morning in the hope that, if luck was on our side, he might capture a Royalty barbel on film.

The rolling master.

I first met Ray on the banks of the Great Ouse and since then we have become good friends. I like characters and Ray is certainly one of these. You've only to see how he dresses - from head to toe in camouflage and with all his tackle strapped to various parts of his body – to realise that. Ray's love other than the Great Ouse barbel, which had filled his time in recent years, is the famous Royalty Fishery on the Hampshire Avon. What he doesn't know about the venue could be written on the back of a postage stamp.

After a spell of wet, warm rain, Ray was on the phone to see if I fancied a day out on the bank. I knew there was every chance of a good fish, as the Royalty hasn't

Bleary eyed from the early start, I cut across Salisbury Plain out of Wiltshire and into Hampshire for our 7am rendezvous at the café. I pulled up to find Ray tucking into a full vegetarian breakfast. I find his attitude towards things like pork and beef very puzzling when the only bait he uses is luncheon meat! After the normal leg pulling and hearty 'Full Monty' fry-up we headed a few doors down the street to get our day tickets at the local tackle shop.

By 7.30am we were in the car park and Ray was delighted to see a tinge of colour pushing down the river. These are perfect conditions for his rolling meat approach - a technique which sees a matchbox-sized

lump of meat bouncing down the river's bed, mimicking a free offering with the aid of the flow. Now, I always like a bit of banter with Ray and rather foolishly challenged him to a match.
"If you can roll lumps of meat I can do the same with boilies," I said. The gauntlet had been well and truly thrown down – it was meat versus boilies. As I wandered up the bank along the famous stretch I wondered if I had been a little hasty. After all, I thought, Ray knows this water like the back of his hand. I was sure that my old mate wouldn't stitch me up though!

My first choice was just beyond the railway bridge, while Ray plonked himself a further 100 yards above. Tackle-wise, I opted to combine a fixed spool reel loaded with 30lb braid and a 1lb 12oz test curve barbel rod. The terminal tackle was simply a size 4 hook, on which a fishmeal boilie was side hooked. For casting weight I grouped several swan shot together, adding or subtracting weight to allow the bait to trundle slowly along the river bed. Ray, on the other hand, opted for a rod bearing his own name, along with the famous Ray Walton 'Rolling Pin' reel. This he had loaded with 30lb braid. At the business end he adapted a size 4 hook with a small piece of shrink tubing placed on the shank containing heavy metal putty. This provides not only

casting weight but ensures that the meat trundles along the gravel naturally. If additional weight is then required a lump of brown modelling clay is squeezed onto the braid approximately six inches from the hook.

Ray really has mastered the art of rolling and I doubt there is a better exponent of the method in the country. Flicking his bait upstream and allowing a subtle bow to form in the line, the meat slowly began to trundle down the gravel run. Ray carefully studied its path until the braid pulled taut, with the meat now well downstream. Reeling in, I noticed him make an adjustment to the small lump of modelling clay pinched on the braid. A tiny bit had been removed to speed up the rate the meat travelled through the swim. On many occasions before Ray had stressed the importance of his bait behaving as naturally as possible, much in the same way that a match angler would adjust and fine tune his float tackle.

From my position downstream I watched as Ray once again flicked his bait upstream before standing heron-like as he concentrated on its path until it was directly in front of him. Suddenly he swept the rod backwards and the braid whooshed on the surface as it pulled taut. Walton was in. A short but spirited fight ensued and

within minutes a fish of about 5lb was being drawn over his landing net. At this point Ray loudly pronounced he was one-nil up, much to his amusement.

As I headed back to my swim I thought I had better get a move on. Ray had other plans though, and no sooner had I picked up the rod than I heard the words: "I've got another one." Turning on my heels I reached him again to see a similar-sized fish pop in the net and listened to: "2-0."

That was it. Drastic situations call for drastic measures so I did what any right-thinking anglers would do when faced with a hiding - I decided to poach Ray's swim! But for all my trying with a boilie the fishing gods weren't smiling down on me and I could not get a pick up. Twenty minutes later Ray felt I had slogged away enough and suggested we go and try the famous 'Pipes' swim. He assured me that I would get the prime spot this time.

Standing just yards apart we laughed and joked as we flicked out our respective baits. Surely, I thought, if there was any self-respecting barbel out there it would choose a juicy boilie over an old lump of meat. What do I know? Just seconds later Ray struck into a fish again and I was left holding my head in my hands. A smile as wide as the Avon crept across Ray's face as line fizzed from his reel and he did battle with what was obviously a good fish. I had the job of being his netsman and within minutes I scooped up what was clearly a cracking barbel. The scales offered confirmation and settled on 10lb 3oz. A Royalty double is to be cherished but something else gave Ray even more satisfaction – the fact that he had won 3-0!

The little honour I had retained in defeat evaporated when I was forced to beg him for a piece of meat. The lesson? Modern designer baits, while very effective, are not always the be all and end all of fishing. To add to my humiliation Hugh had captured the whole event on film and I was left to ponder a simple truth - you never stop learning in this sport.

The greatest ever chub swim?

A Lea monster.

What an enjoyable day that was, with lots of banter and the best of competitive spirit, the sort that is just for laughs. Life is fun when you fish with friends, and Martin's next call was to Jerry Hammond, the kind of mate we'd all like. He's an ex-stunt man and extra from feature films with a fund of stories. But he also has a house on a River Lea weirpool full of big chub. Our next *'Impossible'* target was a 7lb chub and Jerry had recently caught a monster of 8lb 10oz so it wasn't long before we were heading round the M25 with a van full of optimism.

One of the best things about making our films was the interesting characters we had met along the way, each having walked a different path in life. At first glance they would seem to come from different worlds but there is a single passion that unites them all – a love for fishing.

It was a pleasure then, to meet the latest, Jerry Hammond, who runs Carthagena Fishery in the Lea

Valley Park. This complex comprises two lakes and three-quarters of a mile of the River Lea, including a mill stream and a gorgeous weir pool. The lakes are made up of a syndicate fishery – Carthagena – with carp to nearly 40lb and a day-ticket lake – Brooke – containing fish to over 30lb, along with a good stocking of crucian carp, tench and bream. It was the river though, that really grabbed my attention, having already produced giant chub to over 8lb. With a fish of 7lb being our *'Impossible'* target, Carthagena seemed as good a place as any to start our quest. But before we began fishing we got to know a bit about Jerry and there is certainly more to him than meets the eye.

For eight years he was a physical education instructor in the army before he left to seek his fame and fortune. Now, for most of us this remains a pipe dream but for Jerry the glitz and glamour of Hollywood genuinely beckoned. Working as a stunt man and actor he performed in movies such as 'Saving Private Ryan' and 'Gladiator', as well as TV shows like Band of Brothers. As you can see he certainly picked the big ones! There was a danger that life as a fishery owner could seem tame after such adventures but Jerry wouldn't change it – he now lives his original boyhood dream. But could his venue help produce us our latest *'Impossible'* goal? Like everywhere else that seems to throw up monster chub these days, a high-protein diet of crayfish fuels the growth of the Lea's chub. The potential for an 8lb-plus fish is easily within the grasp of this river, so I was rather excited when the time came to begin fishing.

The first thing we did was stare into his weirpool and to say it took my breath away would be an

understatement. Dozens of big chub lay in the tail of the white water in little more than a couple of feet of water. If this didn't get me drooling then their reaction to a handful of dog biscuits certainly did. It was like a shoal of piranhas during a feeding frenzy! I had little doubt that this was the greatest chub swim in the world. If that seems like a bold statement it had to be seen to be believed. The average size seemed to range from 4lb 8oz to 5lb 8oz but sat in among them were two monsters that were not only longer than the rest but with the width of a house brick. If we could tempt one of these I felt sure another 'Impossible' would be a formality.

I began fishing with a simple paternoster rig supporting a size 6 hook and a big lump of paste flavoured with a spicy prawn additive. The plan was that Hugh would film while Jerry and I took it in turns to catch chub. Unsurprisingly, the first few casts produced immediate bites but although these fish looked easy it wasn't long before they began to melt away. The shallow, clear water was doing us no favours in holding the shoal together but it was hard to be disappointed with half a dozen fish to half an ounce under 6lb. What had been particularly interesting was watching the chub suck in our paste hookbaits without registering the slightest tremor on the quiver tip. It just goes to show how many times fish escape with a free lunch leaving the angler oblivious to the robbery.

Day two dawned once again under a clear November sky. The initial bite of dawn was soon replaced by the soothing sun and with our midday deadline approaching we hoped that one of the real monsters would pay us a visit. Alas, with only half-an-hour left we remained fishless. The vast shoal of the previous day was no longer present, still stung, I'm sure, by our plundering. Hugh made one final suggestion and asked if I could cast over to a raft situated on the far bank. Once it had been filmed it could then be edited into the earlier fish-catching sequence. As I released my trigger finger from the spool I just knew it was a perfect cast. Like a golfer's hole in one, it sailed into the tiniest gap between the floating debris and was sucked deep down by the river and into the shadows. I'd obviously taken some kind of aim but for it to hit the bull's eye was more by luck than judgement.

I now faced a quandary. Hugh required me to 'fake' a strike for the benefit of the film but how could I shift my bait after making such a perfect cast? I just had to get a bite. Resisting Hugh's instruction for as long as I dared my reward came with a savage wrap of the tip. I made immediate contact on the strike and an unseen force did its best to smash me in the trailing branches. Experience tells you when you have something special attached and this chub left me in no doubt of that.

After several minutes of stalemate 12ft of carbon began to tell and it was a huge relief when my opponent entered open water. It did its best to bore under the nearside bank but all that was required was a cool head and one of the two monsters we had seen yesterday would soon boil in front of me ready for the net. I was so close to winning I could touch it. But the fish had enough energy for one final charge and my rod suddenly sprang back straight as a poker and the line hung limp and distressed. To have the hook pull out was a cruel, cruel blow. Jerry did little to take away the pain. "You've just lost one of the big girls," he said. I didn't need telling. All I could do was throw the rod down as the dark clouds began to gather in my mind. I knew an '*Impossible*' had just slipped through our fingers. Driving home, I hoped the storm would soon blow over with the arrival of winter. Or was it just a prelude to what was to come? Only time would tell.

Not good enough.

Missing Monsters

ONE of the *'Impossibles'* that was going to prove a huge challenge was a 30lb pike. A fish of this size is one of nature's rarest creatures and catching one on camera probably would be impossible. However, a monster like this would look so impressive to our audience that we had to try, and with winter just around the corner it was time to make a start, but where?

A piking interlude.

It is often said that you can't catch a fish that isn't there, and though obvious, finding out where big fish live requires the right personality and attitude. Martin has these qualities in abundance and having spent his lifetime searching for big fish, his bush telegraph is hot-wired. One of the golden rules in information gathering is to be discreet, the other is to give as much help as you receive, and on these scores Martin has great integrity. So we were hoping that Martin's reputation would lead us to a giant pike. Pike require a lot of food to grow big and fat so one of our most likely locations would be a lake into which the owners stock lots of trout. Some of these trout will die of course, and pike like dead trout! Nutritious, and requiring little effort to eat, trout enable them to grow rapidly. These pike often become obese, making them delicate and likely to die after capture, so finding a large one before anyone else is the challenge.

One of the locations Martin had been told held big pike was a large trout lake in the Cotswold Water Park, so on November 1st our quest began. The lake was large, shallow and weedy and the swirls of rising trout suggested there was plenty for the pike to eat. Maybe too much, because after ten hours of wobbling dead trout and casting lures all over the lake, we hadn't had a single take. Either they weren't hungry or there weren't many pike. However, we only needed one - so long as it was over 30lb! Two days later, we had indeed caught one but that weighed just 4lb, and it coughed up a pike the size of a pencil. It seemed we'd arrived too late. If small pike were eating even smaller pike, perhaps the big girls were dead.

The following week we were in Yorkshire, roach fishing, trying for a big one of course, and we caught plenty of average redfins which we stored for a few hours in a keepnet. The pike here were certainly hungry – the net was soon surrounded by toothy critters that periodically lunged at the occupants inside. It was a wonderful sight, five beautifully marked pike close to us in the clear water. The trouble was the largest was only about 10lb, so we were back on the road once again.

One of the benefits of fishing for pike is the characters you meet on the journey and among these is Nige Williams. He has a pike fishing CV second to none, and with hundreds of 20lb pike to his name, along with twenty one thirty-pounders up to a best of 41lb 4oz, we were fortunate that he agreed to help us find our monster. He'd heard about a trout water in Yorkshire that held a lot of big pike and having been granted the privilege of trying to catch one by the owner, we gathered there on a cold November day to

Beady eyes.

Watching us blank!

assess our chances. The scene was bleak. Brooding clouds scudded across the black cliffs of the old quarry in which nestled three dark lakes, the surface broken by rain drops and rising trout. We retreated to the cafe for tea where the owner showed us a video of a recent netting of one of the lakes. The nets bulged with very fat pike and some looked big enough to be an 'Impossible'. Suitably excited by the film evidence, Nige and Martin had baits in the water before their tea had time to go cold. The expected takes never materialized. Nige knew every trick in the book but after three days we remained fishless, the only highlight of the visit being a beautiful peregrine falcon that sat on the cliff above, watching us blank!

Another of angling's great characters is Bob Church, a fly fishing world champion and gold medal winner several times with the England team. But Bob is one of those rare anglers who fishes for everything, a successful all-rounder with big tench, barbel and carp to his name, along with pike. Luckily, Bob had agreed to help us catch a big pike, preferably on a fly, and he had some special places to try.

Hidden away in the county of Bedfordshire is a lake secluded from the world. Shrouded by a veil of trees, it's free from prying eyes and unaffected by the passing of time. In this time-warp few can wet a line but fortunately for us this magical place had opened its doors, with Bob Church arranging two days of pike fishing. We hoped these types of lost venues would bring mystery to the series and perhaps even a few of the monsters we so desired.

As always Bob was brimming with confidence and pronounced that catching pike on the fly would be 'no problem.' If enthusiasm and optimism were tangible commodities then Bob would have enough of both to set up his own shop. The lake in question was wooded along its banks and broken up by an island at each end, its stock relatively untouched, save for the odd previous sortie by Bob. It provided then the perfect habitat for neglect-loving pike and that fact, together with Bob's tales of fly-munching predators, ensured I was full of excitement for the days ahead.

Now I'm no fly angler so I knew I'd need plenty of assistance from the master. Casting large predator

The hustler.

flies is far harder than a nymph or dry fly so tackle needs to be stepped up accordingly. The reel in particular must be of a wide arbour variety which is specially designed to prevent coils forming in the thick line and inhibiting casting.

A 20lb flurocarbon leader was attached at the business end with a short wire trace. We could then clip on an array of weird and wonderful flies - white, orange and blue to name a few. Some had buoyant heads and some had enormous eyes, so there was plenty in Bobs' box to tempt me, if not a pike.

and forth and in a well drilled routine the fly flew effortlessly through the air with a straight line shooting behind. Mine, meanwhile, collapsed into a crumpled mess just past the boat, the fly crashing down with little finesse. In a series of steady pulls, Bob worked life into his offering until half way through the retrieve a set of jaws sped up from the depths and took hold. With a rapid strike, line shot out from his hands as a pike zoomed away in alarm. Bob, the crafty old fox, had drawn first blood.

Drawing on his years of fly fishing experience he slowly gained the upper hand, even when a series

The yellow peril.

Now, I noticed at this stage that Bob selected the only yellow pattern in his collection but its importance was lost on me at the time. I chose an orange creation with giant teddy bear eyes and with that it was time to go afloat and begin the search for our dream. The use of a boat would allow us to seek out all the pike's haunts and, aided and abetted by an echo sounder, all the underwater features that provide perfect predator haunts could be located.

As we slowly drifted into the bottom bay our depth-finding gadget revealed a constant seven feet. Bob, keen as mustard, was already wielding his rod back

of acrobatic leaps from his foe tested him to the full. An angry, shaking head soon slid by the boat as I prepared to glove it out, its jet black eye staring back at me in defiance. Bob, though, was not to be denied and as we hoisted his prize aboard he knew immediately that he had cracked the double-figure barrier. But this was only the beginning of a lesson from the 'master'. While I failed to get a sniff another eight pike fell to Bob throughout the day and with each one the word 'yellow' was bellowed out in a kind of victory salute. To be fair though, I think his success was more down to skill than the colour of his fly. Still, I vowed to keep my eye on him in future.

Day two found us once again afloat on the lake but the action was as gloomy as the weather. Only a solitary pike came our way but at last it fell to my rod, saving me from another blank. It felt the right time to say goodbye to the water - we had a feeling that nothing more could be achieved and with time a precious commodity a change of venue seemed in order. The pike we hoped for might be just around the next corner and so with Bob in tow our search for the 'Impossible' thirty-pounder continued. We tried lures and jerkbaits in a nearby lake but only caught pike to 16lbs, so continued our search.

A trout lake near Earith was our destination. The owner, Ray, who was also a friend of Bob's, had given us special permission to target the pike which had grown fat on his rainbow trout stocks. He gave us the impression that not many predators were present but the ones that were there had grown to giant proportions. It seemed that we may only need one bite but that, as always, was going to prove tricky.

We slipped out onto the water aboard one of the resident boats, carefully charting the venue's topography via the echo sounder. But the problem that lay ahead didn't need the latest gadgetry to find – the naked eye was more than adequate. The lake was so weedy it looked more like the centre court at Wimbledon and I knew from experience that this wouldn't help the fishing. Wrapped up in the green duvet the pike would have little reason to move, save for snatching the odd passing trout. Still, you have to be in it to win it as the saying goes, so we rigged up a couple of livebaits and began to slowly troll them around the lake.

With virtually seventy five per cent of the water weeded up our efforts had to remain in the only open water available – in the centre. As the day wore on, confidence slowly sapped away as our heads began filling with doubt. Then, out of the blue, my float bobbed and sailed under – was this our big chance? I swept back the rod...and struck into thin air. Despondently I reeled in convinced that I had blown an 'Impossible'. My mood though, was lifted somewhat when I inspected the bait and discovered a couple of tiny puncture wounds that are the tell-tale sign of a small jack pike.

There was, I'm afraid, no further action to report and with night falling we gladly accepted Ray's kind invitation to join him and his family for dinner. Suitably refuelled it was time to head to the snooker room and take my revenge on Bob for his yellow fly escapades. "You're the youngest hustler in town!" he declared, as the black ball fell into the pocket, drawing another day to a close.

So dawned our final day in the company of Mr Church. I have to say that a nicer, more generous man you couldn't wish to meet and he has the enthusiasm for the sport of a man half his seventy odd years too. He really is one of fishing's great characters. Bob and I continued our search of the lake, fishing live trout under large floats in the hope that one would attract a pike's attention. Alas, by mid-afternoon the writing was on the wall and we both accepted that this was not to be the trip that

saw the monster banked. Perhaps we would return once the weed had died away and winter had taken much more of a grip.

Reluctantly I shook Bob by the hand and I thanked him for his efforts and company before I undertook the long journey home to Wiltshire. Interestingly, although we never found time to return to Earith, it did produce an absolute giant just a few months later when one lucky angler took a 39lb pike. Proof, if it were needed, of how unpredictable our sport can be.

Our quest for the pike was now bordering on an addiction. We both knew that a 30lb-plus fish would almost certainly be the hardest of all fish to catch and, if we were lucky enough to achieve it, it would be the most important capture of the series. Ask any non-angler to name a big fish and they wouldn't say carp, barbel or bream. No, stories of duck-eating pike abound in urban myths and would be expected to be found in any fishing tale like

Bob strikes again.

A legend.

ours. So it was on with the search and the next stop was as unlikely as it was intriguing - a canal!

The Kennet and Avon Canal is typical of this type of waterway, being full of locks and barges, and not the type of place you expect to encounter a monster pike. But my ears pricked up when I had heard a rumour of a fish being caught that measured a staggering forty six inches long. Sadly it was never weighed but I knew if the measurement was true it would certainly be of the proportions we were looking for. Experience told me that tall tales and pike go together like strawberries and cream but on this occasion I was confident of my source. And anyway, we had nothing to lose but a morning of our time, as Hugh was already in the area editing a BBC film about the Arctic.

I have to admit that as soon as my deadbaits hit the water my confidence began to drain away. Occasionally I get a feeling that it just isn't going to happen and it's rarely wrong – my sixth sense has become acute over the years and I have come to trust it implicitly. Perhaps I think myself out of success but the many hours I have spent on the bank has taught me to follow my instinct. Dodging between dog walkers, boaters and cyclists we leapfrogged up the canal and, save for a single jack, there was little to brighten up the morning. We called it quits and I vowed to keep my ear to the ground in the hope of hearing of the pike once more. If I did, we intended to return and attempt to explode the myth.

 We'd now done four months filming and had already accumulated a lot of material so the pressing matter of editing started to raise its head. It would take four months to complete each programme and the only way I could make our meagre finances stretch far enough was to do most of it myself. So with a new powerful computer installed we took a week out from filming while I learnt how to use it. Jill Garrett, a colleague from my wildlife film-making days and ace editor of many fine programmes tried patiently to teach an old dog new tricks. One thing became clear - we already had some beautiful scenery and exciting action shots of fishing, let alone some awesome fish - I just had to learn how to put it all together. However, our long journey was well underway.

Martin is related to Britain's most famous angler, TV star John Wilson, and characters don't come any bigger or more generous. So we were delighted when he agreed to try to catch us a large pike from the Norfolk Broads, preferably a thirty-pounder of course! This would be a trip down memory lane for me. I'd grown up fishing the River Bure for big roach and bream, and paddling around Hickling Broad in my little boat in search of tench, rudd and pike. That legendary Norfolk angler Dennis Pye became a friend and was the subject of my very first movie at film school. It told the story of the capture of a

Dennis Pye's pike.

famous pike and Dennis caught it for me too, all 26lb of it. I just wondered if lightning could strike twice and John would pull off that stunt once again.

 "This county really needs a motorway," I cursed as I found myself struggling along behind a tractor in Thetford Forest. Four hours is a long time to be stuck behind the wheel of a van, especially when the last third of the journey takes longer than the rest put together. But John's house, at last, beckoned and so did another adventure.

The plan was to meet with Hugh before adjourning to the local pub for dinner. Luckily, we had planned to stay for a couple of nights in the same location, allowing us to enjoy a glass or three of wine, something John and Hugh took great advantage of! Over our pub meal we debated where our piking sortie should commence the following day and eventually settled on a free stretch of water called Oulton Broad. Is there a finer way to spend a winter's night than talking about successful fishing adventures past and hopefully those still to come? From beside a warm log fire we arranged a rather bold and chilly 6am rendezvous, but before he left

Kingdom of the Ice Bear.

us John agreed to pick us up, with his boat in tow, to make the hour long journey across Norfolk.

It was still dark when my alarm call dragged me from my slumber. I quickly readied myself and stumbled downstairs, not sure if the other two would have shaken off the previous night's excesses. But, true to form, the two old pros were ready and eager, their urge to go fishing still burning strong after all these years. We raced across Norfolk in a bid to beat the break of day because, as any pike angler worth his salt knows, old esox enjoys his breakfast even more than we humans. Dawn had just broken when we pulled up at the slipway. John backed his boat into the water before we set about loading her up for the day ahead.

Although catching a fish was important, having fun was the first priority, as Hugh was keen to capture on film the camaraderie that exists between anglers.

So it will hardly surprise anyone to learn that there was more food onboard than tackle! John had promised to supply freshly-cooked bacon and sausage rolls to make up for the early start and he duly obliged. The smell of a full frying pan can make the bleakest of mornings seem enjoyable and even though our mission throughout was to catch fish of 'Impossible' sizes, nothing could replace the joy of fishing with friends.

The engine slowly ticked as we pushed out onto the broad. The weather was unusually kind for the time of year, with the water calm, inviting and free of even the slightest ripple to break it's glass-like appearance. It was perfectly still and quiet, save for the seagulls that squawked in annoyance as we unwittingly disturbed their morning. To the left a typical reed-fringed broads scenery filled the horizon but on the right was a less traditional scene – the lights from bankside warehouses, homes and hotels still glowing in the half-light.

We decided the reeds would offer the best area to start and we were soon anchored up twenty yards from a bed of them. My rods were 2lb 12oz tc models loaded with 40lb braid and on both I opted for static deadbaits - a herring on one and a lamprey on the other. John also chose a lamprey, but went for a smelt on the other rod. As is often the way for the professional angler, pleasure was combined with work and John had a new 12ft pike rod to put through its paces and we both hoped it would get a severe workout. While I had chosen braid, he went for 15lb mono instead and for casting weight attached three double swanshot before finishing his rig with a 30lb wire trace attached to a set of size 8 trebles.

Although the lack of wind provided us with a glorious dawn, the conditions did not bode well for sport. For many years John has made trips to the Broads but very few, he insisted, had ended in success when it was so calm. Still, we had the fry-up to look forward to and plenty of friendly banter to keep us entertained. Many people ask me if John really is as enthusiastic as he is portrayed in his numerous TV programmes? Well, I can confirm that it really isn't an elaborate act and John's love of this wonderful pursuit runs deeper than most men I know. He is definitely one of the lucky few who has combined the love of his life with his profession.

Following the predicted script, only a jack each provided any sport and by lunchtime a move of location was on the cards. Interestingly, the echo sounder had shown that no bait fish whatsoever were present and these are a vital ingredient in any successful pike recipe, especially in a large, open expanse like a broad. We upped anchor and headed towards the town in the hope of finding a sign of life.

Herrings and smelts splashed down on the surface and we kept our fingers crossed that an esox would hear the call. Alas, they attracted little attention, with only John tempting just a single small fish. The boat though, gave us total freedom and a move was once again on the cards.

The three of us made the decision to head back out of the town and, at last, we got the break we needed, even if it came from the most unlikely source. A cormorant, normally the bane of all anglers, popped up onto the water's surface before taking fright and flying

Broadland dawn.

Normally, in my experience, the bright lights always seem to be a magnet for fish. Quite why I'm not sure as the water temperature is exactly the same, but perhaps they do in fact enjoy the company of humans after all.

As we zig-zagged slowly down the broad we kept our eyes peeled on the echo sounder. We all knew that if we found the prey fish, the predators wouldn't be far away. But nothing so much as flickered on the screen. Where exactly were they? Reaching the end bay we decided to drop anchor and fan out an array of baits.

off. Now, although we had the latest modern technology in the form of an echo sounder, it would have been foolish to ignore the possibility that the cormorant's inbuilt fish-finding device was better than ours.

As we cruised into this area the lights on the echo sounder lit up brighter than those on a Christmas tree. Amazingly, a vast shoal of bream and roach seemed to be at home in an area that we would, in all probability, have passed by. Mother Nature really does have all the answers; you just have to learn how to read the signs. `

Silver fish, as explained, equal pike so, unsurprisingly, we dropped anchor and set about getting the rods out. The day had reached the point where it was do or die - there seemed little point in moving off the area so we settled down with some mince pies for the wait ahead.

Perhaps half-an-hour had passed when John's free-running multiplier spool ticked into life - the lamprey section had been grabbed some 15 yards behind the boat. He slowly and deliberately engaged the reel and swept the rod back firmly...only to be met with a brick wall. John allowed himself a characteristic chuckle before setting about gaining some line. The fight wasn't spectacular, instead a dogged heavyweight hung low down in the water, remaining completely unseen for quite some time. All we could do was wait and see. Finally we got our first sighting when we glimpsed a tail pattern – boy, John was attached to a very big fish!

Immediately I threw away the glove I had on in preparation for chinning the fish and reached for the net. There was no room for error. It never ceases to amaze me how your luck can change so quickly. For the best part of the day we had sat without a bite, each passing minute adding to the growing despondency. Then, out of the blue, our world had turned upside down and dejection had turned to joy.

John clamped down on the spool and the pike was pulled upwards through the gloomy water. Collectively we held our breath as a huge, mottled green back broke the surface – this was a kipper! I gently scooped her up and John let out a bellowing laugh. What a jammy devil – the old pro had come good for a TV camera once again.

Both of us guessed she would be a good twenty pounder but when I lifted her we had to revise that a little. She was one big girl and the scales settled on 27lb 8oz.It was John's biggest pike for a decade and his joint biggest-ever on film. Magic stuff. The anchor was immediately pulled up and we headed to the pub for celebratory drinks. Toasting

John's success I decided there and then that if I ever needed anyone to catch a fish to save my life, I would definitely choose John. With the job essentially done on the first session and with a specimen we never expected, we decided to spend the next day on the lower Waveney. Unfortunately, as much as Lady Luck had smiled on us while we'd been on Oulton Broad, she now frowned in equal proportions. In calm, overcast conditions we flogged away for a single pike. John's assessment was that sport had been affected because of the unusually high tide, which had meant that the river ran off for most of the day. The fish, therefore, had spent the entire time fighting the elements, not feeding.

So for our final day we headed back to the broad and the scene of our success. We went without any expectations of another big fish, instead it would give Hugh a chance to get the extra shots required to build a better sequence. For me this unseen work had been a hard learning curve. The angler in you wants to do one thing, but often the film may require you to do another. Attention to detail is the reason for Hugh's great success and this project demanded a lot of attention to detail!

Still, the job once again provided more than its fair share of pleasure as we hit into a number of double-figure fish and captured plenty of extra footage for the film. This time the long journey back west was made a lot easier knowing that another piece of the jigsaw had been fitted. Would this turn out to be our biggest pike? Only time would tell.

 What a result - a fish so close to our target and caught by the legendary Mr Wilson himself. So lightning can strike twice - and our epic journey, not long started, could hardly get better. So with a big pike in the can we all looked forward to a Christmas break, especially as I was also able to indulge in my first love, trotting for big roach on the Hampshire Avon - and on Dec 22nd I got my Christmas present, a beauty of 2lb 3oz . Now it was time for turkey and relaxing with family and friends.

Jammy old bugger.

Heads You Win - Tails You Lose

 THE Christmas break from work was over all too quickly but we still had our New Year gathering to look forward to, a tradition that has lasted for nearly thirty years. Two film-making friends and their families always join up with us to celebrate the past and the future in each other's homes - and I suppose the surprise in this day and age is that we are all still married to our first wives!

As good as it gets.

Why roach – and I'm talking big roach here - have become appealing to so many anglers is a mystery but maybe it's just their air of the unknown that makes them so highly coveted. All of us would-be redfin catchers have experienced days when you can be in what you think is the right swim in the right conditions but don't catch. It happens so often that being driven crazy like this becomes the norm. But when that trotted float finally disappears and you feel that unfamiliar thumping of a big roach in the current you are cured .....until it rolls off near the net and a nervous breakdown follows.

In my wife Sue's case it is a bit of a miracle. Not only does she have to put up with the long absences of a wildlife film-maker but also those of a keen fisherman! On this particular occasion we gathered to celebrate and view our snow leopard film on ITV, a Himalayan marathon that had been seven years from inception to completion. Then the Asian tsunami hit and our film was postponed. However disappointed we all were, it was inconsequential when compared with the tragedy and suffering of so many people.

Sue knows I'm a long-term sufferer and realises that I'm a lot easier to live with (not much she says!) if I've been roach fishing, so puts up with my obsession. Even just a few hours fishing cures most ills and if I've actually caught a roach I'm a happy man. If that roach happens to be over 1lb then that's a good one, though one of more than 2lb is always the target.

Back in the world of the keen angler, Martin and I were excited because it was winter and time to add yet another challenge to our list of unfulfilled dreams - a 3lb roach. I was still a child when I caught my first big one, a fish of 10oz, which, following the minnows, gudgeon and small perch us boys had initially caught was stupendous. I became a roach angler for life and every winter that is pretty much all I ever fish for.

When roach breed, a female lays at least 200,000 eggs. Most of these offspring die before they are a year old, let alone survive to school age and grow to weigh a pound, so if one lives to be a teenager she will not just be 'a fish of a lifetime' but a fish in a million. It is easy to understand that a roach of 3lb is indeed 'Impossible'. However, creatures of that size do get caught occasionally, particularly from a certain lake in Oxfordshire and even I managed to catch three in just three visits from that particular roach heaven. Martin and I planned to visit there, with our cameras of course - we even felt that if we did fish there our 'Impossible' target would be too easy. So to add the essential madness to our quest Martin suggested we try to catch a three-pound roach - from a river!

Dream roach.

A bridge too late.

Even non-anglers are aware of the dangers of pollution and dredging, of storms and floods. If the problem of flocks of predatory cormorants is added to this roach-killing recipe then it is easier to understand how a 3lb river roach has become one of the rarest creatures in Britain. They don't get mentioned in wildlife programmes because no one knows they exist. But one or two still do, so within a few days of the New Year celebrations Martin and I were heading towards the most famous big roach swim in southern England, Ibsley Bridge, on the Hampshire Avon.

Almost every year for the past few years, this spot had produced a roach of over 3lb so we hoped that it was only a matter of time before Martin caught one - but just how much time? I have been lucky enough to catch two 3lb river roach but I've been fishing 35 years to do so. Unfortunately, we didn't have quite that long! But leaning over the parapet at dawn we could see that the river was up a little, was carrying a tinge of colour and that the gentle breeze was blowing upstream. It was also overcast and mild - perfect conditions for a big roach - any roach, in fact. But after skillfully trotting a float

through the hot swim from dawn to dusk, Martin failed to entice even a hint of a bite. I tried several swims on both float and ledger and the result was the same. We tried the area on several more occasions when conditions were right, along with other stretches too, and all we caught were chub. We were not alone - nobody we knew caught a roach - not one.

Captivated.

The prime time.

Reinforcements.

We decided we needed to enlist some help, so friends Terry Lampard and Tim Norman joined our quest for two of the river 'Impossibles', both the 3lb roach and the 7lb chub. Tim and Terry have probably achieved these 'Impossibles' more often than any other anglers in the country, so despite the enormity of the task we felt we had a chance of catching at least one of them. So on a sunny day in mid January we met on the banks of the River Stour not far from my home.

Terry knows this stretch of delightfully wooded river really well. He has caught several 7lb chub from it in the past and he kindly led us to one of his most productive swims. Upstream the river runs through a narrow gap between trees, which increases the flow and funnels it under a large willow which sprawls across half the river - a classic chub swim. Terry generously donated the downstream cast to Martin so his bait - a secretly-flavoured chub cake - could lie right under the branches. Terry was using his deadly Nutrabaits Trigga paste which the local chub love, but it was Martin's tip that pulled round first. Sadly, it was a mere 2lb fish that was quickly followed by a three-pounder for Terry. As if to keep honours even, each then caught a 'four, so we were

heading in the right direction, and all the while the river was falling in level and clearing in visibility. Our chances were improving but the fish went off feed and despite trying a variety of delectable looking swims downstream, neither caught another fish - and it was lovely light for filming too.

Next day was dull and drizzling and we were back at the fallen tree. Very little happened despite the improved conditions, just a few twitches of the quiver tips. Then at mid-morning we saw the possible cause, an adult female otter drifting downstream. On seeing us she snorted and dived, then we heard the splash of what sounded like another otter under the tree. No doubt our presence drove them off but we hoped our chances of a big chub hadn't been scuppered (or eaten). However, seeing an otter in broad daylight was a real treat.

The next hour was uneventful until Martin had a little twitch on his quivertip followed by a sharp pull and a strike that met with solid resistance. This chub was obviously of a serious calibre because Martin's rod took on an alarming curve as the fish tried to drag his tackle into the tree roots. Judging by the heavy thumps he was sure this was our seven-pounder, but just as hopes were raised they sank. The chub reached her sanctuary and everything went solid. Steady pulling, even slack line, did nothing apart from move the branches of the tree so Terry, who can't swim, ventured courageously out onto the flimsy branches with a landing net handle in the hope of freeing the fish from the snag. All that achieved was to confirm that the fish was still attached, so as desperate situations require desperate measures, I nipped home to get a pruning saw. If we had to land both chub and tree then that's what we would do. But when I returned the chub had already gone and Martin was inspecting his frayed line with a tear in his eye. Our *'Impossible'* fish had become just that, and despite trying a few more swims, our hearts weren't in it - we'd have to try another day.

Our filming now went through a whole series of failures as we chased our elusive dreams. If river conditions were right, we'd try for roach, if the water was clear we'd try for chub, and if it was

Searching for silver.

warm I joined Pete Orchard for some river carping. He is the keeper on the famous Longford beat on the Hampshire Avon and being a keen and expert carp angler he landed some beautiful commons for the camera up to 14lb or so. We were after a twenty-pounder of course but the gorgeous colours of the carp's golden scales made up for their lack of size.

On one notable day he caught three lovely carp, making the most of one of those perfect days when everything in the river was biting. In between his carp catches I had to have a few casts and trotting casters down mid-river with a small topper float I caught eleven chub to well over 5lb, some clonking dace and, joy of joys, a 2lb 5oz roach. However, as those who know the Hampshire Avon well, it can be a moody river and on most occasions it seems lifeless. Our attempts for our giant roach were fruitless despite thousands of biteless trots and hours of unquivering tips.

However, on any days that seemed suitable I'd join Terry on the River Stour in the hope of catching our giant chub. We fished lots of promising looking swims, all of which had produced impossible-sized chub for Terry in the past, but all they yielded this time were 5lb fish. Then, on a lovely sunny day in late February, with the river running low and clear, we all met at the bridge with renewed enthusiasm and Terry scrambled down the bank to fish the fallen willow swim. This time though, he was on the opposite side of the river from where Martin had been smashed up.

Trotting a float down to the offending branches and spraying maggots every cast, Terry was soon catching chub, but only 3lb fish. However, we hoped a big one might be tempted out from its secure lair under the tree and on the next trot down I zoomed in on the float as it approached the branches.

The timing was perfect. The float plunged down and on striking Terry felt the solid thumps of a good fish. He quickly became disheartened by the lack of weight, then delighted when it rolled on the surface

Happy snap.

connected with something serious under the tree and it was a case of 'hang on and pray'. The rod kicked violently two or three times, a barbel crossed our minds, then the crisis was over as the fish kited across the current and out of immediate danger. The fish stayed deep for a while and headed upstream towards the snags under another tree, but Terry soon convinced the battler that it was losing the war and it rolled on the surface, a huge chub the likes of which I

to reveal red fins and silver sides. It was a pristine roach which when finally landed weighed 2lb 2oz - a lovely fish and a lovely bit of film. Terry continued spraying maggots and on his next trot down the take was so violent that the chub 'straight-rodded' him and smashed the line, much to the amusement of Tim and Martin who were quick to offer advice such as Mr Crabtree's, "now Peter, keep the rod up"! But the last laugh was Terry's, for he soon

had never seen. There was a bit more give and take, then it was in the net and gently weighed - all 7lb 4oz of its bronze beauty. Photos taken and congratulations accepted with a warm smile, Terry slid his 'Impossible' chub carefully into the current and with one wriggle it was gone.

Terry comes good.

Make or Break

 DESPITE our success with Terry's giant chub, Martin and I were aware that time for our first winter's filming was flying by and though we had almost always managed to avoid working weekends in the interest of family harmony, we had been flat out during weekdays. Apart from the filming, Martin had the demanding task of producing a big fish, good photographs and a thousand-word story for his Angling Times feature every week. There was no let up whatsoever.

Crystal clear.

We also had a series of films to complete before the turn of the next century and we still had most of our species to catch. Two of these are classic winter fish and we'd set our sights on a 1lb dace and a 3lb grayling, both rare fish in a climate of declining rivers.

Fortunately we both had friends who might be able to help us with the location of these monsters and mine is a river keeper on a beautiful stretch of the upper Kennet, Rob Starr. These delightful crystal clear chalk stream might be suffering from years of abstraction and drought but they still provide some of the most desirable trout fishing in the world. What sets Rob's beats apart from many is the enlightened policy of leaving the coarse fish to swim free in what is essentially a mixed fishery. He argues that predators are more likely to catch roach or dace than his prize trout, so they help maintain the balance of nature. What is more, the roach and dace produce numerous young offspring, providing fattening meals for the native brown trout so everyone is happy.

This enlightened attitude also provides additional income for the estates that practice this thoughtful river management, because once the trout season is over they can let out the beats to anglers who enjoy fishing for coarse fish or grayling... and this is where we hoped to benefit too. Rob knew of several places where he'd seen grayling that might fulfil our dreams, so when it was too cold for us to continue blanking with big roach we were invited up to see if we could catch one.

 The first thing that struck me was the water's clarity. 'Gin clear' is a phrase often used within the angling world but never could this have been more appropriate to describe the picturesque tributary of the Kennet called the Lambourne. The midday sun illuminated the shallow gravel runs stripped bare of weed by the grip of winter and each stone shone out brightly. It was a pleasure to just walk the bank and the occasional brown trout darted off in a startled fashion as they desperately tried to find cover. The surrounding landscape was certainly worthy of adorning any Christmas card.

Such was the icy air temperature that every breath I drew in was cool, crisp and clean, while every one I exhaled caused billowing steam to rise in the air as if my mouth was a smoking chimney. It was a day that made me glad to be alive. Feeling suitably stimulated by the fresh conditions, I was really looking forward to an afternoon's grayling fishing.

Unlike many fish in the UK, this species has no fear of the cold, in fact they positively relish it. As long as the river runs clear the 'lady of the stream' can be relied upon to play ball. Our main challenge was to locate their whereabouts and once this had been achieved I felt certain success would follow. Even though they are magnificent creatures with power in their tails to spare, grayling aren't the brightest of fish and have among the lowest IQ of all our freshwater species. Fortunately for the angler, their stomachs rule their heads and finesse is not normally required.

As already explained, with the shallows bare it didn't take a genius to figure out where our prize would be

hiding – the deep pools which give cover from the beady eyes of predators such as cormorants. Our first port of call was a tumbling weir pool that spewed white water from its sill. I suspected this is where the grayling would be hiding and I just needed to whet their appetites with a starter of red maggots.

To introduce my feed by hand would have been pointless. It would have been dragged in all directions by the flow and I suspected barely a grub would have found its target. Instead, I felt it was best to reach for a tool called a bait-dropper. Once filled up, this container of maggots can be lowered through the surface chaos and into calmer water at the river's bed. And when the contraption touches the bottom the hinged door springs open and releases its cargo exactly where you want it. Half-a-dozen droppers later and I was confident that my free offerings had aroused some interest - it was now time for the tackle.

Usually I trot for grayling but in such conditions I could not be certain of my positioning in respect of

the loosefeed. Therefore I opted for a little practised method called stret pegging. While the float's bulk shot is placed hard on the deck, the float itself is fished over depth, allowing an underwater bow of line to form. Once a bite causes the shot to move the tension is transmitted to the surface and the float submerges in a traditional manner. By fishing a static bait like this I could be certain of its placement over the free offerings. With a few turns of my centrepin's drum I lowered the hookbait into position – if grayling were present I suspected it wouldn't be long before I found out.

My suspicions proved to be well founded and seconds later the float dragged under – I was into my first grayling of the day. The battle with this dynamic fish can be a long one, primarily because it is blessed with a huge dorsal fin that, once erected, it uses as an underwater sail to catch the river's fast flow and kite from left to right. But that's not all. Even when manoeuvred into calmer water, its wiry, muscle-bound body can produce powerful surges that can test an angler's skill to the very limit. It was just a case of being patient and allowing my

tackle to take the strain until at last I netted our first grayling. Being nearer 2lb than 1lb it was a pleasing start and as their greed overcame them, another half-a-dozen fish made my wrist ache. However pleasing as this was they fell short, by some distance, of our 'Impossible' target so Hugh and I felt it was time for a move – new ground had to be searched out in our quest.

After a long stretch of shallows the river bore sharply to the right and disappeared momentarily under a foot bridge. From here it re-emerged into a narrow neck before pouring over a concrete sill into a pool. I could not describe it as a weir, more of a disturbance, but either way it was to the grayling's liking and sitting stationary with their heads facing into the flow sat at least a dozen fish. Like a giant magnifying glass, the river's clarity allowed us to observe every detail. These, we immediately established, were definitely bigger fish.

Just like before, I enlisted the help of the baitdropper, not this time to counter the turbulence but because of the sheer power of water that was

Dorset Frome.

A lovely lady.

pushing in front of me. My float could now be slid down into a trotting position, cocked by three swan shot and connected to 3lb line. A size 18 hook, carrying a couple of red maggots, finished it off.

As the pool was no more than twenty feet long I held the outfit back hard as I tried to maximize the time my bait was in the zone. With each trot I increased the depth until the maggots hit the spot and my float buried without ceremony or warning. My success though, was short-lived and before I had time to celebrate the grayling had gone. Minutes later we re-enacted the same scenario. I would have been glad to take the blame if it had been my inadequacies but grayling are masters at shedding the hook and losses are an occupational hazard. On the third trot down I at last struck lucky and I was finally able to sample the delights of the pool. Awash with pinks and purples, I hoisted a classic example of the species ashore and admired a true winter's gift. At 2lb 4oz it was not a fish to be sniffed at but when blinkered by targets I couldn't help but wonder if our *'Impossible'* fish just wasn't in the swim. And so it proved.

As the dying embers of sunlight bled from the sky I enjoyed the company of a few more ladies but the giant we so craved did not appear and I felt a thousand casts would not find one. Not on this river anyway. We needed to journey south and fish a place many believe is grayling utopia – home of monsters and, perhaps more importantly, the stomping ground of an old friend.

Tumbling down through the deepest reaches of Dorset is a river which for some reason produces grayling of Jurassic proportions; quite why I am not sure. Perhaps it is the exceptionally high quality of the water that holds the key to their success. Perhaps too it is the natural larder packed with shrimps, leeches and molluscs, that help in their exceptional growth rates. Or maybe the simple truth is that so few coarse fish share their home that they are able to gorge without hindrance. Whatever the truth, if you want to catch a monster grayling then the Dorset Frome is the place to be.

By the time of our arrival my companion for the day was already in position. In the distance I could see

Simple and stout.

his silhouette breaking up the contours of a sweeping bend, while in front of him water sparkled in the dappled half-light of daybreak. As I crept along the river a flock of white geese watched me closely from the far bank, barking their disapproval – they hadn't expected to be disturbed so early on a winter's morning.

Before I had a chance to say hello, the angler swiftly lifted his rod into the air before it lurched over and he connected with what was obviously a good fish. As expected, the fight was savage and

the grayling strained every sinew as it twisted and turned in a vain attempt to shed the hook. But to no avail. A gorgeous grey flank soon hit the surface and within seconds it found itself within the mesh of the angler's net. I arrived just as the weighing scales settled on 2lb 2oz and made my acquaintance with the captor in the most fitting way possible – by sharing a magical fishing moment.

The lucky man was Pete Reading, a true gentleman of the piscatorial world. Not only is he adept in the art of trotting, but in all the skills needed to tempt big fish from his favoured counties of Dorset and Hampshire. But the reason why I have such respect for this man is not because of his impressive list of specimens but for the fact that he is one of the few men who puts more in than he takes out. Local angling clubs and, more recently, the Barbel Society have benefited from his conservation work. In this day and age, when time is so precious, it's rare to find a person who cares more about wider environmental issues than personal gain. On this occasion though, Hugh and I had decided to call on Pete's skill and knowledge to help us in the pursuit of our *'Impossible'* – 3lb grayling and with the

Grayling weather.

pleasantries over I headed for the swim above him to try my luck.

For this type of fishing I needed little more than a couple of pints of red maggots inside a bait pouch and a very simple tackle set up. A 13ft rod was combined with a centrepin reel and loaded with 3.2lb monofilament connected to a large loafer float. Fancy shotting patterns have no place in the world of grayling so the bulk was set at three-quarter depth followed by two dropper shot. The first was a No 6 and the second a micro swivel – a great little trick that prevents the hooklength from spinning up in the fast flow.

As with most forms of float fishing, I opted for a little-and-often feeding approach that I hoped would trigger the grayling into taking the bait and after half-a-dozen trots the bulbous fluorescent float tip was dragged under. The first few seconds of the battle were typically erratic before the fish swung out into the faster flow and erected its huge dorsal fin to strain my hook hold to the maximum - and

beyond. Once again I found myself a rather frustrated angler with the rod now straight and line hanging limp. It was a typical start to a grayling day.

Once the shoal had found a liking to the maggots I knew another encounter wouldn't be far away. A spooked fish re-entering the shoal won't prevent their urge to gorge, indeed it would come as no surprise to discover that the same individual specimen had begun feeding again. When the next bite arrived I was careful to steer my competitor away from the quicker water and allow it to tire itself in the slack. Eventually the fish rose upwards and its body became exposed to the air. For this individual its life span was nearly over. Not that I had any intention of ending it prematurely, it was just that the normally grey flank had darkened to be nearly black – a key sign of old age. For this fish, its seven year cycle from birth to death was almost complete.

I coaxed my prize into the waiting landing net but struggled to grab hold, such was the power still present. Slowly I lifted it close to my nose, taking in a deep breath - but I'm afraid the smell of thyme eluded me. The grayling's Latin name is 'Thymallus Thymallus', a name given to it for the herby smell it exudes when freshly caught. And although this older specimen had lost its aroma it was still a handsome creature at 2lb. None the worse for wear from its close encounter I slipped it back and continued with my trotting. Pete and I plundered many fish that day along the pools and runs but it wasn't until the last swim, a small weir pool, that he wielded the dreaded swim

But, for me, it's this banter and leg pulling that makes a day on the bank with a friend so special and is often more important than what is actually caught.

Anyway, Pete was having none of my protests and explained the turbulence within the pool would not allow a bait to be fished successfully in any other manner. At this point I decided to protest no longer and bow to his superior knowledge as, after all, he has caught more grayling than I've had hot dinners. Gently the hookbait was lowered into position by an

Close enough.

feeder in an attempt to catch us an *'Impossible'*. How could he even think about using such a monstrosity?

Grayling, as we've already established, are not the sharpest pencils in the box when it comes to guile and by using a float as a means of catching them seems to somehow even the contest out. Using a swimfeeder, as I jokingly told him, was akin to shooting chickens in a battery farm. Either way, to a non-angler we must have appeared mad to even be discussing the merits of a guaranteed fish-catching tactic on such a cold and difficult winter's afternoon.

unrepentant Pete. The flow grabbed hold of the line and pulled tension into the quivertip – the tool which would now supply the bite indication. Less than 60 seconds later the tip was savagely dragged round as the maggots were devoured with gusto. Pete commenced battle with a good fish and the risk of a hook pull was only too apparent as the grayling spun like a Devon minnow in the fast flow. His tiny hook was the only thing that was keeping him in contact with what was obviously a very big fish and the tension of the situation was etched all over his face. Was this the *'Impossible'* we dreamed of?

After a minute or two I was able to carefully slip the net into position and Pete drew her up into the mesh. It was total vindication for choosing the swimfeeder and with genuine delight, and not a little relief, we shook hands and gently lifted the prize onto the unhooking mat. She looked stunning as she lay there, her torso dappled with such vivid colours that they almost burst from the canvas of small grey scales. It didn't seem to matter that at 2lb 12oz she was a fraction away from our goal. Frustration gave way to wonderment as we stood and admired her in the late afternoon sun.

Starting its life in the Marlborough Downs, the Kennet winds its way through some of England's finest countryside. In the upper reaches the chalk-filtered water sparkles over meadows and feeds countless carriers no more than a foot deep. This landscape may at first seem natural but over the centuries has in fact has been shaped by man and, for once, his meddling has been to the benefit of fish.

Dotted along these waterways are tiny pools that form where sluices and weirs spew out their liquid

The best way to spend a day.

Having enjoyed such great company in the stunning countryside it was impossible to be disappointed at the result. Instead it was a reminder that we needed to put our targets into perspective. Although they remained important to the success of the project, we couldn't let them become the only factor that determined whether a day had been enjoyable or not. It was time to shake hands and head for home. The winter was passing us by and it felt as if we still had everything to do. Roach and dace were on our radar now and a return to Berkshire seemed the best place to try.

treasure and it's here, perhaps unsurprisingly, that the trout holds sway. Brownies and rainbows jostle to be top dog, eagerly awaiting the next unfortunate fly or fry to feed their voracious appetites. But hidden within these waters are creatures much more special to me, creatures that have far more worth than those sought after with intricately-tied daddy-longlegs or Buzzers. Fly fishing may be for gentlemen but give me a roach or dace any day of the week.

Go back twenty years to the 1980s and this place was truly a theatre of dreams. Roach to 3lb and

In you come.

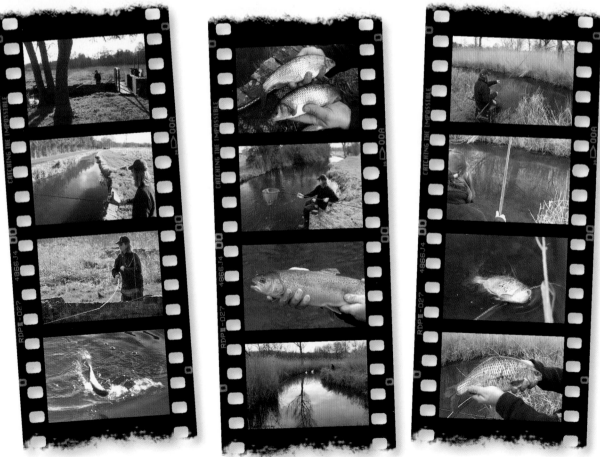

dace topping 1lb grazed through silkweed, feeding at will in their rich, plentiful environment. Alas though, this was a period when I had yet to acquaint myself with the finer things in life and was probably lost to carp in a bivvy on some windswept pit. How I wish I could go back in a time machine and fish for those magnificent, yet tragically rare, creatures.

The intervening years have not been kind to the upper Kennet. Pollution and cormorants have reduced the silver fish stocks dramatically, leaving the real giants in such short supply that they are like finding a needle in a haystack. But who really cares? This is some of the country's finest fly fishing water so surely nobody is bothered if the roach and dace populations are in short supply? Well, Dave Culley and Nigel Wilson care. They care deeply. Both are river keepers and these guys live and breathe the Kennet, putting countless hours in to ensure that a small slice of heaven is maintained. Due to their efforts the coarse fish are finding a foothold once again but knowing they are there is one thing, catching them is another altogether. Could we do it? Only time would tell.

The weather had at last provided us with a window of opportunity so it was with haste that we headed to the river. With thick cloud cover and mild temperatures it was the perfect fish-catching day so when Hugh and I arrived on the banks of the Kennet we hurriedly searched for treasure coated in scales of silver. We left the tackle behind and crept along the bank, peering into every nook and cranny but all we could find was clean gravel - there seemed to be no sign of fish life whatsoever. The once abundant coarse stocks had clearly been decimated but we remained convinced that, somewhere in the crystal clear water, there had to be something, somewhere. We continued our hunt to find creatures that had avoided man's ever growing lust to destroy Britain's waterways.

Two hours later our prayers were answered. A shoal containing a dozen roach and a dozen dace

headed upstream, dividing into two at the fork in the river. Both groups, probably the last remnants of a bygone era, held station over lush green weed and hung there oblivious to our presence. It was doubtful that any of the roach hit the magic 3lb mark but neither of us was going to turn down the chance of a two-pounder. The dace though, were true goliaths and there was every chance that an 'Impossible' was present.

On this occasion we decided to double our chances and Hugh left the camera behind in preference for a rod. He decided to take the downstream fish while I hid myself in a reedbed ten yards above the second group. Both of us opted for 11ft rods combined with ultra-light glass quivertips. A simple link-leger with just a single swan shot to hold bottom was coupled with hooklengths 5ft in length to avoid alarming our quarry. For an hour I steadily trickled in a stream of red maggots which had been laced in a secret additive. Would this make a difference? I couldn't be sure but like so many anglers I was willing to grab any possible edge available to increase my confidence. Slowly the grubs began to stir the fish below, their

Silver darts.

Willing roach for a change.

fins twitching as excitement levels increased. It was clearly noticeable though, that it was only the roach that were making these movements. The dace, I suspected, were already in the throws of passion. Had the mild conditions triggered the spawning ritual? Would they be more interested in procreation than feeding?

Whatever my chances, it was time to make a cast. Feathering the line, the rig gently broke the surface and I allowed a bow of line to form before watching the flow tension the tip. Shadows still lurked downstream – the dace hadn't scattered in alarm. A handful of maggots headed their way to calm any anxiety that they may have felt from the disturbance. It wasn't long before my tip began to tap before being dragged round and I was quickly on my feet with my rod arched as, in typical fashion, a roach swirled below before hitting the surface. Hook pulls are a fact of life in the soft, white mouths of these beautiful creatures so the fight is always fraught with tension. But on this occasion I was lucky and 2lb 4oz of silver scales soon sat beaten in the bottom of my net. Unsurprisingly for a fish of that size it was an old warrior but where big roach are concerned you cannot afford to be choosey.

It came as no shock when my shoal scattered at the commotion so I crept round to see how Hugh was faring. Already sitting in the landing net was a plump roach of 1lb 6oz and in the slightly deeper water the group had remained intact. Were they willing to feed again? The answer was a resounding 'yes' as his tip pulled round. Why do big roach always boil on the surface when hooked? I don't know but true to form this one did too. We could both see the fish spinning in the flow, trying to gain its freedom but the soft rod absorbed the tension and enabled Hugh to slowly gain the upper hand.

Another good fish soon found its way into the landing net and pulled the scales down to a hefty 2lb 5oz. With two specimens banked we would have had every reason to be happy but I couldn't help feeling a little disappointed. While the roach of our dreams wasn't present the dace certainly were and we had failed to make the grade once again.

'Failed' may seem a strong word but this is how I felt .Was it my lack of ability or Mother Nature cruelly conspiring against us? One thing was certain though, the pressure of filming suddenly hit me like a ton of bricks. We needed a breakthrough and with only pike and perch left on our agenda in the winter months, the tide needed to turn and turn quickly. To end the season with only one *'Impossible'* – Terry's chub - was a prospect not even worth thinking about.

Many days had been spent in pursuit of our film during the winter months and while far from successful in a fish-catching sense, I could, at least fall back on the fact that the methods we were employing were enjoyable. But I'm afraid what follows couldn't be described as fun.

'Ten rod Nige'

Nige Williams is a man who could catch pike out of a swimming pool and his tally of monsters is unsurpassed in angling history. So when the need for a thirty-pounder arose we knew who to call. But great angler though he is, I make no bones about saying that Nige is a pike fishing pirate. Bending of rules are his speciality, in fact Hugh's wife Sue nick-named him 'Ten rod Nige' during the filming and there is little he wouldn't do to catch a big pike. However, in the same way as Captain Jack Sparrow,

the star of Pirates of the Caribbean, is a loveable rogue, Nige is exactly the same.

So, promising to be on his best behaviour, we entrusted Nige to come up with perhaps the most difficult task of all – locating a giant pike. Such is the rarity of the species, we knew this could be the toughest of all *'Impossibles'* to catch on camera. Nige though, came up trumps. Typically of this larger than life character, he didn't just find a lake that held a

It's good to suffer.

'thirty', oh no, he dared whisper the word 'forty' too. Surely not?

We weren't about to question a man with a nose so well tuned to sniffing out huge predators so, like treasure hunters following a forgotten map, we became instantly captivated in the quest and set forth immediately to the sleepy village of Haslemere in Surrey.

I had become so intoxicated by this adventure that my mind had somehow conveniently pushed to the back what really lay ahead. I hate sleeping in a bivvy during long, dark winter nights and somehow I had agreed to do six of them with little more to do than shelter from the cold and wait for our giant pike to feed. I could now re-tell the story with a day-by-day account of how my spirits began to sap away in a manner more akin to Captain Scott but I won't, as I personally don't want to revisit the nightmare. A special mention has to go to Nige and the lake's owner, Robin, for being such wonderful hosts as they tried to encourage me but I'm afraid my heart wasn't in it. Dark, cold nights should be spent in bed cuddling up with my wife and not laying under a sheet of condensation-riddled canvas

in a bloody field. Call me a wimp if you like but I started to question the whole thing. "If this is what it takes to make a fishing film, you can keep it."

Hugh had told me it was good to suffer on a project like ours but I am afraid those thoughts haunted me as the rods were finally put away. Since my early twenties I have been self-employed and having to factor in someone else's opinions and requirements was proving difficult for me to cope with. But above all else the mantle of trying to catch '*Impossibles*' was weighing me down and if I failed I felt as if my confidence would be gone forever. As you might have guessed, the pike never did make an appearance and we left licking our wounds.

A week later news started to filter through on the grapevine that the big girl had been caught. As if to rub salt into the wounds, as well as prove how cruel the angling world can be, it had fallen to a carp angler fishing a boilie of all things! In short, a complete and utter fluke. I didn't know whether to laugh or cry!

Contrary to Martin's impression, I found the wait for Nige's giant pike to bite a bit of a laugh, for it wasn't all mud and moaning. In fact, the banter between Nige, Martin, Robin and myself was highly amusing at times, and I also got to do some roach fishing.

Robin's lake is very beautiful, surrounded as it is with birch trees and rhododendrons and it provided some cracking roach to long range feeder tactics. I could see Nige eyeing them covetously for pike bait but no roach of mine is going to end up being munched, so much to Nige's frustration, he was stuck with sea fish as my roach swam off unharmed.

Apart from good roach fishing, we were entertained by a pair of great-crested grebes. They had evidently decided that winter was over, for their summer plumage was already resplendent. They waved their russet crests at each other, then stood upright beside each other in a courtship dance, running across the surface of the lake with beaks full of weed to indicate that nest-building should commence immediately. This behaviour is one of the most impressive ornithological displays of all but if we needed any further convincing that we had run out of time with our winter dreams, a flock of swallows arrived from Africa to skim insects between the pike floats.

Despite the many attempts, our quest for a giant pike had failed and the enormity of our task was suddenly apparent. We had caught only one 'Impossible' fish all winter and now it was nearly spring.

Spring Struggles

 THE last two weeks of the traditional coarse fishing season are usually a banker when it comes to catching fish - but not for us during this year when we needed it most. We were at a low ebb but felt sure we could still catch one of our 'Impossible' targets, a 4lb perch.

Martin has caught more 4lb perch than any angler in living memory, even taking into account the famous catches of Les Proudfoot on Oulton Broad. Les caught twenty three but at the last count Martin had recorded twenty eight, mainly from the upper Great Ouse. He had also helped others fulfil a lifetime's ambition, but make no mistake, a 4lb perch is a huge fish. For many years in the 70s and 80s you'd be lucky to catch a perch of any size due to a disease that had almost driven them to extinction. But now they are back with a vengeance and lots of anglers are catching perch of over 3lb, even if a genuine four-pounder remains a very rare fish. Thankfully, Martin knew where a few of these monsters might be hiding and he certainly knew how to catch them. However, the pressure to succeed was increasing with every passing day and as a result our dream was turning into a nightmare. We had just spent two days on the Gt Ouse and failed to attract even a bite.

 I couldn't believe it – the 4lb perch had managed to slip through my fingers once again! Catching a big fish is all about confidence, something which all who know my psyche would agree I thrive on. Tip me out of kilter, however, and I struggle to operate. The films, or should I say the noose around my neck, had thrown me off balance. I admit that the pressure I felt was all of my own making but if you start off with the word 'Impossible' in the title it's never going to be easy. Of course it's great when you achieve your goal, not so good when you don't and I knew that unless I reached these 'Impossibles' I would be broken.

For the first time I can ever remember I no longer wanted to go fishing – the series was in the balance and I don't know if Hugh ever realised how close I had come to walking away. Perhaps he felt the same and who could blame him? Being very independent, I struggle to cope with working closely with anyone else. I needed to trust Hugh more and perhaps he needed to do the same with me. If left to my own devices I was sure I could deliver but this was not an option, because you can't make a TV series without a camera. For the film, having an angler as the cameraman is a godsend but for the angler being filmed it can be a nightmare. It felt like a critic was watching my every move and it was horrible, especially to a person like me who, I freely admit, hates criticism and doesn't like being watched! Sometimes you have to make mistakes to eventually achieve success – I just needed some space.

To help me with my soul-searching I sought the wisdom of the only two men that I knew had experienced these quandaries – John Wilson and Chris Yates. Both men provided the shoulder I needed but it was perhaps Chris's words which guided me the most. "Allow Hugh to work his magic and all the hard times will be worthwhile," he said. He should know, having trodden the same rocky road that eventually led to 'A Passion for Angling.'

I hoped that the spring would see a new outlook, where my insecurities would be banished and my mindset return to how it was before filming started. I would catch these fish but I would do it my way and in return I would trust that the film, under Hugh's guidance, was going to be a success. If we could just get the film back on track everything would fall into place. Both Hugh and I are 100% men and surely between us we could save this sinking ship.

 Knowing that Martin was struggling was no surprise given the size of the challenge we had taken on and it reminded me of a quote that I'd copied into my journal: "Success is not the key to happiness, happiness is the key to success. If you love what you are doing you will be successful."

THE WILDLIFE SPECIAL
WITH DAVID ATTENBOROUGH

TIGER

Natural History Unit

I knew that we both loved what we were doing and that given time, we would be able to mend the leaks in the sinking ship, even if it was the weather and river conditions that were the true cause of our problems.

As all anglers are aware, fishing success is dependent on reading the signs and signals nature gives us, and as I'd spent nearly fifty years making wildlife films, I guess my instincts might be finer tuned than most. So, at least one of the things I have learnt over the years is the value of patience and perseverance when conditions are conspiring against you.

For instance, while filming tigers in India for a BBC David Attenborough special we were seriously hampered by bureaucratic politics but patiently manoeuvred our way around the obstructions to win an Academy Award for the finished film. In South America's Andes Mountains we had to suffer the tragedy of poachers killing our big cats in the National Park. However, we persevered and luckily the mountain lion that I'd spent four months habituating to my presence survived to become our star. I named her Penny. Then while filming snow leopards in the Himalayas we twice had to evacuate our cameraman from high in the mountains due to altitude sickness and if we hadn't succeeded he'd have died. In comparison, our failure to catch large fish when the weather was against us was comparatively easy to put up with, even if it was frustrating at the time.

One of Martin's greatest assets is his professionalism so I felt sure that he would quickly regain his composure and confidence, especially as another of his great assets is his determination. So, as expected, within a few days he had recovered from

Looking for lunch.

Penny the Puma.

Snow leopard tracks at 17,000ft.

CASHZONE

```
DATE       TIME   SEQ NUMB  ATM ID
08\02\21  16:15   8390      E014898
COOPERATIVE DA5 1BT     BEXLEY HEATH
CARD NUMBER: XXXXXXXXXXXX2225
AID: A0000000291010
WITHDRAWAL      :  £30.00
```

ACCOUNT BALANCE	£3169.02
AVAILABLE BALANCE	£2094.62

DID YOU KNOW BALANCE ENQUIRIES ARE FREE?

PLEASE RETAIN OR DISPOSE OF THOUGHTFULLY

his recent frustrations and we were back on the trail of our giant perch. Hope springs eternal, especially in an angler and there were no shortage of places we were assured held huge perch. In fact it seemed that almost every water in the country had a story about four-pounders. But which ones were true? An angler who has a lifetime's experience with big fish, like Martin, grows cynical of angler's tall stories and the accuracy of their fish-weighing skills. That's not to say fisherman are natural liars, they are just imaginative with the truth!

Anyway, we'd been told about an old gravel pit in the Cotswold Water Park that had an enviable reputation for big perch, so once the river season had ended we arranged to meet our informant on its wooded banks, a great friend of Martin's - Terry Theobold.

Theo is one of the most enthusiastic anglers I know, always trying to grab a few hours to wet a line in between his job on the railways. He is also a generous friend who, over the years, has put me onto countless big fish. Ever willing to help, Theo was on hand to pick me up from my failure to catch a 4lb Ouse perch and he had just the tonic – a pit on the Cotswold Water Park which perhaps had hidden within its depths the stripey of our dreams.

So shortly after the rivers had shut down for the closed season we accompanied Theo to the water in question to continue our quest. The pit was typical of other venues in the area, windswept and crystal clear, its rich aquatic life and surrounding fauna testimony to the creation of something positive after intrusive gravel extraction. The whole of the water park, even if a little raw around the edges, will, I'm sure, go on to provide anglers with a wonderful environment to enjoy, especially as per square mile there is more water here than in the Norfolk Broads!

Luckily we had been given the use of a boat which would help us search out every nook and cranny of its six acres. During the previous evening at the local curry house we had formulated a plan, instead of worms or fish baits we'd attempt to use spinners and plugs to begin with. This mobile approach would allow us to cover a large area quickly and should we be lucky enough to locate a shoal of perch, the bait rods could then be used to target a specific spot.

Slowly but surely we tracked around the lake, investigating every likely looking feature that we highlighted on the echo sounder. Occasionally a pike would raise our hopes, snapping and snarling at the artificial; we also had a rather bizarre encounter with a carp. While retrieving a silver spinner a fish of well over 20lb followed it in alongside the boat. In the gin clear water we could make out the flank of a mirror carp but unfortunately it drifted away and we were never to see it again. The lure had obviously triggered an aggressive response - highly unusual for the species.

By mid-afternoon I was worn out. Hundreds of casts and retrieves had failed to turn up a single perch so I felt it was time for a rest. Putting down my rod I reached into the rucksack for my flask of soup. Theo, meanwhile, had taken a shine to my multi-bladed spinner and asked if he could have a cast. What did it matter? I had covered the water a dozen times, he could waste his energy while I enjoyed a warm drink. But yes, you've guessed it – before I had time to savour the tomato flavour the rod bucked in Theo's hands.

"You jammy so and so," I exclaimed, while all he did was grin! A 2lb perch hit the surface and whacked its tail in anger. The clear water of the lake ensured the colours of the fish were intense and vivid, with jet black stripes tipped with blood-red fins lying on an emerald flank. In short, it was magnificent. Also, and more importantly, it gave us a spot to target with baits. As a shoal fish, where you find one perch, you can nearly always find a few more.

I would now like to be able to recount that I re-took possession of my lure rod and on the very next cast banked a monster. However, Theo took it upon himself to put the spinner into a snag and lost it! Who needs enemies with a mate like that? Still, we were buoyed by the action and with twilight fast approaching the worm rods were readied in the hope of capitalising on our quarry's prime feeding period. We had moved to an area close to some overhanging bushes and I continued to pull Theo's leg over his errant casting, despite him really being the one who had the bragging rights.

Our banter was cut short, however, by a savage bob on his float before it slid away. Once again Theo was into a perch and by the healthy bend in his rod a good one too. Slipping the net into place I waited patiently until the pressure told and the fish surrendered. This too was as exquisite as the first, but a touch bigger at 2lb 12oz. Alas, this wasn't a prelude to greater things. Instead it drew our perch action to a close for the day and, for that matter, the year. With spawning just around the corner it was time to leave them alone and all we could hope for was a better result the following year. Yes, it hurt to finish with a failure once again but for now there was nothing I could do to put it right.

As one door closed another opened. For an angler who follows the seasons, there is never a period in the calendar when one fish or another can't be targeted, so with the sun shining longer northerly winds switching to the south our thoughts turned to spring. Catfish were just one of many targets but as they awoke from their winter hibernation with hungry bellies we wouldn't have a better time to snare one - our goal being a fish of 40lb.

Roy Parsons of Linear Fisheries in Oxfordshire had bent my ear on several occasions about the monster moggies which live in St John's Lake. So it was here that the spring of 2005 began for Hugh and I, with two nights in pursuit of a whiskered giant. The cats in this lake had grown to over 70lb but not on a diet of fish as you may suspect. No, carp anglers had supplied something much more nourishing – pellets by the wheelbarrow load! Appealing to the catfish's scavenging behaviour, their large mouths could mop up vast quantities and should an angler get in the way, well, they were simply smashed up by these powerful creatures.

Fully aware of this behaviour, I laced my swim heavily with halibut pellets before presenting

Time for stripes.

deadbaits and worms over the top. My tackle needed to be strong so I opted for 40lb braid and purpose-made catfish hooks, which would have been more at home in a butchers! All I could do now was wait and hope that a moggie awoke from its slumbers.

To while away the hours Hugh and I were joined for a spot of early season tenching by my good friend John Everard. Equally spaced along the bank, our floatfished baits were presented down the marginal shelf. If the cats weren't playing ball the tench certainly were and it was good to see spring properly heralded in with a string of tincas. Linear also has the added bonus of being an incredibly social environment and rarely did an hour pass without a visitor or two. Peter Drennan, of tackle manufacturing fame, and his daughter, Sally, came to lend support while Roy and his assistant John Newlands not only enjoyed gently winding me up, they also supplied bacon sarnies and endless encouragement.

The cats? Well, they seemed to prefer sleeping and ignored my best endeavours. Even though success had not been achieved I left with a smile on my face – it was good to remind myself that angling is so much more than the fish you catch.

Even if the cats were still hibernating, spring is obviously a time when everything is waking up or arriving from foreign parts. On the last day of the traditional river season a chiffchaff celebrated its safe return after crossing the Sahara, a blackbird started to sing for the first time and on April 4th a mallard hatched thirteen ducklings on our garden pond. The minnows in this pond had already migrated up the stream to spawn and the first big hatches of grannom had fluttered into the air from the Hampshire Avon. Underwater life was stirring everywhere, and there is no better time to bank a big carp than April, particularly if the sun shines.

This is what it's all about.

Carp are now the UK's most popular fish, largely because so many waters have been stocked with them, making them accessible to all. This has been to the detriment of many other species and aquatic life in general but at least carp grow big and fight hard and with the minimum of effort, using the standard bolt rig, they are easy to catch. We naturally wanted a big one for our series and settled on 40lb as our target. Though this might not qualify as an '*Impossible*' in serious carp fishing circles it is still a very big fish and the fact we wanted to catch one from the most beautiful location we could find just added to the challenge.

Martin's friends had told him about a gorgeous lake that nestled in the hills of Shropshire. It is surrounded by woodland and wildlife and holds carp big enough to fulfil our dreams. What is more the owner, Rob Hales, generously allowed us the privilege of fishing it for a few days in mid-April, so we hoped we could repay his kindness by doing justice to his beautiful corner of England.

Some carp anglers might question why we'd chosen this particular lake when other more famous waters were closer to home. The answer is simple and serves to highlight what we hoped to achieve in the TV series. Our intention throughout was to try to portray angling to the general public in the best possible light and we didn't think that carp anglers blanking while living in a bivvy for a year on a gravel pit under the Heathrow flight path quite cut the mustard! So we chose a lovely lake where wildlife abounds and where we could show how an angler becomes immersed in nature. And maybe we'd catch a big carp too.

The dew-filled meadow shimmered almost white with ground frost, providing a visual reminder that the overnight temperatures had approached zero. Cloud had now filled in the clear night sky, creating an almost claustrophobic feel to dawn. Still, with rods in hand and a bucketful of bait we told ourselves that it sure beat working and we headed purposefully towards the waterside.

The rolling hills and woodland of the Shropshire countryside held a jewel within it – and we intended to enjoy every last second of our trip to the mere. Very few had sampled its richness and those anglers who had knew of its monsters. Carp, but not just any carp, lurked within its depths and

The Shropshire mere.

these huge fish had a beauty to match their size and we hoped that at last an 'Impossible' could be achieved. However, our wished-for sun had eluded us once again, replaced by a chill more reminiscent of February than April. I told myself, however, that out there somewhere would be a carp willing to feed and with three days ahead of us there was plenty of time for the weather to change.

Rob Hales, the owner of this magnificent lake, had kindly taken time out to show us the favoured spots but, as always, priority had to go to the swim which offered the best camera angles. Halfway down the bank was a pitch nestled under an old chestnut tree and from here the lake splayed out on both sides. The far bank was in the shadow of a wall of trees, giving an amphitheatre effect to the mere. If you had told me that we were in Canada I would have believed you and so our camp was chosen and lines wetted. With deep water situated to the left and shallows to the right it seemed a

perfect ambush point for that fat old carp we hoped would cross our path.

My three rods were positioned at approximately seventy yards where the lakebed fell away to 8ft, giving a hard, smooth substrate and each one was laced with half a kilo of prawn-flavoured boilies. When carp awaken from their winter slumber I prefer to use boilies as opposed to pellets or particles. These man-made round balls give a hungry fish a quick fix, stemming the famine suffered in cooler times. Carp are greedy creatures so in my experience it's always best to give them plenty of food in spring. What we needed most though was some sun.

As the first day slipped by and the second arrived the canopy of clouds refused to budge. Occasionally a carp would roll on the surface along the deeper dam end as if to torment me. So why didn't I move? Well, filming fishing isn't quite the same as a

normal pleasure trip. Sure, we may have caught if we moved but then our splendid backdrop would no longer be in place and for every fish caught at the dam end it would only make the task harder in the original spot.

You see filming is a compromise between beauty and success. After all, we were not trying to make any old film, but one that captured the very essence of angling. It takes incredible self-control as an angler not to follow your nose and even now I often find myself in turmoil. Patience is the key and as the afternoon of the second day arrived the weather suddenly warmed up.

The wind dropped away and a weak, but distinct, ray of sunshine broke through the clouds. Once penetrated, the gloom offered little resistance as the light values rose. A fly hatch emerged and buzzed in celebration of their freedom. Nature was at last awake and when my bite alarm screamed it heralded the carp's arrival. Before I could reach the rod, line

was torn from the spool. Tempted by those prawn boilies, the carp's natural caution had been replaced by greed and now she was panicking.

With my rod arched the line cut hard right, pulling through the water like a wire through cheese. The atmosphere had changed completely in the blink of an eye and it's at moments like this that I realise why I love fishing so much. A yellowy flank of a big mirror carp rolled, sending ripples across the calm surface as the tackle took its toll, sapping energy away from her enormous rudder.

When the time came to take possession of my prize I gently slipped the net into position under her. My commentary for the camera had long since dried up, only being reinstated as a huge flank fell over the cord and relief flowed over me. It was big, there was no doubting that, but was it 40lb and an 'Impossible'? My suspicions were justified with the scales weighing 36lbs. Soon I had her back in the water and with a single flick of her tail our time together was over.

As quickly as the lake had opened up for us, it once again shut under another bank of cloud. It was time to leave but I felt the groundwork laid on this trip would be rewarded should we ever choose to return. Other species now called and our attention fell further south to targets that I felt were getting closer. My confidence was, at last, beginning to rise.

A boilie feast.

 Despite Martin's success and his more positive frame of mind, our visit to Shropshire just proved to us how vulnerable we were to the fickle English climate - we could so easily lose weeks of filming at critical times of the year. Pressure was mounting on us all the time so we were relieved that we'd given ourselves four years to complete the series.

Summer was approaching fast and this was confirmed during a brief holiday on the Scilly Isles. Migrants were pouring across the sea from Europe and Africa to take advantage of the insect bounty in our green and pleasant land. We counted dozens of species, most numerous being the hirundines - swallows, swifts and House Martins, but most memorable was the Hobby, a small bird-hunting falcon that migrates north with it's food supply. It was spectacular watching it chasing a House Martin above our heads, until it finally caught the unfortunate bird over the sea. As the hobby flew on to England I imagined the bass below, moving towards the shore with the incoming tide and felt sure our freshwater fish would be moving with intent too. It was time to start our summer campaign.

Confidence rising.

Tinca, Tinca

 IF there is one species that heralds the coming of summer more than any other, it is the tench. Ever popular with anglers due to its love of warm weather, its good looks and tenacious fighting qualities, the tench is affectionately nicknamed 'tinca' after its scientific name tinca tinca. If I'm not fishing for roach I love fishing for the red-eyed tench, perhaps because, at times, they share with roach that quality of being fiendishly difficult to catch. When I was an inexperienced angler, I'd be delighted to catch a tench of any size and still have vivid memories of those special dawns when I caught one of over 4lb. In those days the record stood at 8lb 8oz and even Dick Walker would be delighted if he caught a five-pounder.

How things have changed. If I go tench fishing now I can realistically hope to catch a seven-pounder and I've caught eight-pounders from many waters around the country, even beating the old record several times.But when you consider that the record now stands at a mind blowing 15lb-plus, you start to wonder how even the average tench has grown so much - not that any anglers are complaining of course! The growth in the popularity of carp fishing and the huge piles of nutritious food they use to tempt their quarry must contribute to the growth of tench. Then global warming and the advent of longer summers and milder winters gives tench more time to feed. Add to that the digging of numerous gravel pits to provide materials for housing and motorways and the improved tackle and tactics of anglers and maybe the catching of bigger and bigger tench isn't such a surprise. However, a 10lb tench is still a rare beast and would certainly provide Martin with a substantial challenge.

Though we had a good choice of waters to try, we wanted to catch a double-figure tench on the float and this raised the target towards the 'Impossible' category. However, Martin had achieved this feat only the previous year so with the kind permission of fishing film-maker Len Gurd and the tireless help of bailiff Roy Parsons, we returned to Linear Fisheries near Oxford. Luckily Martin's chosen tench swim was vacant but what a difference a year makes - his hot swim was cold. In the spot where Martin caught countless tench last year we blanked! We were suffering a late spring and the water temperature was so chilly that the tench never came anywhere near the bank. We tried other swims too but the result was the same - not a single tench caught.

Martin could have caught if he'd cast a feeder 40 to 50 yards out into deeper water but sometimes I had to handicap him in the interests of 'art'! Filming float fishing is a lot more attractive than legering and we were keen that all methods would be featured in the series, so he had to suffer. And while he was blanking I made the first tentative steps towards finding out what was going on below the surface. We were hoping to illustrate the underwater world of an Oxfordshire gravel pit and the results were a revelation.

Finding a quiet corner of the lake and using a tiny colour camera on a landing net pole, I could see into the depths. The visibility wasn't great but after a time I could make out the ghostly shapes of carp and tench and by dropping maggots and pellets near the camera, I could draw them in. It took a few hours to win their confidence, but then the carp started drifting through the swim, looking at the camera with inquisitive eyes. The tench were bolder and started picking up a maggot or two and after coming and going for an hour or so they really got stuck in and hoovered through the silt and debris, taking in great mouthfuls and spitting out discarded sticks and leaves with great force. It was amusing to watch but also an education because they managed to avoid Martin's baited hook completely. So we made progress filming the underwater world but not with the catching of a 10lb pound tench. We needed to try another lake with greater potential and Martin knew of just such a water nearby.

The cool spring had certainly made the 'Impossible' monster tench on a float a tricky one. With them unwilling in cold water temperatures to venture into the margins and gorge on bloodworms and snails, I had become frustrated by the lack of action on my local waters. We needed to get in among them quickly if we were to stand a chance of tempting that 'double', as once spawning commenced our chances for the season would pass through our hands quicker than sand.

I'm often told that all the best waters are private and while, of course, they hold their fair share of fish, more than one surprise exists on open access club waters. Both Hugh and I did not want to be elitist, so these types of venues would feature in the series as much as syndicates. Newlands Angling Club in Oxfordshire is an organisation that has one such venue in its portfolio. With a steep marginal shelf slipping into deep water, I hoped this lake would provide the action we desired, even if the sun refused to shine.

Margin munchers.

margins failed to awaken. Apart from the odd small perch I struggled to tempt a bite. At this point you are probably asking yourself why it mattered. As long as I was catching, what was the problem? Both Hugh and I wanted to capture the very essence of angling and a stream of wailing buzzers could never achieve that. So we had to suffer for our art - which is fine in principle until you have to do it! How could the weather, the tench and the world, come to think of it, be so bloody cruel? For season upon season I had enjoyed catching big tench on the float and now the moment the camera arrived I couldn't manage it!

Yes, feeder fishing is a successful method but a tench on the float, to my mind, is worth so much more. It's not just a romantic notion to use such a method either, because when the tench are within range its effectiveness is unrivalled. By fishing over depth and cocking the float via tension in a lift method-style, every knock or twitch is clearly visible. Although modern tactics such as bolt rigs have aided the angler you should never under-estimate the traditional methods, as there are still plenty of occasions when they are superior.

Our plan was to camp by the lake for three days, with the chosen swim being a peninsular jutting out into the main body of water. Between a couple of overhanging trees to my right was where, I hoped, the action would take place. By regularly dosing the gravel slope with micro pellet, hemp, caster and red maggots, I felt sure the tench would give themselves away with a stream of bubbles popping to the surface.

To while away the hours and meet my ever demanding Angling Times column, an altogether different approach would commence out in the lake at sixty yards. As a Method ball crashed down I surmised that there was more than one way to skin a cat. The script, I'm afraid, played out once again like my previous sorties and while tench began to fall to the uncouth Method ball at range, the

Rome wasn't built in a day and, I told myself, patience is a virtue, so I counted to ten and tried to remain positive. It's funny though, how the harder you try, the luckier you get and our reward for

Crude but effective.

patience finally came on the last morning. The sight of frothy bubbles on the surface at dawn led me to believe that below swam at least one tench, scoffing on the banquet.

Lights, camera, action – it was time to catch and I did not fancy messing it up after such an investment in time and effort. One bite is all that may be given and I couldn't afford to miss it. At first the crystal waggler lay flat before semi cocking under the weight of two swan shot. With a tick of the centrepin's drum I sunk the float still further, inch by inch until only the tip remained on show. A scattering of maggots finished off the preparation – all I could do now was wait.

The calm before the storm is always a tense affair and while I needed to exude an air of peace and tranquillity for the film, inside my stomach churned. A single bob was the only foreplay before the float tip left fresh air behind. My strike which followed made a connection with a muscular, green-flanked creature and it wasn't pleased. The rod bucked while the pin's ratchet sang its song again and again. The tench may have been silly enough to eat my bait but it certainly didn't want to meet me! Luckily summer had yet to arrive and the banks of weed my opponent desired to find so she could bury her head and smash the tackle were absent. Provided I stayed in contact and allowed the line to take the strain I felt sure I would end up the victor.

As the surges relented and the ferocity of the tail slaps subsided I crouched down ready with the net. Her flank was broad and laden with spawn - could this be our '*Impossible*'? With one final turn of the drum my landing net was filled with the prize and it was clear I had caught a very large tench indeed. Gently I lifted her from the water and felt the weight for the first time. It was close to our dream. The scales spun and settled the issue – 9lb 4oz. How could I be disappointed when we were just 12oz short of our target? Luckily Hugh felt the same and as I slipped her back we agreed that while our quest for the double wouldn't relent we no longer needed to be so uptight about the method used – the float, after all, had proved its worth.

When I needed to come up with another venue that could possibly produce a double- figure tench for the camera I knew who to call - Chris Logsdon at Mid Kent Fisheries. He controls superb places such as Larkfield, Milton, Stour and many others and although the fishery is perhaps best known for its record carp, Chris has a policy of welcoming all types of anglers and supplying venues to match.

So it was for this reason that Hugh and I made the long, arduous journey into the 'Garden of England' buoyed by the prospect of adding to our 9lb tench on

sat either side of the hump. The terminal tackle was a combination of Method feeders which had been encased in balls of softened halibut pellets and sprinkled with casters and hemp. A very short hooklength of no more than a few inches hung off this, made up of 12lb fluorocarbon. Finally a very strong size 14 hook sat at the business end, hair-rigging three rubber casters. Once I was satisfied with the position of each rod I marked the spots with a fluorescent piece of pole elastic by simply tying a stop knot on but leaving one tag end trailing by an inch. This was then placed in the spool clip prior to recasting to ensure pin-point accuracy. Although the area had been pre-baited I decided to spod a dozen times over each rod with a combination of pellets, casters, hemp and red maggot.

Like a TV studio.

Our arrival had been in the evening, so with darkness fast approaching and tench not being the greatest nocturnal feeders, I felt the following dawn would give me the best opportunity of opening

the float. I had arranged to rendezvous with two local lads who had become friends during my last visit to Kent. Owen and Paul were there to greet us when we pulled up at the lake. The lads had really done us a huge favour, sacrificing their own sport to keep two very productive areas free of disturbance and baiting them liberally for over a week. The phrase 'above and beyond the call of duty' sprung to mind but like many people who have assisted us with our filming all I can say is 'thank you'.

My swim was made up of a series of bars and a gravel hump to the right. Under Owen's instructions I placed one rod forty yards out over the back of the second bar in 6ft of water, while the other two

my account. The 4.15am alarm call saw me drag myself from my bed and get on with the job of tempting a fish. Tench are funny creatures, who can be frustratingly shy biters, but they do seem attracted to commotion and I was going to give them exactly that. Reeling in all three rods I re-baited with a fresh Method mix and crashed them back down on the water's surface. This was swiftly followed by numerous spods of bait over each one. "That will wake 'em up," I thought, as I clipped on the bobbins.

Sky TV were coming along today to record Hugh filming me for its 'Tight Lines' show, so the pressure was really on to produce the goods. The banks of

Kentish dawn.

Pan Lake would be reminiscent of a film studio! I needn't have worried, as an hour later the line began singing off the reel. On connecting with the tench I became acutely aware how savage those gravel bars really were. The grating sensation was resonating down the line onto the rod so I quickly held it as high as I could and pumped the fish over the top. It's at times like these that you need total confidence in your tackle, as no matter what I fish for there's nothing worse than losing a big one.

The first green back of the session rolling on the surface is always exciting and this time was no different. A big yellow belly then popped up and into the net. At over 8lb it was a dream start but proved to be just a prelude of things to come as a steady flow of tincas began making the journey to my landing net. The incredible factor was the average size. I can honestly say 75 per cent of the fish were over 8lb and in my opinion this is unmatched by anywhere else I have ever tench fished in the country.

A key part of consistently tempting a shoal of tench is to feed regularly during the session. I'm never afraid to re-spod or groundbait over their feeding heads when I'm getting action as tench seem to become mesmerised by the noise. Remember as well that to fish the Method to good effect needs regular casting. Once the ball had fully broken down the number of takes dramatically reduced. A good tip for ensuring your Method ball remains intact during touch-down with the water's surface is to glaze it prior to casting.

Simply squeeze on the groundbait as normal then wet your hands and run this around the ball. Cracks will then be removed, stopping it from breaking up.

Packed with particles.

Although the sport was tremendous I was acutely aware that we had set ourselves a target of filming a double-figure fish - a rare beast indeed. I strongly felt though, that over the next couple of days we would never have a better chance. Tuesday dawned and I became connected to a big fish. During the entire battle I was sure that this may be the special tench we desired and on landing I knew it would be close to our goal. The scales though, had other plans and read 9lb 10oz - close but not close enough! It could only be a matter of time now though.

Half an hour later I was away again and the solid resistance indicated another big fish. For five minutes it battled like a Trojan in the margins and I held my breath. Like only tench can, it slapped its huge rudder on the surface time and time again as it powered away. This was not a good moment for anything to go wrong and I offered up a quick prayer to the fishing gods.

At last I could celebrate victory and hoisted a monster onto the mat. It was huge in every dimension, a true goliath of a fish. This time the scales wouldn't deny me and the dial spun round to 10lb 7oz. At last, after

so many long months of struggle, we had again attained one of our goals. Ecstatic, Hugh and I shook hands – this was an epic moment in our quest to produce 'Catching the Impossible'.

This was to spell the beginning of a tench dream with 8lb-plus fish coming thick and fast. The pick was one of 9lb 14oz and another 'dodgy' 10-pounder. I say dodgy only because an exact weight sits uncomfortably with such a monster. Perhaps we should call it 9lb 15oz as it mattered little and joy should never be counted in ounces, especially after banking our double. In total nineteen tench were banked over 8lb, whilst the majority, incredibly, were over 9lb!

With the job done it was time to celebrate with the people who had been equally, if not more, instrumental in our success. It was good to share a glass of wine with Chris and his wife, Lynn, together with Owen and Paul. We could only thank them and hope we had made their efforts worthwhile.

At last!

The perfect perch.

 What a wonderful catch of tench and in a beautiful landscape too. What's more we'd had some gorgeous dawns and glorious light and the wildlife had performed for the cameras as well.

Memorable were the pair of tame great crested grebes, tame because they had become used to seeing harmless anglers on the bank. Once a rare bird, and usually shy, I was able to film them fishing close to the shore and even passing right under Martin's rods. The pair evidently had breeding in mind because on several occasions they indulged in their delightful courtship display, facing each other with plumes and necks extended, shaking their heads in between bouts of preening. They provided an elegant interlude between the tench.

Equally entertaining were the starlings. Now, you might think of starlings as mundane black birds, but get close to them and their plumage glows with irridiscent blues and greens. And these starlings were indeed close - perched on Martin's rods, when they weren't bent into a tench of course! Several starling families had recently fledged youngsters and they were evidently delighted with the perches Martin had provided close to the 'left-overs' from the method balls. Great gangs of them would sweep in, landing on the rods and noisily demanding to be fed

by their parents. Their Latin name "sternus vulgaris' seemed highly appropriate !

The gods had certainly smiled on us in the 'Garden of England' and we wondered whether we had now turned the corner in our struggle to catch *'Impossible'* fish in the most beautiful places we could find. We wanted our series to be a celebration of the British countryside and its wildlife as well as showing angling in the best possible light and our visit to Kent had certainly achieved that. We also wanted to appeal to a wide audience and felt this could best be achieved by inviting some of angling's 'characters' to take part. Martin has a friend who is certainly a great character and we were keen to spend a few days with him - Des Taylor.

Following Des's car, we pulled off the main road and down onto the estate. Straining for a glimpse, I caught the first sight of water through a row of ancient oak trees. With the car park situated alongside the dam

bank I would soon get a full view of the 'secret pool'. I, like many people, had read Des's description of this place in his Angling Times column and I wondered if it really was as beautiful as he had claimed. Well, I soon confirmed with my own eyes that a jewel hidden in the Shropshire countryside did exist. At six acres the peaceful lake was shrouded from prying eyes by enormous oaks which had seen many decades pass. Anglers had come and gone until the lake fell from grace and nature took it back for its own, wrapping her in a blanket of reeds, bushes and wild flowers. There she lay while the grass carp and a few commons gorged amongst thick weed beds, growing fat in this bountiful larder.

Des and his friends had only recently tried to re-stake a piscatorial claim. To their knowledge at least twenty grass carp had lived out their lives here, growing to an incredible average weight of over 30lb! A possible record was mentioned in hushed tones. "It's a case of when", the big man boomed out in his confident fashion. Could we be the lucky ones?

Des is an outspoken man and even though he puts both size twelve feet where angels fear, his passion for angling was clear to see from the glint in his eye that the pool had re-ignited. After a whistle-stop tour Des

The big man.

The secret pool.

pointed to the two swims he had selected for us at the shallow end. The water in front resembled the colour of the Lord's cricket pitch such was the extent of the weed. "Hit and hold 'em," he said, "and they'll not get away."

Not totally reassured by Des' confidence, I proceeded to assemble my tackle - an arduous task but one which needs to be done correctly. I placed each bait carefully, ignoring Des' movements in the next swim until there was an almighty crash in the clearing out to my left. What was Taylor up to? I clipped on my bobbins and walked up to find Des with a rod sitting vertically 5ft off the ground with the butt in a rod rest! "I didn't know there were any cod in here?" I quipped. He replied in an instant. "That, young man, is the beachcaster rig and I was making a video about it when you were still in nappies!" That well and truly put me in my place!

The aim of the method was to suspend a floating dog biscuit on the surface for, hopefully, a passing grass carp to feed on. Perhaps this was the way forward as they have a penchant for surface baits. Interesting as Des' approach was I had to report that by close of play on the first day it had done little to trouble the scoreboard. Des did his comedy routine over a bottle of wine that evening and by the time I went to bed my sides hurt from the laughter. If there's ever been a better story-teller in angling than I've not met him. Fishing is so much more than catching, with friendships formed that last a lifetime and these prove to be far more valuable than any fish caught. How else would I have met this larger-than-life Black Country boy who has more gags up his sleeve than the best stand-up comedian?

Overnight, the clear skies gave way to a thick bank of cloud that was laden with rain but this didn't stop my bite alarm shrieking at dawn. Following Des' advice I clamped down and the weedbed rocked. If I allowed the carp to bury its head there would only be one winner and that wouldn't be me! Rolling the fish over with the strength of my tackle, I quickly plunged the net into the water and scooped everything up. Parting the weed I confirmed that it was indeed a carp but alas it was of the common variety. Still, at over 26lb it was not to be sniffed at.

After replacing my corn hookbait it was only twenty minutes later when it was taken again. This time I failed to make any inroads and sickeningly I could feel the line grating before snapping as if it were cotton. Des also didn't miss out either, with two commons up to 23lb coming his way. But where were the grassies?

Evening saw the wind switch one hundred and eighty degrees and begin to blow into the dam end - it was

time to move for the final night. If we were going down we would do it fighting. Eager to follow my new plan I woke Des from his afternoon nap. The thoughts of moving in the rain did little for him. "That's a young man's game," he said, "once I was a warrior running around like you but now I'm a chief and I just sit back and watch!" With that he rolled back onto his side and closed his eyes, reminding me of a big grizzly bear. Unsure what his words of wisdom may have meant, I shrugged my shoulders and got on with the move.

Hard work, in my experience, is nearly always rewarded and indeed, two more carp fell to me but again they were commons and not the desired grass carp. Netting the last fish I tried to bite my tongue but couldn't. "Des," I said, "are there actually any grass carp in here? You do know the difference between a common and a grassie don't you?" Well, the reply was unprintable and, sadly, our target failed to show. We did, however, hope to return at a later date and settle the score, so with handshakes all round Hugh and I headed back down south.

Where are the grassies Des?

Searching For Gold

 IF there is one species that challenges the tench as the epitome of summer it is the rudd, that golden jewel of a fish that would look more at home on a tropical reef. Lovers of warm, weedy water they have become as rare as the clear, unpolluted lakes in which they used to thrive. Martin and I felt it was one of the most important species to include in our series simply because a non-angling audience would be blown away by their beauty - but where could we catch a big one?

When I was a child the answer was simple - the Norfolk Broads, where summer holidays were spent paddling about Hickling Broad and Heigham Sound in my little dinghy. I'd row miles a day along the reed edges and into the backwaters and because the crystal clear waters allowed me to stalk the rudd, bream and tench, I'd make some memorable catches, usually at dawn and dusk.

One in particular remains etched on my mind. It was the summer of 1957 and on this particular afternoon I'd located a huge shoal of big rudd in a distant corner of Hickling Broad. I returned in the evening and casting breadflake close to the reeds from as far off as I could manage, I landed twenty two rudd over 1lb 8oz, with ten over 2lb and the best being 2lb 4oz and 2lb 5oz. Only the onset of darkness stopped me catching more, and in order to get a picture in daylight, I flooded my boat with water and used that as a keepnet. It worked well, the gorgeous fish unmarked when I released them soon after dawn. Sadly, the catches of rudd from the Norfolk Broads are a distant memory - the fish all but gone due to killer algae, encouraged by eutrophication, the enrichment of the once pure waters by increased pleasure craft and agricultural run-off. Another childhood water full of wonderful rudd disappeared for different reasons.

Landbeach Pits were a twelve mile cycle ride from my school in Ely, but their crystal clear waters were a magnet for two fishing mad boys because the shoals of large tench and rudd had my mate 'Purdey' Hawkes and I goggle-eyed. We'd think nothing of pedalling over there for a few hours - cooking moorhen's eggs in an old can for lunch and climbing trees to gaze down in wonder at the rudd as they cruised between the weedbeds. Dropping breadflake down from our perches would have them circling below, huge green backs, golden flanks and crimson fins just a few feet away. We couldn't wait for the start of the season on June 16th, as we thought they'd be easy to catch but they too must have had a calendar, because on that day they were gone! We did eventually catch several up to 2lb 7oz but not the 3lb giants that they grew on to become. By then the waters were out of bounds to small boys, ownership changing hands to a syndicate,

and fenced. But worse was to come. I drove past the lakes just the other day and was deeply saddened to see that what was once a glorious wildlife wilderness is now a science park and covered in concrete. And they call that 'progress'! Martin also has childhood memories of giant rudd, true stories of catches that would make our 'Impossible' target of a three-pounder seem easy.

Golden as any crown and with fins the colour of blood, the rudd is a truly magnificent fish. Its bottom jaw protrudes beyond the top and like a trout it rises continuously on the evening's fly hatch, supping down tea. Occasionally it will porpoise, revealing its back and forked tail, a sight that provides the angler with a sure sign that summer is here.

Unfortunately, there is now an ever dwindling number of venues for the rudd enthusiast. Small pockets hold on throughout the country but it is a worrying affair with cormorants and hybridisation taking their toll. For me the heady days of Elstow - arguably the greatest rudd water ever - is but a distant memory. The crystal clear brick pit held some true leviathans and perhaps at the time I didn't savour the moment long or well enough. I used to creep alongside reed beds and watch giant fish to well over 3lb devouring maggots with glee. I lowered in my hookbait and watched as an upturned mouth took up the invitation before a golden flank twisted and turned as a strike hit home. Personally I don't think a similar venue will ever come my way again but it won't stop me trying to find one.

The university counties of Oxfordshire and Cambridgeshire are two of the last bastions of rudd fishing in the UK and so it was to these places that we looked for our 'Impossible'. Carp lakes, however unlikely, appear to have provided a saviour. Lots of ever-present anglers bivvied up 24/7 keep the cormorants at bay and with an apathy for anything other than mud-suckers, the rudd's genetics remain pure, with little

Paddling for rudd.

enthusiasm for stocking roach. Linear Fisheries is one such complex, with rudd present in most of the lakes. But the first we would look at was Unity, a pretty ten acre gravel pit sculpted into the countryside near Witney in Oxfordshire.

Late afternoon saw the challenge commence with little more than a bait apron bursting with maggots, a float rod, catapult and landing net. Although it was now 5pm

On the drop.

the sun still burnt down fiercely on the calm surface. Wandering around the margins we reached a reed-filled bay - rudd country if ever there was one. Flies had begun emerging for the evening hatch and they buzzed over the pool, playing daredevil as they pimpled the surface. Occasionally a kamikaze pilot would be held by the surface film's suction and there it would struggle in vain until, propelled by the tow, it would eventually reach the entrance to the reeds where it would be gulped down by a rudd. From my vantage point I needed no further invitation and peppered the surface with the first catapult full of grubs. For five minutes I kept up the rain of bait. The rig I intended to use comprised a puddle chucker float with 3.2lb line linked to a 2lb 12oz hooklength and size 16 spade-end hook. My shirt button-style shotting pattern was made up of micro shot, with the remaining bulk around the float's base. A13ft float rod and fixed spool reel finished off the outfit perfectly.

Punching the float out I failed to keep my bottle and touched the spool too soon. Six feet away from the reeds was 6ft too short. I knew from previous experience that while the sun still hung in the sky the fish would remain in their cover so I reeled in, recast and corrected the mistake, feathering heavily to prevent the loaded float from diving deep. I spun the handle once to straighten the rig and allowed the maggot to fall but halfway through its descent the float bobbed and slipped away. I responded immediately and lifting the line from the water, felt the carbon bend in my hands. Gaining the upper hand was vital and I risked a hook pull as I withdrew my prize from its sanctuary. For a few seconds it was heart in the mouth time but the tackle held firm and once in open water I was able to take control. Allowing the tackle to take the strain, I readied the net. At last I had her, a magnificent creature that surely matches the beauty of anything else a summer's day can offer. I took a long lingering final glimpse at 2lb 9oz of rudd perfection and then I allowed my fingers to open while she slipped back into her home. It was certainly a big fish but short of our 3lb mark – we needed to look elsewhere.

Spurred on by this success, Hugh and I decided to target another pit in the same Upper Thames chain – Andrew's Lagoon. So a few days later we pulled up in the car park and surveyed the scene. A large expanse of water spread out before us, with the occasional tench meandering along the marginal shelf. However, it was the opposite side that drew our immediate attention. A south-westerly blew into a bay banked on one side by reeds which was perfect for rudd, so eagerly we headed

off and positioned ourselves at the bay's entrance. Steadily I trickled in maggots about thirty feet out. Also included were some floating casters and these would be swept down into the bay, hopefully drawing up any rudd which were out of catapult range.

As the minutes passed by I scanned the surface, hoping to see a sign. On a vast expanse of water it's easy to be a long way from your target. This can be intimidating for many but it shouldn't be. Simply break the area down into bite-size chunks and slowly disregard zones via the same watercraft you would use on a smaller water. By following this principle, large waters become an easier proposition - or so we hoped! The first rise happened thirty yards downwind. I noticed a flat spot in among the ripples and with rudd being very obliging fish, I knew once located I was in with a great chance. A bold statement I know but, as always, confidence is as important as any item of tackle.

Following the casters, the shoal soon came face to face with the maggots and my hookbait. Due to the surface light conditions I had opted to use a black tip insert in my puddle chucker. It's amazing how few people use a black tip but I use one for at least 50 per cent of my float fishing, as it's far easier to see in bright conditions. The first rudd was a handful and over 1lb and then for

An Oxford degree.

the next hour I stood thigh-deep in water spraying bait, casting and catching good fish. From across the bay I could see Hugh was also enjoying a similar experience (for once the camera had been put down in an effort to asses the venue's potential quicker) opting for flake in an attempt to catch a bigger specimen and he ended up taking them to 2lb 5oz. All too soon though the pressure of catching so many fish pushed our shoals out of range but it was certainly a slice of special fishing that we had enjoyed. You never know, perhaps I will once again stare down on a three-pounder. However, as with all our 'Impossibles', only time would tell.

 One of the delights of John Barnes' lake, apart from the rarity of shoals of large rudd, was the crystal clear water and prolific weed beds. This didn't just make it rudd heaven but also an ideal place to try to film fish behaviour underwater. Martin and I spent several happy hours in the sunshine, paddling in its warm waters, armed with our little camera, surrounded by gorgeous rudd and plump tench. They gorged greedily on red maggots as we captured some lovely images for the film. However, we were about to achieve even better results.

One of our original ambitions for the series was to film the natural behaviour of Britain's freshwater fish underwater, and we'd made an encouraging start but in early June we took a big step forward. A friend who had made a major contribution to my Snow Leopard film in the Himalayas was also an ace diver - Doug Anderson. All those who saw the BBC's Blue Planet will have seen his work, and I was delighted to find that he had a couple of days free in his busy schedule to film for us in a flooded quarry in the Midlands. It is crystal clear and by using a re-breather, a brilliant but dangerous apparatus that doesn't produce fish-scaring bubbles like a normal aqualung, Doug was able to get really close to shoals of roach and perch. He even managed to fin gently up to hungry pike.

had conclusive evidence that they can be eaten by even a moderate- sized perch.

Doug's film sure was a bonus, but more good underwater footage was to follow. Martin's hunt for a giant rudd led him to a crystal clear lake in Cambridgeshire, and when his close friend Jacko called him to say that the rudd were around, we were there like a shot. While Martin tried to relocate the rudd with Jacko and get them feeding, I gently eased my camera into the lilies - and the scene was simply beautiful. Rising like a forest of trees above the camera, the lily stems and leaves stretched six feet up towards the sky and the water was so clear I could see many yards into the distance. It was like a clearing in a sunlit jungle. Small fish cruised around the stems and when a large carp swam through the scenery the beauty was complete. It didn't take many handfuls of pellets before I had the carp and tench feeding greedily in front of the camera and I decided there and then that filming fish underwater was every bit as exciting as actually fishing for them. Several hours slipped by as I watched my video screen, fascinated by the calmly grazing tench and the sometimes nervous but eventually greedily truffling carp. Then a whisper in my ear jerked me back to this more familiar world. Martin and Jacko had found the rudd.

He phoned me after the first day and reported on the good progress he'd made, but in doing so he mentioned that there were lots of crayfish crawling about (the non-native, American signal crayfish). Knowing that perch love eating crayfish I asked him to try to film this behaviour, an 'Impossible' to say the least - but blow me, he got it. When I received the video recordings back from Doug we could see clearly how the perch stalked gently up to the crayfish, but if they got even a hint of the predator's presence they would quickly swivel round and threaten the perch with their large claws. This defence strategy worked for a time until two perch combined forces, one distracting the crayfish from the front while the other sneaked up behind it and with one powerful suck, swallowed it whole. The perch swam off with the tips of the claw still protruding from its cavernous mouth - it looked rather smug. Wherever signal crayfish have colonised waterways the perch have grown huge, and having seen the film, it's easy to see why. It had often been doubted that perch could eat an adult crayfish but we now

I crept round with them and peering carefully through the willows there was a scene as if from my childhood - a shoal of giant rudd circled just below us, all eye-poppingly large. There were fourteen in the shoal, all over 2lb, the largest maybe 3lb, but before Martin was allowed to attempt to catch our target fish he had to feed the shoal with maggots while I tried to film them underwater. We risked everything by poking a camera on a pole at them and no doubt it was frustrating for Martin - but it was worth it. The rudd were nervous at first, but Martin tempted them closer and closer to the camera. After an hour or two we had film of the most glorious fish in Britain, golden scales and crimson fins glowing brightly in a sea of pale blue. It was a scene of great beauty, but one which would only be complete if Martin managed to catch one!

A bag-full of beauty

 Fishing does funny things to me! It can turn me into a quivering wreck, with adrenalin coursing through my veins, making the experience nerve-jangling to say the least. The whole situation is then compounded further when I can actually see my quarry in front of me! To a non-angler this reaction is perhaps one that's hard to understand, but to us more enlightened souls the wide-eyed excitement of boyhood stays with us for a lifetime. So, shaking with excitement, I fumbled on a maggot and tried to keep my composure - at last I was allowed to fish. Hugh's underwater filming was finished and despite the disturbance the shoal of monster rudd had continued to gorge.

A catapult full of maggots went out first, followed by a cast beyond the area and then another pouchful of grubs. Swinging round, the shoal of gold homed in on their target but this time I gently teased my hookbait into place. Finding it hard to hold the rod steady, I knew the bite would come as

each and every maggot fell into their mouths. Then it was my turn – and the float jagged under. The strike, woefully inadequate, saw the rig sail past me into the bushes. What a clown! This whole performance was then re-enacted another three times as the giant rudd laughed at this fool. I needed to calm down and think things through. If I waited for the float to submerge I was a second too late and the maggot was already on its way out of the rudd's mouth. They may have appeared to be feeding with gay abandon but these fish were certainly not as simple as they looked.

"Watch the maggot, watch the maggot," I told myself over and over again, focussing intently so as not to lose it in among a dozen free ones. From my right a large underslung mouth homed in and with a single suck my grub wafted momentarily upwards before being dragged backwards and disappearing. Striking, both of us froze for a split second, unsure what to do now before my opponent flashed its gold flank and began to dive. Shaking its head vigorously a few feet down, the rudd tried its best to free the hook and when this didn't work it bored down to the weed-coated bottom. On very light line I put the brakes on this manoeuvre as best as I could, luckily stopping it in time. Next the reeds to my left would provide an ideal place for the rudd to break the line or transfer the hook to a stem but with sidestrain and a thumping heart another obstacle was overcome.

Rolling directly in front of me, every golden scale shone, flexing in the sun as the tail, blood red and magnificent, splashed against the surface. Praying was a good call now, but I needn't have worried as the tiny spade end had found a strong hold – at last we had her.

Gently I lifted her up onto the unhooking mat and parted the mesh. Every scale was perfect so I didn't want to be the cause of putting one out of place. She was easily the length of two hands and we clearly had a very big rudd. At 2lb 11oz the scales stopped short of the 3lb barrier but neither Hugh or I could be

disappointed. Yes, the capture of an '*Impossible*' would have been great but a superb setting, an exhilarating capture and a beautiful fish was much more important. With my eye in, so to speak, this wasn't to be my last encounter. Further fish weighing 2lb 11oz, 2lb 9oz and 2lb 5oz all found their way into my net, which is tremendous fishing in anyone's books. Eventually though, it was inevitable that the small shoal would drift away to pastures new. But we had been treated to one of nature's finest sights.

Hugh had captured some wonderful images, both above and below the surface, and I had captured the rudd to boot but it was my mate Jacko who had been the real star. Like so many before him he had selflessly sacrificed his own fishing for our film. With handshakes all round, we left Cambridgeshire behind, leaving Jacko on watch. Should those rudd ever reach 3lb before our filming comes to an end it would be difficult not to return.

Wow!

Bernard's Carp

 THE question asked as a result of the success of my previous series, 'A Passion for Angling,' more often than any other is: "Will Bernard Cribbins be narrating this new series?" His voice is wonderfully distinctive and he is the ultimate story-teller, so it was difficult for me to consider making these programmes without him. Martin was enthusiastic about the idea too so when Bernard agreed to join us we were delighted.

Picture perfect.

Battles in the pads.

Bernard's enthusiasm is infectious, his sense of comic timing instinctive, and with an age difference between Martin and Bernard of about 40 years we felt there was mileage in the 'lad out with granddad' scenario, especially as Bernard would probably teach Martin a thing or two about fishing!

Like Martin, Bernard started fishing when he was a young lad and we can't do better than to allow him to tell his own stories of childhood.

However, I'd always been keen that 'Catching the Impossible' wouldn't be seen as just 'Passion Two', so we had to make this series different in every possible way. Firstly, we didn't have the Bob and Chris duo carrying the story. Secondly, we would add all the underwater fish behaviour, and thirdly, Bernard would actually get to fish. Most folk know that Bernard is a star of stage and screen but many don't know he's a mad keen angler and has been since childhood. What's more, he is very able at all forms of angling and when I proposed the idea to him the bite was immediate and decisive.

"Someone once said that the first fish that most anglers catch is a perch and certainly they are very accommodating creatures when approached by a small boy with a bent pin and a worm, but my first fish were sticklebacks.

I come from Oldham, in Lancashire and my fishing began with a net and jam jar in the local ponds and streams, especially a place called Hollow Brook. This was an overflow from a reservoir on the edge of the Pennines. Part of it ran underground in a tunnel about six feet high.

He's a good ghillie.

This was a great place for large sticklebacks or "Jack Sharps" as we called them.

Then one day I saw one of my mates with a rod and line complete with a red-topped float and a real hook! Well that was the end of the net wasn't it - off it came and instead tied on the cane was a length of cotton thread with two spent matches tied on as a float. I didn't have a hook and somehow a bent pin detracted from the delicacy of the outfit, so I came up with the idea of tying the worm on. It was an unqualified success! The worm was heavy enough to cock the "float" and the very best bit was catching TWO sticklebacks at the same time - one on each end of the worm! The hardest part was getting the worm to keep still long enough to get a slip knot round its middle - that was more fun than fishing !

It was about this time that my mate Jack Rigby and I became professionals. We had heard that a man who had an old porcelain sink in his back yard, which he used as a pond for goldfish, was in the market for new stock. So we arrived at his home with jam jars full of prime, red-breasted tiddlers. I seem to remember he was a bit amazed at the sight of these two scruffy kids with fishing rods and loaded jam jars - but he said he'd have them and we got sixpence between us - a fortune in those days.

Not long after this, Jack and I graduated to fishing for gudgeon in Alexandra Park Lake with more sophisticated tackle bought for tuppence. This was a cotton line, a piece of peacock quill for a float and a hook to gut, with a couple of lead shot - complete with winder. By using this and a slightly longer cane we were able to reach over the railings round the lake; with bread paste for bait the gudgeon didn't stand a chance! The only trouble with fishing the park lake was that a certain large policeman called Bobby Finney would suddenly appear from nowhere. He was a huge man and I'm sure a totally benevolent, old-fashioned bobby, but we never found out his views on the finer points of the "Gentle Art" because we were too busy legging it to the exit trailing fishing rods, bait and various other bits and pieces in our wake.

It seems that around this time a lot of my fishing was illegal - I remember that some very good carp and goldfish could be caught in the mill lodges alongside the many cotton mills, which were the main industry of Oldham at the time. These lodges were small reservoirs that supplied the water for the mill boilers and the recycling system meant the water was warm and the fish thrived. There always seemed to be a gap in the railings and one could squeeze through and fish very happily until someone started shouting to clear us out or until the dreaded cry went up, "Cops are coming!".

My younger sister Kathleen was a very good lookout - she was quite small and nippy and once we got her trained to SAS standards she was invaluable. I'm quite sure that it was all this early speed training that helped her to become a good hockey player and captain of the town netball team.

My fishing since those days has covered coarse, game and sea - from sticklebacks to sharks, taking in on the way salmon and trout and the lovely grayling - bass in

A flowery walk

the surf in November on Irish beaches, when one day was summer and the next cold and grey with driving snow flurries - rainbow trout 10,000 feet up in the mountains of Ethiopia - Nile perch and tiger fish in Lake Chamo whilst dodging hippos - stingrays and squid on the jetties of Glenelg near Adelaide - chub on the fly at the bottom of the garden - and blissful days on the Test and Kennet learning about chalkstream fishing from my good friend John Goddard.

It is a wonderful sport, art, pastime - call it what you will - and I'm forever grateful to those bristling, red-breasted little warriors - the sticklebacks!

Martin and I had been filming for eleven months when we decided it was time to get Bernard involved and so we devised a sequence for the start of the series in which he would be seen carp fishing with Martin. We hadn't scripted any of the previous sequences because we never knew what was going to happen but on this occasion the words were carefully written and plan of action laid out.

The sequence required Martin and Bernard to stalk carp using floaters in the lilies of a beautiful estate lake. Martin would miss or lose a fish, then take Bernard to a pre-baited spot round the lake where he would catch an 18lb common carp. Sounds simple when written on a script, but I'll describe what actually happened.

We tried to pick a hot summer's day because the carp would be more active in warm sunshine. Luckily on the day we chose for filming the sun shone down from a cloudless sky. We arrived at dawn, so while waiting for the water to warm and the carp to rise to the surface we indulged in a bit of tench fishing. The action was splendid, Bernard catching several rotund specimens that fought hard as they attempted to reach the lily stems. Martin caught too, while also acting as ghillie for Bernard. It was the perfect start to what we hoped would be the perfect day.

Having tested their fishing skills, Martin led the way through head-high wild flowers beside the lake while Bernard spoke eloquently to camera about Martin and the whole concept of why fishing is a magical experience - or can be if you get it right! Martin then tried to attract the carp into a small clearing in the lilies with a shower of dog biscuits while whispering to Bernard about driving them 'barking mad'. The joke worked because it wasn't long before three large mirror carp were slurping down the free offerings.

It was now time for Martin to cast, and despite being one of the finest anglers in Britain, it took several attempts to hit the spot - much to Bernard's amusement of course. It is strange how a previously simple action can become difficult when a camera is recording your every move, but most people who have appeared in front of a film camera know how the pressure it creates can play tricks with your mind. Anyway, eventually the bait was in the right spot and the carp were able to recover from the dodgy casts.

The tension increased because the carps' feeding intensified as they approached the hook bait, with Martin and Bernard's whispered observations increasingly excited. Zooming in with the camera, I saw the carp approach and take the bait and could also see quite clearly that Martin struck too soon. Martin's hunting instincts had been taken over by an adrenalin rush and he was mortified at his incompetence. But when I congratulated him on his professionalism in following the script perfectly he felt a little better. It was now Bernard's turn to fish and the script demanded he catch an 18lb common carp. Needless to say, Martin hadn't left anything to chance so I'll let him take up the story.

 After messing up my chance on camera it was Bernard's turn to be put to the test. This was to be our first time angling together either on or off camera, so it would be interesting to see how we faired.

The previous week had seen me on a scouting trip to this beautiful old estate lake with my good friend John Everard. He had been kind enough to point out a swim which had been producing carp for him regularly and

that would supply that all important 'wow' factor for the film. As always, John was incredibly kind in helping us with our requirements. In fact, he volunteered to pre-bait the area a couple of times prior to our arrival. Also, during the first day spent preparing and capturing the initial floater sequence, I had continued to feed the hotspot, so by the time it came to show Bernard, I was confident that he would be excited by what now lay in front of him.

Sunlight failed to penetrate the canopy as we crept through the wood. Under each footstep the floor cracked and crunched, brittle and lifeless, testimony to the dense leaves above our heads. It was hard not to let the carp know we were coming but Bernard and I edged ever so carefully closer. A shard of light illuminated the brown ferns framing a window on a brighter world ahead. Both of us slowly rose into the opening and from this side it was hard to appreciate that the rhododendron bush was in full bloom, supplying a colourful garland around our heads. It wasn't the purple flowers which drew our attention. No, in only a couple of feet of water were half-a-dozen carp feeding greedily. Tails waving, causing vortexes on the surface, there was no doubting that they had found the pre-bait. Bernard now had a choice of fish. Mesmerised, we whispered excitedly to each other, pointing out the sizes as if wanting to increase the adrenalin levels still further.

The rig I had readied for Bernard was an uncomplicated affair, combining a short, soft rod with a centrepin, both helping in the close quarters battle which we hoped lay ahead. Three grains of sweetcorn sat on a hair in conjunction with a bolt rig. There was no room to strike - the carp would hopefully hook itself, but before we could lower the trap into position we needed the fish to back away a little so as not to risk spooking them. My trick here was to scatter the surface with a couple of handfuls of pellets, enough for each fish to back off but remain unfazed. Quickly, the corn swung out onto the gravel and was soon lost to the eye among the stones. Gradually the line sunk but before it could drop on the deck a very big mirror sidled up and as the line hooked on its dorsal we watched in horror. Had we blown it?

Luckily, on some days greed overtakes natural caution and today was such a day. Three carp - two mirrors and a common - headed up the shelf, mouths going like hoovers. They were now right over the hookbait, but which one would take it? For a second there was a pause before the common rose off the bottom, shaking its head from side to side. The line lifted and I shouted at Bernard –"she's hooked!" What came next took him a little by surprise, as I all but pushed him into the lake! From our hidden pitch there wasn't enough room to raise the rod, so bursting out into the daylight like two madmen, we chased the carp down the slope. Bernard now had a chance, but with snags to the left and right it was by no means a certainty.

Failure wasn't an option because after this commotion no self-respecting carp would return here for days. We had only one chance and this was it. The carp plunged towards the roots before veering hard left and being a ghillie was worse than holding

the rod as I was helpless and unable to dictate proceedings. I shouldn't have been so concerned though, as Bernard is a more than capable angler and stayed in control.

"Try him, try him," were his words as I made a scoop and found the net full with Mr Cribbins' prize. With a shake of the hands we had triumphed together. A common of 18lb insured the script had been followed to the letter. The fish gods had certainly been watching over us. Now, I was not the director and I'm certainly no expert on making films but to me the chemistry between Bernard and I felt right. A vital ingredient in 'A Passion for Angling' was the bond between Chris and Bob – could it work for the two of us in the same way? With plenty of trips planned it would be fun finding out.

Wet but happy.

Planning a series of programmes can be tricky when you have no idea of what might happen or what you'll catch, if anything at all! However, Bernard's opening sequence for the series had gone like clockwork so now we could press on with some of the other elements we needed. Despite the unpredictable nature of angling we had a plan for the story and content of each film, the *'Impossible'* fish we wanted to catch and the guests we wanted to film catching them. But, as we've said already, there's a lot more to fishing than catching fish and one such event proved the point.

Martin had been trying to catch tench at Linear Fisheries near Oxford and I had been nearby, filming tench underwater, feeding enthusiastically. It was a perfect summer's evening so the perfect time for a party and the food and wine were to be provided by long-time friends Peter and Francis Drennan. They had been generously helpful and supportive ever since our project started, so it was a treat to sit beside the lake and share the evening with them, along with yet more friends Roy Parsons and John Everard. Even if we couldn't catch any tench in

between the glasses of wine, the evening was a tribute to the wonderful atmosphere that angling can create and the happy memories it leaves us with.

I guess every angler has his or her own vision of what makes a perfect day's fishing. For instance, some enjoy hauling endless small carp from a puddle in the ground and good luck to them. Others, like Martin and I, prefer the more traditional mist-shrouded pool on a summer's dawn with, if we're lucky, an occasional big fish. We felt it was important for our series to show all aspects of the sport, not just the atmospheric weather and lovely light but the sheer joy and humour created when with friends by the waterside. We would give 'carp puddles' a miss but we certainly needed a misty pool to set the scene for the giant crucians we'd caught the previous August. But where?

Luckily, Martin had been tipped off about a lovely lily-lined lake which was home to big crucians, so that was our chosen location. However, the ideal weather eluded us and it seemed that every half light of dawn of July 2005 found us looking sleepily out at grey skies. It was tiring and frustrating but on

Carp puddles could wait.

Little and large.

alongside the float. Not long after, the red tip was pulled gently under and the strike met with a wild resistance. This was no crucian but instead some demented fish that threatened to smash Martin's rod, let alone his line. Despite being snagged in reeds, then tree roots, he eventually extracted what turned out to be a beautiful, rotund tench of about 4lb. Safely netted and carefully released, it was time for a cup of tea and a couple of hours recovery from the days of sleep deprivation. The ultimate dawn sequence was 'in the can' and Martin could now join famous angling author and previous carp record holder Chris Yates for a crucian carp fishing match.

the unlucky 13th a rather haggard, unshaven pair woke to the perfect dawn. Martin was fishing well before the sun came up and I think those images of his silhouette as the golden orb rose through the mist-shrouded pool encapsulated everything we feel is special about angling. Even the fishing had that essential unexpected quality as Martin's float sat contentedly by the rising bubbles of feeding fish. It was classic 'Mr. Crabtree' but the baby rudd that followed were not and neither was the carp that smashed Martin in the lily roots.

Eventually Martin's jangled nerves calmed down and what appeared to be perfect crucian bubbles rose

Finding a water which contains true crucian carp is no easy matter as Hugh and I found out on the quest for the Eversley monsters. For this trip though, we required something altogether more sedate, especially as the co-star would be a certain

Boyhood memories.

Mr. Yates. I'm afraid, however, that even with all my contacts up and down the country I drew a blank on a suitable venue, such is the scarcity of these magnificent creatures. Fortunately my two companions had fared better, befriending a gentleman called Peter Rolfe, a student of crucians if ever there was one. Based in sleepy south Wiltshire, Peter retired from teaching to commence a small aquatics business which encompassed two estate lakes and two medieval ponds. A love affair then began with field ponds and so a desire to find an ideal stock fish.

Unsurprisingly, he arrived fashionably late, but only by five minutes, showing how keen he was for the day ahead. A Kelly kettle in one hand and split cane rod in the other, his gangly frame danced down the path, eager to sample the delights on offer. There were handshakes all round before we headed off in an angler's convoy to, the home of a crucian or two.

It was decided that Chris and I would duel it out side by side, separated by only a bed of lilies in a 'crucian match to the death'. Peter, meanwhile, wisely tucked

Yates strikes again.

Way back in 1965, he had obtained seventeen small crucians and from this brood a staggering fifty thousand spawned and were seeded locally. These, of course, provided the ideal inhabitants for the field ponds. With a clean gene pool (confirmed after dissection of one of the crucians), the area, thanks to one man, is a hot-bed of crucians and more importantly, wonderfully secluded from the cut-throat world of the specimen hunter.

So with two full summer days ahead Hugh and I arrived at a lily-fringed canvas of water to meet with Peter, and hopefully harvest some of the fruits of his labours. A man genuinely in love with his subject greeted us, his enthusiasm typical of someone whose passion runs so deep. But where was Chris?

himself in down the bank, away from the affray. We both assessed our swims and then glanced at each other like two gun slingers in the Wild West, trying to mentally gain the upper hand. Surely the battle could go only one way? I had some of angling's finest modern tackle and bait while Chris aired his Edger Sealey Spanish reed split cane combo paired with a Carter Dragonfly centrepin.

The bait came transported via an ancient metal tub, with its contents looking almost as old - red maggots with a secret flavouring to send the crucians into a culinary stupor, or so he claimed. Now came the terminal tackle. The text books say finesse is crucial when crucians are the target and I have to say, I agree.

But Chris instead opted for a hand-crafted porcupine quill with the Yates universal shotting pattern underneath, which has stood him in good stead from boy to man. Finally at the business end sat a hook which probably would have looked more at home in a butchers. With a gentlemanly handshake the angling commenced. My pole float sat dotted so low even a fly couldn't find a pitch, while Chris' quill lay flat, hopelessly over depth - or so I thought.

The piscatorial genius had devised a cunning plan, one capable of fooling these shy-biting creatures into complete bamboozlement. He convinced them that no angler could surely be responsible for such poor

detailed conversation it may not be just a simple case of avoiding commons and goldfish. The lakes and ponds under his management are constantly monitored. Periodically, the water is drained and the stock is cropped, returning only the larger fish to prevent over population. He is convinced that the modern scene may have missed a link made by Victorian biologists. They felt that in fact two types of crucians existed - the pond crucian (lower back) and it's much larger cousin, the lake crucian (higher back). Like mirrors and commons, are there various strains of the same species?

Peter hopes either to prove the Victorian's finding or really put the cat among the pigeons and discover one is

A cauldron of bubbles.

presentation! It was sheer brilliance and something only possible to execute in the mind of someone working on another plane to a mere mortal. Chris' bites resembled ones caused by sharks while mine bobbed minutely; my jaw touched the floor. Had the crucian world gone mad or was Chris truly a genius? "Enough," I cried falling twenty fish behind - I could take no more. Licking my wounds I retreated to Peter's swim to try and gain a better understanding of the crucian - it appeared I needed too.

His real love is in the scientific study of the species. Hybridisation is a word to be feared but on a more

in fact a hybrid. More of this work is carried out at another of these wonderful Wiltshire ponds, so when he invited us along there for the following day's filming we all jumped at the chance. I was hoping that bigger crucians read the text books I had studied and not those in Chris' head! For now though, I had to suffer the mickey-taking, proving that we can all have a bad day at the office.

Another splendid sheet of water sat before us on the dawn of our second outing and Peter kindly placed me in his favourite swim. This was the lake that held his biggest crucians and he whispered the words '3lb and over'.

Redemption.

After yesterday's humiliation, I redoubled my efforts, smelling revenge in the air. It might have been a bit unfair as Chris had yet to arrive - but I needed all the help I could get! My 12ft rod was combined with a centrepin that had been loaded with 3.2lb monofilament. Then onto this sat a small pole float, a barbless 18 hook to 2lb hooklength. For bait I opted for sweetcorn, with a groundbait of liquidised bread to provide the finishing touch.

I love watching a stream of bubbles heading towards the float before it bobs, dips and then sails away. I struck and the long length of carbon keeled over in

response. The fish held deep and in typical crucian fashion circled continuously around on itself. As the pressure told, the coloured water was suddenly illuminated with a flank the colour of bright gold. Eager to touch this prize, I strained the tackle a little too keenly and as I desperately thrust down the net the hook flew out. Cringing, I drew it back towards me and there, like a shiny new penny, sat my prize - 3lb 7oz of pure crucian.

For me the day was already complete but while they fed it would have been rude not to continue! Another three-pounder and five over the 2lb mark followed and all before my nemesis of the previous day arrived. Sleep, you see, and Mr Yates are good friends and even a fishing trip rarely gets in the way. Still, it mattered little because when he finally arrived we feasted on tea and cake far away from the real world and it was good just to be there. Who caught the fish was irrelevant and I couldn't think of a better way to while away the day.

Revenge was sweet.

Going Against the Flow

 AS already mentioned, part of our mission in this series was to reveal to a suitably astonished public the size, variety and beauty of our freshwater fish. We also wanted to give them an understanding of why they lived where they did and how they survived, so Martin and I were constantly on the lookout for places where we could film them underwater. We had already captured some good images in still water but rivers were trickier if only because a heavy camera on the end of a long pole was difficult to hold steady in powerful currents. What's more, we were keen to film barbel and they prefer the strongest flows. We needed clear water too.

Luckily some good friends came to our aid. John Everard is one of the finest anglers in the country and saviour of the lovely River Windrush in Oxfordshire. Threatened with crippling water abstraction, the river flows strongly today only because John and his fellow protagonists fought a long battle to protect its clear waters. Recovering now, the river is famous for barbel and big roach, so it seemed like a good place to start filming. It was certainly exciting to carefully slide the camera into a gravel glide under a tree and reveal a world that few ever see.

Shafts of sunlight penetrated the water through the willow branches, creating a lovely scenic view, soon enlivened by hordes of minnows and dace that relished the food particles stirred up when I manoeuvred the camera on the gravel. Martin then lowered a bait dropper full of hempseed in front of the camera and it wasn't long before a shoal of good sized chub came to investigate. They were wary of their reflections in the camera's lens at first, but in time they grew confident and started to feed. Then several barbel ghosted out of the tree roots and shouldered the chub out of the way. Even a good perch, ever inquisitive, swam out of the bankside cover to investigate. Capturing such lovely images was encouraging, but our series was about big fish and none of these were giants, so we had to moved on.

One of the principles we said we'd stick to was not just to film all our underwater scenes truly in the wild, wherever possible, film the fish we were attempting to catch in the location we were actually fishing. So having already caught a giant barbel of 15lb in the Great Ouse we travelled there to see if we could film one of the fabled giants underwater.

Martin knew the river well, having caught numerous monsters in the past, not only his ex-British record of 16lb 11oz but since then up to a massive 17lb 3oz. So I was confident that once he'd prepared a swim under a tree and I'd placed the camera, a giant would appear. It was a long wait and after a couple of hours the screen was still empty. Then, suddenly, a huge barbel appeared, its whiskery face filling the frame, its long body tapering off into the distance. What's more, on later inspection of

the shot we were pretty sure it was the 15lb barbel that Martin had caught the year before, affectionately nicknamed 'Liner'. So we had well and truly honoured our principles on this famous waterway.

Another historic river we wished to celebrate in our series was the Hampshire Avon - indeed, we'd decided to commit a whole programme to its fishy characters. The journey would run from source to sea and we'd call it 'Going Against the Flow' because for a fish, a lot of their energy resources are burnt in trying to combat the strong currents. These powerful flows were a problem for our underwater camera too, but one of our good friends was barbel expert Pete Reading and he felt sure he knew of a swim where barbel would be in residence and where I might be able to hold my camera still enough to get good shots. Having walked across the sun-

drenched water meadows to the swim, it was soon evident that Pete had chosen well, because several barbel drifted in and out of the ranunculus and one or two were big. After last year's failure Pete was well aware that he still had to produce a double-figure barbel for our film, so it must have been doubly frustrating for him when I banned him from casting until I had captured the underwater images of his quarry.

On the Avon.

Sliding the camera carefully into the depths, there was every chance that I would spook his fish into the next county, but we shouldn't have worried. The scene was wonderful, huge fronds of ranunculus waving in the crystal clear water and clouds of minnows busily pecking up the hemp that Pete had deposited in the swim. Then the barbel drifted out from their hiding place under the weed and homed in on the camera where Pete had scattered some boilies. Their feeding was rapacious and, contrary to expectations that the camera would scare them, they were actually pushing it out the way in their eagerness to feed. We were so excited by capturing such lovely images that we even felt that filming fish almost beat catching them - but not quite! There was at least one double-figure fish out there, and Pete had to try to catch it.

While Pete assembled his trusty Avon rod and centrepin, I left him in peace and went to explore a series of chub swims up river with a loafer float and maggots. The barbel, meanwhile, had indeed found the pungent aroma of his creamy boilies to their liking, so when a handful of broken pieces were thrown in, a series of shadows moved out from the streamer weed and began rooting up the bottom. Pete's hookbait was accompanied by a stringer of freebies, offering an 'hors d'oeuvre' to any willing recipient.

In such clear water, fish can be far from foolish, spotting an angler's tackle well before a mistake can be made. Pete needed to make the barbel compete with each other if he was to tempt our target, because if two mouths went towards the hookbait at the same time perhaps caution would be overcome by greed. A trickle of feed and a good deal of patience was required and I only knew of its success when Pete shouted up the bank that he had made contact. My arrival met with a large, bronze flank rolling in mid-river, followed closely by a huge tail slap as the barbel charged under the cover of a weed bed. Fortunately, his line strength was suitably matched and with a crank of the 'pin a barbel once again found itself rising towards the surface. It appeared to be a good fish but not until the battle had drawn to a close did we

realise how good. There in the bottom of the net sat the prince of the river, weighing in at an impressive 12lb 10oz. We both admired him for a moment before once again letting him go back to his world. A handshake was the least I could offer Pete, who is not only an excellent angler but a true gentleman of Wessex.

Pete had finally delivered us a lovely barbel but we now had to rely on another Pete to help us with a river carp - Pete Orchard. The fast-flowing waters of the Hampshire Avon are a long way from most fishermen's idea of classic carp habitat but escapees from flooded lakes have colonised rivers in good numbers, and they've thrived. One of their major strongholds is the beautiful waters of the Avon south of Salisbury at Longford Castle where Pete Orchard is the river keeper.

I've been a rod on this delectable fishery for nearly 30 years and actually made a wildlife film about it for the BBC in the early 80's with famous river-keeper Tom Williams. His assistant Mike Trowbridge took over when Tom retired and he had a highly successful spell during which the river's fish stocks blossomed.

When Mike retired in 2004, Pete took over and he's proving to be not only a fine keeper like Mike but as he's

A true gentleman

Bridge at Longford.

an experienced fly fisherman and carp angler, a helpful ally in our attempts to catch a river carp. Pete had baited two swims so when Martin and I crept up to these swims on August 4th it was clear that he had indeed succeeded.

Peering carefully into the depths we could see several big carp, including commons of well over 20lb, maybe even thirty, along with smaller mirrors, a host of good chub and even a large roach. Despite being at risk of spooking the fish before they could cast, I slid the underwater camera alongside the carp. Much to my surprise they continued to feed so confidently that they pushed and shoved the camera violently (the casing was strong though, having survived a crocodile attack in Africa, with tooth marks for evidence). There were even brown trout crunching boilies and a salmon swam past but eventually I was satisfied we'd done justice to the impressive inhabitants of the two swims and it was time to try to catch them.

Camera attack.

The Hampshire Avon has, along its length, many famous landmarks and stretches - Ibsley Bridge and The Royalty to name but two. However, situated upstream in the county of Wiltshire sits probably the finest - the Longford and Trafalgar Sporting Fisheries. This is hallowed ground for both the game angler in search of salmon and brown trout, and the coarse fisherman who pursues huge roach.

Longford Bridge has seen many a monster fish swim underneath its arches and for those who can remember, it supplied the backdrop for Hugh's film for the BBC 'Tom's River' and the salmon-catching sequence by Tom Williams. It was a great honour then to meet Pete Orchard, the latest in a long line of river keepers on the estate. Arranged for us though, wasn't the pursuit of any of the aforementioned species but instead a modern invader in this clear, chalk-filtered river. But first we stared down into the fast-flowing water as it forced itself around the bridge, providing shelter for a shoal of dace and a lone trout as they jostled to

hold station in the shadows. Pete spoke of his love for the river and his hopes for its future. Being a river keeper must be like taking on another wife - an affair full of trials and tribulations but incredibly satisfying as it develops over the years. We spoke of roach and whispered about three-pounders, we talked of barbel and imagined the prince of the river drifting into view through the lush streamer weed that lay directly upstream.

Conversation then turned back to our adversary for the day. The carp might be an alien to the river but it has positively revelled in its refugee status from flooded stillwaters. It appears that there is no stopping this steam train and hidden in the Avon's majestic waters is another story of success for the species. Arriving with every new flood, Pete described the stock as similar to a box of chocolates. Mirrors, commons, ghosties, fat or thin - you just never know what could appear. They are big fish too, highlighted by Pete's personal bests of a 29lb 2oz mirror and 30lb 10oz common. These fish can be highly nomadic, covering miles of water in a day.

Under the alders.

To help us in our quest of luring one of these beasts, Pete had set about the task three days earlier. Two swims had been selected and at dawn each day they had received a liberal baiting of Source boilies and Marine Halibut pellets. Hopefully their daily breakfast had held them in one area and made tempting one a far easier proposition.

Walking downstream we came to spot number one under a canopy of alder branches. Peering in, a shoal of chub were at home, the magnifying properties of the river making every one look monstrous. Pete was unworried about the lack of carp and instructed me to introduce some more bait and await their arrival. This was to be my swim so while he headed off down river I stayed behind to observe and ready the tackle.

A 2lb test-curve rod combined with a centrepin and 15lb line provided the backbone. Instead of legering though, I opted to use the almost forgotten art of stret-pegging. Six inches of peacock quill connected via float rubbers was fished 2ft over-depth - this allowed a bow to form down between the float and a running ounce lead. The hooklength was then adjusted to 8ins, with a strong size 6 hook sitting on the business end and finally a boilie connected via a hair rig. Sure, a bolt rig may have been more clinical, but to me fishing is not just about the end result. Whenever possible it has to be done with style, giving as much pleasure as the capture itself. After all, you wouldn't go on a pheasant shoot with a machine gun would you?

With everything ready, I looked once again into the water and there under my feet sat a common carp greedily scoffing pellets. With such clarity I could see every movement and while the mouth hoovered up the bottom with huge gulps, its golden flank shone out, with each scale acting like a bike reflector. Experience though, has taught me to temper the urge to cast in such situations and, like a fine red wine, the swim would be better if left to mature a little. So as not to falter, I slipped gently away and wandered down the bank to see how Pete was fairing. By the time I reached him he was lowering his second bait into position. His swim consisted of a clear gravel hole in 8ft of water surrounded on all sides by ribbon weed. Pete's hushes tone indicated that carp were already present, with one particular individual looking very close to 30lb, a a true Goliath for flowing water.

Settling down, he once again emphasised their nomadic summer nature. Winter, he explained, brought with it a change in their behaviour, with the fish preferring to hold up in slacker areas. It has been during these periods that Pete had enjoyed multiple catches, giving diversity to the more traditional pursuits. This was truly pioneering carping in every sense and provided a thrilling challenge, so when Pete's tip pulled downwards I was equally excited. Alas, a bream had intercepted the bait and this was followed by a string of chub. The carp showed their presence during all of this by rolling their broad backs out of the water no further than ten yards away, as if to show their superiority in this game of cat and mouse.

With all the excitement, I had quite forgotten about my swim and when Pete's rod lurched over again it wasn't hard to see why. The clutch screamed and a huge bow-wave headed down river. This certainly wasn't a bream and our first glimpse confirmed it. A shimmering blueish flank powered away from us, while line left the spool at a rate of knots. Pete's insistence in using strong tackle had been vindicated because these creatures would put their stillwater cousins to shame, both in speed and agility. Eventually he gained the upper hand and after one final dash for freedom 19lb of Hampshire Avon carp succumbed to the net.

With congratulations over, I unsurprisingly, suddenly had an urge to try my swim. Creeping back under the canopy, my heart skipped a beat when I saw six tails waving within inches of the bank. Taking a deep breath and with hands shaking uncontrollably, I impaled a bait onto the hair and carefully lowered in the rig. The carp were so close

my float lay flat on top of some loose weed which had been pushed in tight against the bank.

Below, I could see the backs of the carp nudging ever closer, purple flanks of mirrors intermingled with commons that possessed scales as large as slices of apple. My peacock quill repeatedly twitched as the line brushed across their flanks but, unperturbed, they continued their feeding orgy while my heart thumped and butterflies welled up in the pit of my stomach.

An old friend.

Again the quill rose then suddenly buried, holding station under the surface. Striking on instinct, the rod hooped over and a huge pair of shoulders shot off, leaving in its path a large vortex. So fast was its charge upstream that my centrepin nearly smoked and the cork handle creaked. Turning the brute was not an option as it continued its battle, causing a bow-wave across the river.

Again and again the drum spun as the carp attempted to reach the sanctuary of a weed bed some thirty yards away. Clamping down even harder, disaster looked inevitable but, no, at last the pressure told and doing its best to impersonate a salmon, the carp charged back downstream. Frantically, I span the 'pin to pick up the slack and recommenced the battle. Twisting and turning, the flank of the common carp looked huge and I prayed

Stret pegging.

Best bite ever.

for the hook to hold. Over the next few minutes I declared fishing to be too scary for my heart but I wasn't to be denied and Pete arrived just in time to do the honours with the net. I don't know who was more exhausted – me or the carp!

Carefully laying her on the mat, we admired the golden flanks. All I could do now was thank Pete for his efforts and smile like a Cheshire cat with 24lb 12oz of beautiful carp. Hugh had managed to capture the battle in its entirety and I doubted anything could ever match the sequence for sheer excitement.

 The capture of such a beautiful carp was a fitting end to our summer's fishing and we now had a lengthy break while I went into hospital for my second hip replacement. The recovery from the first operation had been comparatively straightforward, having surprised myself by walking out of the hospital after four days with only the help of a stick. Exercise and recovery was fairly pain free - but this was not the case with the second operation.

Both hips had been severely damaged by thirty years of wildlife film-making including following pumas and snow leopards around the mountains carrying heavy cameras. Now I was suffering for the privilege, because the second hip received not only bone damage, but crunched tendons and other bits of 'kit' too. I could only limp out of hospital on crutches and recovery this time was longer and more painful. For six weeks all I could do was hobble to the computer and continue editing our material. However, once healing had been achieved the replacement 'parts' produced a miracle cure, a sort of equivalent to Lazarus in the bible. After years of being crippled it was a joy to be given a new lease of life; we sure needed it too.

The sight of flocks of swallows heading south in mid September reminded us of how time was flying by. There was still an awful lot to do.

Himalayan hardship.

Myth Becomes Reality

 ONE fact that was becoming clear in our attempt to make a series of high quality films on angling was our reliance on so many people's generosity and kindness. This was to become even more obvious in the coming months and one example typifies the effort folk were prepared to invest in helping us succeed.

Stuart Wilson is the London Anglers' Association bailiff on the Hampshire Avon at Britford, immediately upstream of Pete Orchard's beat at Longford. Both stretches are famous for big roach, a species we just had to include in our Avon film and because of its popularity, one we intended to feature strongly in the series. As anglers will know, a roach of 1lb is a good one, a two-pounder frequently described as a 'fish of a lifetime' and a 'three' in the 'Impossible' category. What is more, Martin and I had set our sights on a three-pounder from a river, certainly one of Britain's rarest creatures and clearly in a category that may have been better described as 'crazy'. However, one or two such fish existed in Stuart's stretch of the Avon and I was keen to try to film these underwater.

Stuart had located a shoal of giants in August and phoned me, but due to the river being too coloured for good photography and then my hip operation, it was October before I was able to film again. Meanwhile, Stuart had kept tabs on the shoal and on the 16th October they were still in the same spot and the river clear. So next day I limped down the bank with the help of a stick and, armed with the camera, peered into the swim and - you've guessed it - they were gone! What's more, they never returned that season and Stuart's dedication had come to nothing.

However, he kept on looking and a year later the shoal returned and we were finally able to show what it was like to be a roach in the Avon. The fast flow was their immediate concern because they had to burn fuel to hold station. They evidently preferred fast, gravelly and weedy runs to slow, muddy sections because the current carried food to them. So each roach would occasionally rise up to pick off some drifting insect, or pick over the gravel as the current swirled snails and food particles around. After they had eaten something, each individual would return to the lee of the fronds of weed, but this was not a random process. Their placing was so precise that after every sortie they would return to within an inch of their favourite lie.

There were about fifteen fish in this shoal weighing up to about 1lb 8oz but Stuart had spotted a shoal of

enormous fish in mid-river, two of which were over the magical 3lb. It was difficult to hold the weight of the camera on the end of four landing net poles, in addition to fighting the flow, but eventually Stuart and I were able to admire these giants on the screen of the video recorder. To suggest we were impressed was an understatement. These rare creatures were so big they didn't so much swim as 'waddle'. What is more, we weren't alone in admiring them, because the lady of the house opposite came over the bridge to see what we were up to. When she saw the images of the roach she was amazed at their beauty and asked whether their colour was actually true to nature. It was a moment of real encouragement, because if this lady was impressed by what she saw, then maybe a television audience would be too. Now all we had to do was catch one.

As anyone who fishes for big roach knows only too well, they can be the most difficult of all fish to catch, so Martin and I enlisted the help of two ace anglers in the hope we could catch a monster before our time ran out. Terry Lampard and Tim Norman have been friends for years and had already helped us to catch our 'Impossible' chub of over 7lb; we hoped they might be able to repeat the trick with roach! Sadly, the Autumn passed us by without any significant

roach being caught, so while Terry and Tim continued searching for our elusive monster, Martin and I diverted our attention to a slightly easier 'Impossible', a 4lb perch.

Now, as I've already mentioned, Martin has an enviable reputation as a very good perch fisherman, having probably caught more four-pounders than any other angler, so we thought this particular challenge would be easy. However, we'd already spent one winter failing to catch one, so when we were told about a trout reservoir in Lincolnshire that held huge perch, we had to investigate.

On the evening of November 8th, having negotiated numerous motorways, we looked out over the windswept banks of the vast concrete bowl that stood high above open Fen country. A small flock of Icelandic whooper swans added to the desolate scene, and flotillas of duck bobbed on the waves, but what really caught our eye was the numerous grebes. They were diving for small fish around the boat moorings and suitably encouraged, we surmised that small fish might lead us to large perch.

A bowl-full of perch.

 Over the decades reservoirs and big perch have appeared to go hand in hand with each other. From yesteryear on London's concrete bowls to the trout waters like Chew Valley, perch have thrived in this man-made environment. Why? I don't have a clue, but it didn't come as a complete surprise when a new water was brought to my attention. Toft Newton, in North Lincolnshire, has made its name as a trout fishery and during this time the coarse fish have thrived unmolested. Vast shoals of fry have provided a feast fit for a king and the perch have grown fat on this larder. Recently the reservoir had come under new management, namely Neil Grantham, who is responsible for one of the north's finest match complexes - Lindholme Lakes. Neil kindly permitted Hugh and I to fish for the perch on a strictly one-off basis in the hope of finding an *'Impossible'*.

This was a large sheet of water, perhaps forty acres, and could easily swallow up hundreds of perch. So where to start? No matter how big the venue, the rules of watercraft stay the same. If you were a fish you would seek the cover and shelter of a feature, and two on Toft screamed out - a water tower which had a pipe protruding from it sub surface and a boat landing stage.

In the fading gloom we could make out a glittering shower of fry spraying across the surface with a series of heavy swirls breaking the water close behind, caused by their pursuers. Was it trout - or could it be perch? Creeping closer to the water's edge we hoped to get a better look. Once again, the tiny perch and roach started to become agitated, grouping up in expectation of an attack. Zooming in from the deeper water beyond the boats came the shadows that were clearly striking terror into the fry. Upwards they headed, driving their prey towards the surface for an easier attack. It was now time for the end game. Fish cleared the water in a desperate attempt to escape and then the spines broke the surface in hot pursuit. From our vantage point a wave of striped flanks came into view - it was perch and big ones at that. How big? Well, that would have to wait until morning but it sure fired our imaginations over a pint in the local pub that evening.

It was no hardship to rise for the alarm call the next day and with a hearty English breakfast inside us we headed back to the reservoir. Catching these magnificent creatures on film, feeding in their natural environment was the priority, so I left Hugh at the boat landing stage and headed round to the water tower. My initial game-plan was to fish a maggot feeder combined with a lobworm hookbait, so I set about the task of tackling up. A feeder rod was combined with 4lb mainline. The feeder itself would sit on a paternoster boom, while the hooklength consisted of 4lb Double Strength to a wide gape size 12 spade-end hook. Rigged and ready to go, I picked out a far bank marker and made a twenty yard cast alongside the tower, placing the line in the spool clip to guarantee distance. Surely this concrete jungle would be hiding a group of perch? Or so I thought. But an hour later I hadn't received so much as a rustle on the tip - had I read the situation all wrong ?

Reeling in, I stripped the feeder from my set up and replaced it with a couple of swan shot. I also lengthened the tail, ensuring a slow descent through Toft's depths. This time, on touch down with the bottom, I cranked the bait slowly back towards me. With two turns of the handle the quivertip had just resettled when it tapped and began to drag round and I found myself connected to something which was intent on shaking my hook free of its mouth. By its constant thrashing, I knew what would be responsible. From way down deep in the clear reservoir water I could see those tiger stripes and blood red tail and I marvelled at how beautiful our coarse fish can be. Such clarity had ensured vivid markings and my net soon became home for a fish touching 2lb.

Back out went the worm and once again I received an instant bite. It never ceases to amaze me how fine the line is between success and failure and do you know what, I never got a single bite with my worm laying static on the bottom. Throughout the day a stream of fish headed my way and they were like peas in a pod, weighing from 1lb 8oz to 2lb. It was great fishing, but could a monster be lurking out there? Tomorrow would see us both head out afloat to explore Toft further.

Worm twitchers.

Our host Neil had arranged to take us out for an evening meal, or to be more precise, a Chinese. Being rather tired, neither of us relished the forty five minute journey, passing numerous seemingly suitable restaurants on the way. Neil was adamant though, that the effort would be worthwhile. Eventually we arrived at a rather swish establishment and were escorted to our table by the Chinese equivalent of a maitre d'. All very posh compared to my normal take away of sweet and sour chicken. The food though, was without doubt the finest Chinese either Hugh or I had ever tasted. From spare ribs which oozed Peking sauce and melted in the mouth to garlic prawns which tantalized the taste buds, it was genuinely exquisite fare. Now we understood why the journey had been undertaken. It was worthwhile coming to Yorkshire for the meal alone but as I climbed into bed my dreams were filled with the striped warriors.

When the new day dawned, a fresh wind and a gloomy sky had developed. Rainfall loomed, but at least the perch would find the conditions to their liking. Drifting around in a boat, the echo sounder threw up some interesting features but except for a single fish for Hugh, we failed to connect with a shoal. We headed back to the landing stage bank and as we did a vast drop-off was illuminated on the screen. The

anchor quickly went over the side and tackle was once again prepared. For the umpteenth time I swapped lures, this time choosing a rather obscure double tailed fluorescent green jelly worm. I was positive that it resembled nothing that the perch had ever seen before but luckily you never really know what might work when fishing. With a weighted head, it cast well and hugged the bottom as I slowly jigged it back. A sudden tap was quickly followed by a savage strike and my 7ft rod looped over in victory. With a green tail hanging from its mouth the perch came spluttering to the surface and a rather angry looking two-pounder had been fooled by this green monstrosity.

Once again, like the previous day, a single change opened the floodgates and a procession of ravenous stripeys took issue with the jelly worm. When I swapped back to anything else they would just melt into the shadows. The day wore on into the afternoon and our final casts saw us arrive back at the landing stage. At times a dozen fish could be spotted chasing the lure as it returned to the rod tip. It was fantastic to watch the fish, gills flaring with aggression and dorsal fins erect, snapping at my lure. Hugh, free of the camera, saved the biggest fish until last, netting a specimen that touched 2lb 8oz and drew a fitting close to our adventure. No, we didn't tempt a monster but I

Green monstrosity.

have rarely experienced such frenetic action. Combine that with some superb underwater footage, and the long journey had been well worthwhile.

Once it was clear that the stories of giant perch might have been a little 'imaginative', I left Martin to prove my scepticism was unfounded and started to explore the possibilities of capturing some underwater footage of the fish fry under the boats. As the grebes were still attacking, I might get shots of them swimming past and if I was lucky, even the perch.

I anchored the camera among the shoals, extended the cables as far as possible then hid out of sight. The grebes returned giving me some lovely shots, primarily because the reservoir water was crystal clear and the sun was shining. The perch, however, kept their distance but knowing how they like to hunt in reduced light, I

hoped I could 'manoeuvre' them closer to the camera by moving several of the boats over the lens. By creating deep shade in this way, the transformation was remarkable. Hardly had I started recording them again than the dense packs of fry parted and appearing out of the gloom were about forty large perch, many around the 2lb mark. They swept right up to the camera with spiky dorsals raised, their stripes and orange fins glowing in the gloom. The shoal did this several times, occasionally attacking the fry and it was not just one of the most exciting moments in all our filming but one of the most iconic images of the series.

Having failed to catch our 4lb perch yet again, and with negative news from Terry and Tim about big roach, we decided we'd better see if we could turn our luck around by rising to one of our biggest challenges once again - the capture of a pike weighing over 30lb. This 'Impossible' fish had nearly broken our resolve the previous winter, so when we relieved Terry and Tim of their roach duties and invited them to help us with the giant pike they were delighted, especially as Bob

Handford of Bristol Water had generously offered us a couple of boats on the legendary Chew Valley Reservoir.

In recent years, this vast and beautiful water had produced more 30lb pike than any other and with Bernard also joining us, we had high hopes of success. We had three days to search the water but alas, on day one all we caught was a small jack and several fat trout before we were blown off the reservoir by gales. The wind kept blowing and we had to give up. It had been fun but a failure nevertheless so we needed a new place to try.

Despite travelling all over England for our giant, Martin had a hunch that the lake nearest to his home at Chippenham just might produce an 'Impossible'. Letters seeking permission were sent off, meetings attended and eventually the Marquis of Lansdowne and his daughter Arabella kindly agreed we could film there and even use their boat. It was a great privilege, because the lake in question lay in the beautiful Capability Brown-designed landscape at Bowood.

 The previous winter's piking exploits had been close to breaking me, and I didn't just consider quitting the series, I considered quitting angling altogether. To put it bluntly, I hated every second of it. So if I was to avoid the same fate this time round it was vital that we found a venue which avoided the need to live in a bivvy for days on end. After all the travelling we'd done I was excited to hear of an estate lake only five minutes from my house – Bowood. Could I be this lucky and find the answer to our quest so close to home? Joining the fishing syndicate, I went to explore its potential and when the lake splayed out before my eyes for the first time I knew we had to try and film there - it was magnificent. Surrounded by stunning countryside, it set a scene that would have any angler's heart pounding. I relayed my excitement to Hugh, who in turn wrote to the estate asking if they would assist us in our search for a monster pike. The rest, as they say, is history.

Slipping out from the boat house, the water opened up before our eyes. If it could talk it would have told tales of anglers pitting their wits against the lake's inhabitants for over a hundred years. Indeed Alfred Jardine, that most famous of pike anglers, had found favour here in the late 1800s, lured, like us, by the thought of monster predators. Up on the hill, casting a watchful eye over proceedings, was the stately home of the Marquis of Lansdowne. Its garden had been styled by the indomitable Capability Brown and what vision the man must have had, shaping great swathes of countryside throughout England. For him though, it was a double edged sword. He might have been the creator but he was never destined to marvel at his own spectacle that the intervening years had

A new PB.

produced. If it was a consolation to him, the two men aboard the boat certainly appreciated what he had created as we drifted down towards the dam end, charting a gradual deepening via the echo sounder.

On reaching our destination, a depth of 15ft was recorded, with a grotto and temple sitting to our right, which is trademark Capability. With the shallow end of

Temple of joy.

free of the leeches which had connected themselves to its torso and hoped the lure of fresh fish would prove too tempting after the enforced semi-hibernation during the recent cold spell. That was the hope anyway and an angler is an optimist if nothing else.

Swaying side to side in the gentle breeze, I became transfixed by the two orange tipped floats, until suddenly one was gone. A double take confirmed events and my hand lifted the herring rod from its rest. I quickly checked the clutch before I wound down into a force below, then swept the rod back, setting the hooks. The rod tip thumped with success. It wasn't a huge fish, but it was a start and a pike of 12lb provided a welcome confidence booster. Over the next couple of hours events were to mirror themselves half-a-dozen more times, with each pike acting more angry than the last. And once again, the float slid away but this time there was no kick, just a solid resistance. A bigger pike had grabbed hold. Heading at a rate of knots towards the boat, I struggled to maintain tension, something that's vital if the hooks were to keep imbedded. We recommenced battle under the boat and as the tackle placed more strain, a long green body rose to the surface. Had we

the lake still frozen from the recent cold snap, we reasoned that logically any prey would have sought sanctuary in the depths and were hopefully followed by their nemesis – the pike. So it would be here that our quest would begin.

While I began to prepare the tackle, Hugh worked his magic by recording the lake and its surroundings. I'm sure he would agree that once in a while a place comes along that can only be described as 'special' and this was somewhere that justified such a description. It was a world away from the campaign of the previous winter, no long dark nights and hours of travelling. This was much more like it – a place to inspire, and oh how spectacular it would be to find an *'Impossible'* here. To catch any pike would have made my day but what if the whispers of monsters were true? Could there be a more fitting venue to do battle? We were about to find out.

A lamprey and a herring sailed out and landed with a resounding crash on the water's surface. Fished via a simple float leger system, the ounce drilled bullet pulled the deadbaits down into the depths and a zone where a pike could detect an easy meal. We imagined a monster shaking itself

"It's only a jack".

banked our dream - a 20-pounder from such wondrous surroundings? Alas, the scales told a different story and read 19lb 14oz. But we could never be disappointed and the temple behind us provided the perfect backdrop for our photographs.

A quick committee decision saw us up anchor and head for fresh grounds. The neck of the dam bay had revealed a few dying weed beds in ten feet of water and this was chosen as our next destination. Silently, I crept the boat into position via the electric motor while Hugh, making the most of a lull in proceedings, took an opportunity to wet a line and trolled a cooper spoon under the boat. I don't know who was more shocked, the pike or Hugh when the carbon buckled in his hands. "It's only a jack," came the call, as he cranked his prize upwards. Gloved and waiting I prepared to do the honours but when it came to the surface I told Hugh to think again. "If this is a jack, I'd hate to see a monster," I proclaimed. "I'd better get a net." At 23lb 4oz it gave Hugh a new personal best and it had only taken two minutes to catch. I suppose some things are just meant to be.

After a celebratory toast was made we once again dropped anchor and, as before, a herring and a lamprey sat to the left and right of the boat. Even though weak, the warming rays of the sun had begun to send the ice into retreat. Perhaps more pike would stir. Below the surface the lake's tow had begun to drag the blooded scent down wind, hopefully bringing it to the attention of a set of teeth. Suddenly my float bobbed twice before disappearing. I wound down and as I made contact I was left in no doubt that it was a big fish. Immediately braid was taken from a strongly set clutch and head shaking was replaced by a heavy, dogged resistance. When piking I'm not one for yielding easily, and believe it's far better to lose in a swash-buckling manner than give line and finish with a whimper. Coming under the boat I cranked down hard and tested my tackle. Up she rose, still powerful but facing the inevitable and a huge head hit the air first, followed by a submarine body. It was big, but how big? For the answer I would have to wait a little while longer but fate was to fall on my side. A fish of 26lb 8oz lay in my arms and I'd taken a new personal best, providing us both with a day to

remember. It was more than we could have hoped for. With only an hour of daylight left I cared little for what may transpire and sat back to soak up the atmosphere. However, my daydream was not to last long as the lamprey became engulfed twenty yards downwind of the boat. Things couldn't get any better - could they?

Again I set the hooks, with prior events only to repeat themselves. It was a heavy fish but, if possible, it felt even heavier than before and as it made its way up past us it actually began to swing the boat around in its wake. If I knew at this moment that one hook of one treble provided the fine line between success and failure my gung-ho approach would have faltered. Tightening the clutch, I made my stand as the leviathan below rose upwards. With a huge tail slap she arrived in our universe, soaking us both in the process and if I hadn't been kneeling my legs might have buckled. I have seen many a sight in angling but this was one to savour. "It's not a pike, Hugh – it's a crocodile," I cried in delight. The head was huge and the back wide enough to climb on board and jetski! It was a pike but not like one that I had ever seen before. With my net at the ready I prepared for the final stages - I didn't want to lose this one.

Eagerly I scooped, perhaps too early but my luck held and now lying beside me was the prize. I was wrong, it couldn't be a pike. It looked more like an Alsatian dog, with that huge head swaying gently too and fro. The moment of truth had come and I eased her onto the scales and watched as they settled on 32lb 6oz. Both Hugh and I knew it - this was a momentous moment. Even though we had set an 'Impossible' weight at 30lb neither of us had been holding our breath in anticipation of success. But now, here it lay before us, an incredible fish and for a moment we simply marvelled at the monster with its awe-inspiring dimensions, before slipping her back into her world. I felt immediately that the tide had turned on our project and that now, anything was possible. To record the capture of such a leviathan was a once in a lifetime achievement.

That evening I finally felt the burden of the 'Impossibles' lift from my shoulders and even Jo, my wife, who doesn't share my fishy passion, celebrated the moment. At last I felt I could achieve what was being asked of me.

The ultimate goal.

Impossible Becomes Incredible

 IF there was one thing Martin and I had learnt from finally capturing our giant pike it was the need to stick with that old axiom of the wildlife film-maker - 'keep on trying'.

Chip in his element.

I was reminded of this when ITV finally informed me that our Snow Leopard film was to be transmitted during the New Year holiday. It was a film that for various reasons, including the death of my close friend and intended chief cameraman Chip Houseman, took seven years to make. To capture enough footage of this elusive big cat required four-and-a-half years of gruelling expeditions into the Himalayas. My replacement cameraman, Mitchell Kelly, nearly died of altitude sickness during this filming so Martin and I hoped that catching a 4lb perch wouldn't be quite so hard, or take as long! However, the signs were ominous.

One winter of failure had already passed us by and we were now approaching our second Christmas so were hoping that a trip to the River Kennet, with its reputation for giant perch, would see our problem solved.

The high of catching a 30lb pike had been incredible for a couple of weeks and every time I thought about it I broke out in a huge smile. Wallowing in success though was not allowed because however important that giant was, it was just one in a very long list of *'Impossibles'* which needed to be caught, especially given the poor results of the previous winter.

The perch was a fish I had foolishly taken for granted and my over confidence in expecting to catch a four-pounder easily had well and truly come back to haunt me. I wouldn't be making that mistake again, whether it was on the Great Ouse or elsewhere.

The perch mission was then the next to be addressed and once again my good friend Terry 'Theo' Theobald had offered two new waters which had been kind to him in the past. A commercial lake complex in Wales was suggested, but that adventure would have to wait, as first we headed back to the River Kennet and a stretch which had produced 4lb fish to his rods recently. Prior to filming, Theo and I had been on a couple of reconnaissance trips on a canalised section of river, typical of the Kennet's middle reaches. Although unspectacular, perch to over 2lb did fall to our lobworm baits so a big fish was certainly a possibility.

Day one saw us gather in the car park but with overnight rain staining the river we opted to fish the Kennet and Avon Canal instead. This had remained clear – a prerequisite for good perch sport. Not that our chances of a specimen diminished, as this waterway ran into the river no more than a mile away and it too was riddled with

Lovely camping weather.

Struggling for bites.

Like the previous day, I called upon the pulling power of the pole and began experimenting with a curious contraption called a flat float. This would allow me to fish with all the finesse of a float, while anchoring the worm to the deck in a similar way to legering. The air temperature had taken on a mild feel but alas, the water's didn't mirror this and again the fishing was hard. Theo struggled to tempt many bites while I scraped five fish, including a couple of two-pounders. The worn banks caused by angling pressure were a further sign we were in the wrong place and we knew deep down that any more effort would be wasted. Perch, like all predators, thrive on neglect and it was obvious that word had got out about these fish and we had arrived after the Lord Mayor's Show, so to speak. It was time to head for pastures new.

crayfish, which are the stable diet of a big stripey. Unfortunately for Theo, he found the sport hard going on rod and line, while I luckily had the matchman's weapon to wield - a pole. By presenting a chunk of lobworm close to the far bank I lured 13 perch in total to 2lb but alas never felt our dream fish was either possible or present.

Day two dawned and with clarity returning to the main river we set about fishing two of the swims which had produced Theo's biggest fish in the past.

Keeping a watchful eye.

"Path to the perch".

 With another two days of failure under our belts, we thought we should be close to earning our stripes, but at least it was a pleasure to have a break with the family at Christmas and do a bit of roach fishing on my local rivers, the Stour and Avon. Nothing big came my way and after recovering from the New Year celebrations with friends, I was heading into Wales to join Martin and Theo at a water reputed to hold the perch of our dreams.

It was a journey I'd made many times before. I am a keen birdwatcher and the road led to the Welsh hills and the home of the few remaining red kites in Britain. In those days they were so rare they were virtually extinct, so we found it exciting to camp out in the winter snows we seemed to get regularly in those days and search the slopes at dawn as the kites sought a breakfast of earthworms. They are the most graceful of birds in flight, so it's a real bonus that the successful reintroduction schemes around the country mean that many more people can enjoy seeing them.

One of the best places to see red kites is along the M40 near London, a far cry from West Wales where I was now enjoying their sunlit plumage as they circled above the lakes where perch angler's dreams come true.

 Heading over the Severn Bridge, we entered Wales. Our journey would see us pass down the southern spine into the town of Pontarddulais and from there we would rise up into the Cefn Drum hills. Now, with the River Loughor skirting this area perhaps you are expecting a tale recounting battles with wild sea trout or the like but it may surprise you to learn that a commercial fishery had caught our attention in the continued perch quest - Whitesprings Lakes.

Maybe I need to take a step back for a moment and explain a little of the background. Over recent months rumours of monster perch had rumbled out of the valleys and reached the ears of this Englishman. It wasn't me though that took the initial plunge but my friend and proud Welshman Theo who made a visit to the complex, again keen to help us catch the 'Impossible'. During a cold, miserable afternoon my day was suddenly lit up by a rather excited angler. "I've had thirty one perch and twenty five of them over 2lb," shouted Theo down the phone. "When are we going then?" came my rather predictable reply.

Hastily I cleared a space in the diary and now you can perhaps understand the purpose of our journey, especially given that tales of 4lb-plus fish accompanied the conversation. Could this really be the place our search would reach its climax? I am always very sceptical of such tales but commercial carp lakes are exactly the type of venues where perch can exist unmolested, which is vital to the well being of this species. With a huge larder of silver fish and anonymity from anglers, it's no surprise that they can reach specimen proportions.

As I stared down into a valley awash with water, Whitesprings did not look how I expected it to. The sparse, uniform banks of my mind's eye were replaced by a series of tree-lined, bay-filled lakes that nestled at the foot of rolling hills. Two red kites hung overhead, majestic and graceful, while a bullfinch hopped from tree to tree, displaying its bold plumage. Not the typical dull hole-in-the-ground, then. Instead I was treated to a site presented in the shadow of a bracken-laden hill, its bronzed slopes tracking the sun's movements across the sky.

Vince, the owner, greeted our arrival with a warm handshake and captivated me with stories of huge stripeys. The Canal Lake was to be the destination and once Theo arrived we started our descent into the complex. Vince had certainly got me excited and combined with Theo's tales of the previous week I was almost running for the swim. For now all our suspicions of, let's say, 'over zealous weighing', were forgotten.

Our game plan was to target the area that had produced the thirty-one fish for Theo. Initially we would try using the lake's natural larder as bait in the form of small roach, fished in conjunction with a loafer float. Tackle consisted of a powerful 'carp bagging' waggler rod and a fixed spool reel loaded with 5lb mono. In my experience perch are worthy adversaries in battle and with the chance of something special, I didn't want to take any risks with light tackle.

Fishing from the same swim, we targeted a corner of an island each where the depth shallowed slightly. With no more than three-quarters of an acre to go at in this rectangular-shaped lake, it felt like we could never be too far away from fish and our target. The initial casts were made and I eagerly perched on the edge of my chair, awaiting a response. The first bite on a new venue is always an exciting affair and for this one I didn't have to wait too long. With a single bob and then a slow drag the float disappeared from view. Striking, I made contact with another world, a world full of striped flanks, flaring gills and erect dorsals.

Spluttering and thrashing, my prize hit the surface and revealed what I had expected. She was a good fish, perhaps 2lb 8oz, and carefully she was drawn over the waiting net. As I unhooked her, I threw my terminal tackle into the margin to keep it out of harm's way – but instead it amazingly went straight into the mouth of another hungry perch! I suspected the shoal had followed the initial fish into the bank, agitated by the commotion, and the result was that I now found myself connected to another big perch.

Theo too struck and simultaneously our rods arced against the hill-side backdrop. Within minutes I had tempted two good fish and Theo was the proud owner of a three-pounder. I surmised that we had already enjoyed the highlight of the day but by midday I couldn't have been further from the truth.

It seemed like our rods had been constantly landing perch, with not one under the 2lb mark. Vince's call on the tannoy that lunch was ready rounded off a terrific morning. Perhaps I could get to like commercials after all!

As we tucked into sausage, egg and chips we recounted our battles and hoped for more to come. Two happy, contented anglers strolled back to the lake in the warm afternoon sun and once again endeavoured to tempt a perch. The float sailed away for the umpteenth time and I struck, making the connection. This perch felt heavy as it pulled from side to side, angered by its mistake and unsure of its destiny. My first glimpse confirmed what I suspected as a large white belly came into view and I checked the clutch as I prepared for the end game. With no mistakes my perch was safe - all 3lb 10oz of it.

Rarely have I ever experienced such frenetic action with our list of success resembling a cricket scoreboard and eight perch over 3lb tells its own story. But what of our target – did the lake actually hold a fish over 4lb? Well, plenty of people had caught one so it was hard to explain that no such fish had fallen in both this and Theo's original trip when I would guess the entire population had been banked. Perhaps what I needed was a new set of scales as mine kept weighing less than other people's!

So in a way we left Wales a little disappointed, as we would have dearly loved that *'Impossible'*. In hindsight this was crazy and maybe a little greedy, given what we had actually caught. Theo and Vince, the owner, had gone above and beyond the call of duty, making us very welcome and maybe, just maybe, that cunning old monster we so wanted had managed to out-wit us and keep the goal from our grasp. For now though, a return to England beckoned and the holiest of angler's grails – a 3lb roach.

Theo's call.

Having got some lovely film of Theo and Martin hauling big perch in the Welsh hills, it was becoming critical that we invested some more time in trying to catch a giant river roach. As you may remember, a three-pounder was our target, which was quite ridiculous when it's difficult enough catching two-pounders.

There was a time when a 2lb roach was something of a formality in the area I live in Dorset, but with the dredging of rivers and general environmental degradation, they are rare creatures now. What is more, cormorant predation is so serious in the River Avon and Stour valleys that roach populations are

unlikely to recover. Young ones only survive to about 10oz now because cormorants target the larger specimens - and I do mean large. A few years back a friend watched three cormorants trying to swallow a roach on the Stour not half-a-mile from my house and when the birds gave up after five minutes he went to weigh the dying monster. It pulled the scales down to 2lb 10ozs.

So when Martin came to stay for a few days roach fishing in January our confidence was tempered by reality. However, it had been raining over the weekend so the rivers were coloured but clearing, the air mild, the sky overcast and the wind light. Perfect roach weather but in fact, on day one a long search with

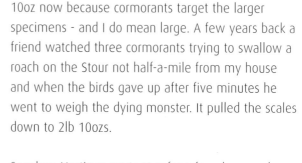
float and leger along the Avon proved fruitless - such is the life of a roach angler !

Day two was even more promising weather-wise and it was clear from the first cast that things were different - the roach were feeding. I'd chosen to fish the swim on the Avon at Longford that fifteen years ago had produced a legendary catch of roach for my series 'A Passion for Angling'. That day had started at dawn with a lucky roach roll that led me to catch four 2lb roach before Bob caught a further ten for the camera, followed by Chris getting one too - it was a good day!

Smiles all round.

Fifteen years later I was light legering this very shallow swim and from the first cast my quiver tip was twitching - there were fish in the swim. Not long after, the tip pulled round and a roach of about 1lb came my way, a cause for celebration because catching even an average roach these days can be a rare occurrence. But better was to follow. Next cast I hooked a more substantial fish and when it rolled at the tail of the swim I could see it was a big roach. A couple of nervous minutes later it was in the net, its weight a satisfying 2lb 3 oz. I phoned Martin to share the moment and he was catching well too, fishing in a gap in some alder trees downstream.

He'd already had good dace and chub and just started to catch roach when his pole elastic was stretched to breaking point by a carp. This large fish trashed his swim before gaining its freedom, so it went quiet for a while. But the fish were obviously 'on' because we

I needed new scales.

both continued to catch chub and the occasional roach all day. We felt sure that our chances of success the next day were high which was great news because we would have help.

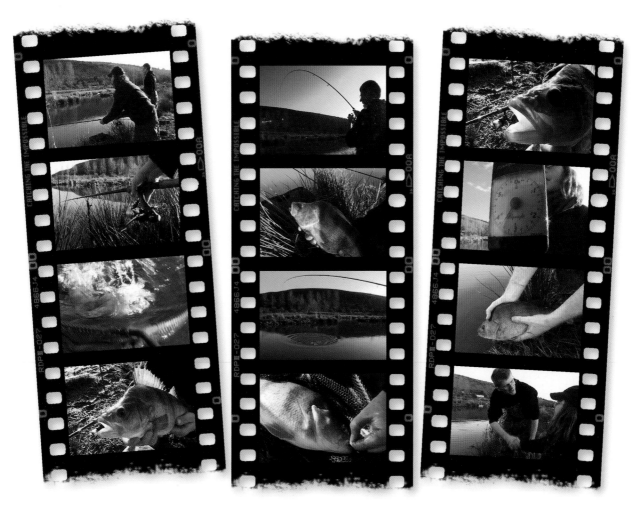

A welcome in the valleys.

 The day had been mild and overcast with the Avon carrying a tinge of colour. In short, perfect roach conditions. Unfortunately I had managed to avoid catching a 2lb fish, let alone an *'Impossible'* and was weighing up whether this was due to one simple fact – my lack of competence. It could have been, but many better men than I have suffered a similar fate. The river Avon can be so cruel and with very few roach present it is easy to sit in a perfect-looking swim that actually contains no fish and then even if they are there, that's no guarantee you will catch one.

Still, with another day ahead I could at least hope to catch a good roach, even if I was less confident of our *'Impossible'* target of 3lb. Therefore, reinforcements were invited, with Tim Norman and Terry Lampard once again agreeing to join the quest. Now, if you are going into battle against a monster roach there are few better men to have on your side. but even with these two heavyweights onside, the chances of catching this *'Impossible'* on film was madness, even if we had a decade to achieve it. A switch of rivers had also been decided upon; the Avon could wait for another day. It was now time to visit the Dorset Stour, home of the English record roach.

Pouring a glass of wine, I scanned over Hugh's library of fishing books, names like Walker, Yates and Crabtree filled the shelves but it was Terry's book 'First Cast' that caught my eye, resulting in me finding a comfortable chair by the fireplace to read it; the page fell open at the White Mill chapter. Here he recounted how the pair of them spent many winters chasing the silver leviathans of the Stour, with both men catching fish over 3lb, the best going 3lb 8oz and 3lb 5oz – certainly enough to endorse their credentials.

Its contents had me enthralled and soon made the pain of the earlier failure fade away. A three-pounder, although rare, was possible and Terry had tempted a total of nine over the magic mark - now

that's just plain greedy! As the chapter continued, the difficulty of the task ahead resurfaced. I shall quote the book directly: "A fish half an ounce under 3lb was my second and last fish of the season, and Tim's season ended completely roach-less from the stretch". And this was from two of the country's best anglers!

Sleep was a fitful affair that night, which is a classic symptom of a fishing trip the next day and I was glad to be leaving the house for a dawn rendezvous with our two new companions. The four of us met on the bridge, laden with a jamboree of floats, quivertips and concoctions to lure our prize. I must admit, the river looked perfect and I half expected to see a huge back roll in mid-river as its owner woke for the morning. Alas, everything else was in place except the roach.

I know I shouldn't have but I just couldn't help asking, "So how close are we to a 3lb roach?" Tim scratched at his beard, taking time to give a full and conclusive answer. "Oh, give or take a bit, I should say ten miles," followed by a bellowing laugh. It made me wish I'd kept my mouth shut.

With the light levels rapidly rising, it was time to call a halt to this bridge conference and get on with the job in hand. I would head downstream while the others went in the opposite direction. We would keep in contact via mobile phone, should the *'Impossible'* become a reality...... but I wasn't holding my breath.

Winter's finest prize.

liquidised bread, blended with 25 per cent brown crumb and a handful of aquarium gravel to ensure a rapid descent in the fast winter flow.

Each had based their swim choice on summer reconnaissance trips when the river had cleared and gravel runs could be located. Thirty yards of unbroken smooth water sat downstream - and hopefully a roach or two. Working their floats and mending the line, it was a meticulous process of gradually increasing the depth until the flake passed within millimetres of the gravel bottom. Half-a-dozen trots later and Terry's float sunk from view. The culprit was only a few ounces but it was still a good sign. Roach are shoal fish and where there's one there will almost certainly be more. Slowly the fish began to grow in size, reaching a creditable weight of 1lb, but the next trot produced a bend in the carbon we all hoped for. Darting from side to side, it tried to rid itself of the hook, but Terry's barb hung in position and allowed Tim to scoop the roach from its watery world. Marvelling at their prize, it was obvious a fish of over 2lb sat in front of them - 2lb 8oz to be exact - a tremendous roach and big enough for it to make a fine capture on film.

Being great friends and happy to share their success, Tim was now to get his opportunity and took over the swim. First run down and his bulbous orange tip buried. Striking, his rod bent over but not in the head-

Quivering with anticipation.

Although trotting is a more pleasurable pursuit, I felt that the lead would offer the best option for a large fish. Roach have not grown big without becoming wary and I reasoned that a float passing over their heads would do me no favours at all, especially with the constant 'whoosh' as I retrieved it upstream. So a 13 ft quivertip rod was combined with a tiny feeder and long tail, on which sat a 20 hook with a single red maggot. Perhaps today would be the day I would make contact with a big roach. Meanwhile, Terry and Tim had decided to set their stall out in an altogether different fashion. 14 ft float rods combined with large wire-stemmed Avon-style floats would prove the mainstay of their attack. Bulk shotted at three-quarter depth, with two dropper shot followed by a size 14 hook. A small lump of soft, fluffy white bread was the bait – an essential for any true Wessex roacher and one the pair swear is more productive than any other. While they set up, both men introduced occasional balls of free feed, a method perfected over winters of similar challenges. The content was made up of 75 per cent

Time to reflect.

Everything but roach.

shaking manner of a roach, instead the rod continued to arc as an unseen force headed back upstream. Somehow Tim had become connected to a pike! A couple of minutes followed, with it doing it's very best to wreck the swim before finally chewing through the mono. Now you would think at this point that fate had dealt a cruel hand to this pair, but destiny was just about to play its trump card.

Unbeknown to the two anglers, while the smaller fish scattered, a monster made up of silver scales and red fins quickly re-took its position at the tail of the swim. With Tim retackling, Terry once again allowed his float to trundle down and guess what was waiting to devour his flake? Initially, its immense proportions didn't become apparent, but gradually as the battle wore on it became bigger and bigger. Both men held their breath as something very special played itself out for the camera.

I only became aware of events when an excited Tim rang to tell me I had better come up quickly. On arriving, I found the pair of them crouched over a net, blocking my view of its contents. As they parted, a fish of Goliath proportions lay before us, pigeon-chested with a silvery, blue chassis that was tipped off with a vivid trim. Carefully, she was placed on the scales and we all waited excitedly for them to read an incredible 3lb 5oz. Amazingly, it was Terry's first three-pounder from the Stour in fifteen years and the *'Impossible'* had just become possible! This was truly remarkable. Not only had we tempted the 30lb pike but the 3lb roach as well, neither of which Hugh or I thought would ever be filmed.

To a non-angler a 3lb roach doesn't seem much, but imagine a creature far rarer than an osprey, otter or golden eagle and you'll understand a little better - in fact, I think you would have more chance of meeting a talking dodo that has a million pounds to give you! Well maybe not quite true, but I'm sure you get my drift.

Thanks to the kindness and dedication of our companions, we had on film the fish of not only a lifetime but ten of them. Catching big fish is about getting on a roll and it felt like we were now unstoppable.

Terry's truly 'incredible' roach.

A River Record

 ONE of the iconic images that all good fishing films should include is a kingfisher sitting on a rod. If it also dives off it to catch a fish, then whacks it on the rod to kill it, so much the better! But where could I hope to film such a crucial scene?

Luckily, being a roach angler means I have plenty of good friends and one in particular is Trevor Harrop. He's a lovely bloke who I don't have time to go fishing with often enough, but when we do it's always a thoroughly enjoyable day, full of laughs. We catch a few fish too, so that's a difficult combination to beat. What's more, he runs our 'local' Roach Club so I had access to a great shoal of 'river informants' including kingfisher spotters. However, it was Trevor who came up with the goods.

When fishing the River Stour for roach, a kingfisher came and sat on his rod, and Trevor was holding it at the time! Doing his best impression of St. Francis, he proceeded to attract minnows under his rod with groundbait so the kingfisher returned and started to fish. Trevor couldn't fish anymore for fear of striking the bird into orbit, so they became the best of friends, with the little fella being christened Neil. Trevor has a way with the birds, or so he tells me.

Anyway, he made us a map with 'x' marking the spot where Neil lived, so a couple of days later Martin and I were set up in Trev's swim, waiting for our proposed star to turn up. Rain had raised river levels and coloured the water so in these ideal conditions Martin started to catch roach. After a while Neil showed up and sat in a nearby bush but the water was too murky for him to see the minnows, so sadly, we never did get to film him on the rod.

Christmas present?

we consider it a bit of an honour that having created the habitat we have managed to attract otters. If only I could have filmed them swimming about in the dark, especially one Christmas, when we had a mum and little cub visiting for several weeks. The fish didn't think it was such a good Christmas present and neither did I, as I had to run around in the middle of the night trying to stop them eating too many of the fish.

It struck my wife Sue and I as ironic that in the early 80's when our children were small, we had to travel all the way to Shetland to find enough otters to make films on them for the BBC. In those days, otters were virtually extinct in much of southern England, including Dorset, but thirty years later they are present in every river in the county. It just goes to show how nature, given the chance, will recover and flourish. It's a good thing we have anglers and the ACA to ensure that there are fish in the rivers for otters to eat!

Enjoying the wildlife of the waterside is just one of the pleasures we get when out fishing. What's more, wildlife was a vital element in our series because it will help make the films more enjoyable, especially for non-anglers. We felt sure that including children and ladies fishing would increase their appeal even more, showing that angling can be enjoyed by anyone, regardless of age or gender.

Reverting to Plan 'B', I set up a rod in one of my favourite perch swims on the River Stour near home. In this spot an ancient willow tree overhung an outflow from the sewage farm. It was a haven for minnows and heaven for kingfishers! What's more, a riverside path with lots of dog walkers ensured the kingfishers were used to people. It was simple for me to set up the camera in a bush close to my rod, conveniently placed just above the shoal of minnows. It wasn't long before the kingfishers started to take advantage of my kindness. In fact, fights broke out amongst all four of them for the best bit of the rod. My only problem was the fishing friends who came along to chat and as a result, frightened the kingfishers off. However, after two days I had the shots in the can.

Trouble is, I needed bigger close ups, so a year later I set up a stick overhanging our pond and hid in the house with the camera. We have a little stream and several ponds in our garden in which minnows thrive, so when kingfishers produce young on the River Stour, they fly upstream to our garden to learn how to fish. Two visited fairly regularly but it took me a month before I had a close-up of one with a fish. Incidentally, one of the kingfishers had broken the tip off the lower part of its beak but it didn't stop it catching minnows.

Herons visit us occasionally too, even egrets, but less welcome are the otters that eat all our big carp! Still,

Kingfisher heaven.

The finest fisherman.

Artic roach.

So we planned to include several ladies, including those who fish competitively in matches, and hoped that Wendy Lythgoe would agree to join Martin on the Bristol Avon; she kindly said yes. You might wonder why we chose Wendy and the answers are conclusive. Firstly, she started fishing as a child, taken out by her dad, the Warrington AA supremo, Frank Lythgoe. She soon got into match fishing, became one of the best lady anglers in the country, got in the England team and then won an individual bronze and four gold medals in the World Championships. She is now the Sales and Marketing Manager for an international bait company and apart from that is as nice a lady as you could wish to meet. So fishing on the Bristol Avon gave me a chance to get to know what made her tick - and to film her catching more fish than Martin!

The contest was staged in Chippenham, a place with lots of roach. Martin trotted a float while Wendy used a pole and while she was catching fish she told me how she got started. At age three her dad said she could either go shopping with her Mum or go fishing with him. She chose fishing and absolutely loved it and soon found she could catch more fish than everyone around her. Taught by her match angler dad, the competitive instincts were strong and, despite competing in a male-dominated sport, she proved that this was no handicap and delighted in beating the blokes around her. She got some stick of course, being a lady among dozens of lads, but being a' northern lass', she was never short of suitable retorts.

While telling me about her life and demonstrating her skills she kept on catching fish, including some netters - but so was Martin in the next swim. However, it was freezing cold and the fishing a struggle so by the time we were all frozen solid we declared honours even and retreated to a warm fire in the local pub.

Next day, Wendy headed back 'up north' but Martin and I had another day's filming planned. With the weather in Arctic mode there was only one species left on our list that we stood a chance of catching in these clear water conditions, and that was our 'Impossible' dace. A 1lb dace is not a big fish but a very rare one. In fact, if we caught our target it would be one of the largest dace in the country. It would take some catching of course, but Martin knew a special spot to try.

 Slowly but surely the lengthening days were sending winter into retreat, even if the New Year had just been and gone. Mother Nature was being urged to prepare for a spring explosion, highlighted in tiny ways which only people close to the countryside notice. And down below the surface of our rivers, fish too were feeling the change. Gathering up and pushing onto faster gravel runs, a shoal of silver darts had begun to prepare for the spawning ritual which would obsess them within the month.

Along the River Kennet the dace, like everywhere else, had started to migrate. These fish though, were more akin to herrings such were their proportions. Their mother of pearl flanks flashed over the gravel as they showed off the bluey-green tint and, unlike the rest of

Ladies day.

the upper Kennet, these fish had avoided the pollution that had ransacked the river less than a decade ago. Nestled in one of the many side-streams, their world had remained unchanged and with the lack of competition and a larder full of rich pickings, life was good. I would guess that perhaps twenty fish still remained and certainly no more, but they were of a size that would make any angler go weak at the knees.

Now, you wouldn't expect these fish to have reached such proportions without gaining a great deal of guile - the reeded far bank of their home was testimony to that. Hanging on stems and separated from their owners were a collection of trotting floats. The temptation to cast too close to the reeds in a desperate attempt at success had proved too much for some. There in full view of the would-be fisherman sat a record fish, something which could understandably drive a man crazy and I was no different, as their pursuit the previous winter had proved. Both Hugh and I had tempted a 2lb roach but the dace remained ambivalent to our efforts.

Such was their lack of interest I felt certain we had arrived too late, their desire to reproduce having overruled their hunger. If we were to catch a really big dace it would have to be a gravid hen fish and this season our timing needed to be spot on. With the shoal size diminishing year on year it could have been our last chance at these fish – we just had to get it right.

Dace fisher's delight.

As we walked down the maze of paths which criss-crossed the water meadows, I was confident in my plan. There was no need for a float, centrepin or trotting rod - I would be doing things differently this time around. Over the years I reasoned that even the stupidest of fish would have become aware of an angler's presence by a float constantly being dragged over their heads, so instead I decided to link leger. My sensitive quiver tip rod was erected to its 10ft length and the reel, loaded with 2.8lb line, was attached. A simple one swan shot paternoster rig was assembled, which was enough to hold station, while a long 1.8lb tail to a 20 hook provided the finishing touches.

Where the river flowed out of a wooded copse and back into the light, a far bank run began to form and there in the shadows sat the bars of silver that we had come for. I know a dace can never look as big as a barbel or carp in the water but believe me these were every bit as impressive. A pound is the magic mark and at a glance every one looked over that weight. As a result, I had an uncontrollable urge to cast out and had to physically

pronounce the words 'don't do it!' to myself. I sat down on the seat box and took a couple of minutes to get my mind together. Avoiding direct eye contact with the fish for fear of falling under their spell once again, I positioned myself well upstream, hidden from view.

I had absolutely no intention of casting out for at least an hour because I had to tip the balance in my favour first. Red maggots would be drip fed constantly down river and hopefully trigger the dace into feeding. Patience was the key here and I nearly weakened on several occasions as time ticked by, not that it was too much of a chore soaking up some of England's finest countryside.

With the tackle now ready and the waiting time elapsed I made an underarm flick into the zone and paid out a large bow of line. This was vital to avoid direct contact between the tip and the fish. Alas, I may have tried to be subtle but the first mouth to gorge the maggot was not! A rogue rainbow trout trashed the swim, sending up puffs of silt as every fish dived for cover. To add insult to injury the line snapped, leaving me one very frustrated angler. I now had to build the dace's confidence up all over again and for a further half-an-hour I followed the routine I'd gone through earlier, all the time having to fight hard to resist the temptation to make a cast. Only when I felt certain that I had gained the shoal's trust did I reach for the tackle again.

First cast, the swan shot landed perfectly and I allowed what little flow there was to slightly tension the tip. Hovering nervously, I held the rod, certain a bite would come - it was just a matter of when. The bait had been in place for no more than a couple of minutes when the tip tapped and then began to slowly drag round. For fear of breaking the hooklength I tempered my strike but still felt the pull of a fish on contact. I knew immediately that it was a dace and although the encounter was never going to be epic I could feel the pace of my heart quickening. Drawing her towards the net I prayed that the hook

would hold and as she reached its embracing arms, I let out a huge sigh of relief.

Still not pigeon-chested but mammoth in both length and width, with its torso shimmering in the winter sun, the scales read 1lb 2oz. The fishing world had gone mad and our *'Impossibles'* were tumbling one after another. All the trials and tribulations of the past where I had begun to doubt if I could even fish were now forgotten and the rewards were beyond belief. The *'Impossible'* tag in the series felt like a badge of honour, not a noose.

I wondered what still lay ahead in the final weeks of the river season? If it was nothing I couldn't complain but that story still had to be written, because we had a date with a stillwater .... and if catching a 3lb roach from a river wasn't enough, Hugh wanted one from a lake.

Record shaker.

 After Martin's great catch the weather remained cold but at least conditions were settled and for me at least, this always seems to be good conditions for catching roach. Despite having already caught our *'Impossible'* 3lb roach and from a river too, we were still keen to visit that lake 'near Oxford' that was Britain's roach fishing Mecca. Celebrating such famous fisheries by including them in our series was important because they have become part of our history. So even if we didn't film at Redmire Pool, at least we could honour Adam's Mill, the Royalty Fishery, and this seven acre lake near Oxford called Willow Pool.

I, for one, had become so mesmerized by this water's succession of 3lb roach adorning the angling press that I had to go to see these wonderful looking fish for myself. I wasn't expecting to catch one but hoped to witness a monster in the hands of an expert. However, much to my delight, I actually caught one over 3lb on my first visit, and one more on each of my two subsequent visits, with a best of 3lb 4oz. It was extraordinary fishing, because I also photographed a fantastic fish of 3lb 10oz for Ron Kettle. These experiences led me to believe that filming Martin catching a three-pounder would be a formality. But maybe the roach would have other ideas...

 Over the years I have been lucky enough to fish a few waters which I'm sure in the passing of time will become legendary. Adam's Mill for barbel, Elstow for rudd and the Upper Great Ouse for perch are all modern day greats. Now we were heading to the home of big stillwater roach, the Linch Hill complex, or to be more precise Willow Pool. This is a lake that will have its place in history long after the last roach has been lured, that much I'm sure. In all honesty I have always looked towards rivers for roach but with big fish becoming rare, I was prepared to eat humble pie and accept that my snobbery could have been misplaced.

3lbs. of silver.

One of the quiet men of the big fish angling world, Adrian Smith, had agreed to be my guru. After tempting a series of monster roach from this venue, I would have been a fool to ignore his advice. Successful tactics had been a combination of 1lb test curve rods with 6lb mainline connected to feeder-fished maggots. By combining very short hooklengths with the heavy feeders, roach, finicky by nature, would give you bites that nearly dragged the rod in. Yes, I'm afraid I was going to be bolt-rigging for them like a carp angler. I was further surprised by Adrian's choice of maggot - the basic white variety. I would have bet my house on them being red in colour. Still, I wasn't going to ignore his advice. I have written it many times before but never be afraid to seek guidance. Only an idiot would ever think he knows everything and as angling is such a vast subject and constantly changing, I suppose that's why I love it so much.

Unfortunately, Adrian couldn't accompany us on our venture to the Oxfordshire venue but he had arranged the next best thing - another companion and a master stillwater roacher, Alan Storey; he would be available to point us in the right direction should we need help. Alan, like Adrian, was a mine of information when we rendezvoused with him on a bitter Monday morning. With the lake's warmest bank busy with anglers we bit the bullet and pitched up in the teeth of a northerly wind – oh, and just to make things even better our bank was almost permanently in shade. It looked like we were going to need every bit of clothing we had packed for the trip.

Tackle was fairly simple: soft tench float rods were combined with small fixed spool reels loaded with 6lb line, while 40gm black cap feeders wrapped with black insulation tape over half the body (to ensure the slow release of the maggots) provided the casting weight. On the business end sat a helicopter rig consisting of two small float stops and a micro ring on the mainline, then a 4ins 3lb flurocarbon hooklength to an 18 hook finished off the rig. Due to the cold temperatures, the only free feed entering the swim would be via the feeder, with regular re-casting every 45 minutes the key.

While white maggots would provide half my feed in each load, I hoped I had a secret weapon up my sleeve for the remaining part - bloodworm and joker. After all, what could be more natural for a big roach? Also, when a match angler is faced with tricky conditions and has to get a bite, this is what he'll choose. Surely these silly old stillwater roach would soon be mine. Well, two days in and I hadn't had a sniff - so much for my plans. To be fair though, I think the near freezing temperatures may have been partially responsible, or was that just my excuse? Alan had managed two fish up to 2lb 12oz, so there was still hope, but only if I could come to terms with this type of angling. Bolt-rigging for roach can be frowned upon by traditionalists and I certainly would prefer to use a more active approach, be it the float or the tip, but two bites in 48hrs puts the challenge into perspective. Trying to concentrate over this period would result in one of two things; firstly you miss the bite and secondly, which is more likely in my case, you lose the will to live and give up. So I'm afraid, if you want a big stillwater roach, bolt-rigging is a method you have to consider!

Day three saw us once again arrive at dawn, hoping to see a sign. Alas, the sight of porposing red fins failed to materialize but I could just feel a slight rise in air temperature; perhaps my luck was about to turn. Unfortunately, Alan's commitments saw him unable to join us so I was faced with a dilemma - go into his swim, the

Theatre of dreams.

Roach food.

Following the same ritual, a light carpet of bait was introduced with regular casting before I settled back in the hope of an afternoon bite. At 2pm my indicator suddenly became unfrozen and jammed against the butt as line screamed off the reel at a rate of knots before everything fell slack. Lifting up the rod, the culprit was long gone and I reeled in a bent hook. Just my luck - I wait ages and a carp decides to suck in my bait. Well, at least the disturbance may have stirred up the bottom and attracted a roach.

Fifteen minutes later and the indicator jagged upwards again and this time there was no mistake. I felt a heavy nod forty yards out and started to wonder if I had at last achieved my goal. With such light lines, small hooks and short tails, patience had to be the key when playing the fish. To rush now would only mean one thing - a breakage and after all this time, with Hugh waiting patiently behind, that was the last thing I wanted to happen.

scene of success the previous day, or stay put. My hunch was that the fish may have begun to move and with my original area normally being very productive, I decided to sit it out. Rods were once again cast out to the side of the island and staggered down the gravel slope which fell away into the depths. The only subtle change I made on the previous days was the introduction of a small amount of hempseed in the feeder mix - its oily properties hopefully drawing a roach's attention.

Gently, I coaxed line back onto the spool until a broad silver flank rolled in front of me. The chore of the long wait melted away as I prepared to net what was obviously a big fish and fortunately everything held firm. At last I became the proud owner of a Linch Hill roach.

Roach anglers mecca.

Its length was huge but the belly sagged slightly, the result, I guessed, of a hard winter. Still, with its huge scales and magnificent blue sheen I was a happy man. Gently placing my prize into a weigh sling the dial spun round to 3lb before slipping back a fraction. We settled on 2lb 15oz and I took one last glance at a roach that from anywhere but Linch Hill would be classed as a monster. It will be hard to believe but I was actually happy that the scales had recorded a result 1oz under an *'Impossible'*.

When we first started out on this long journey both Hugh and I were adamant that the truth was to be told and not just adapted to fit the mission. We were to catch everything we claimed and, critically, every fish would weigh exactly what it weighed. Sure, an ounce could easily have been added but to my mind that would have made a mockery of the whole series. Instead, hopefully the general public would see that there had been no smoke and mirrors used, just bloody hard work.

Another 2lb 4oz fish fell at dusk to give us a fine brace and a chance to notch up my own piece of Linch success. When the history books pass judgement at least I can say I caught a roach there. Also, more

importantly, Hugh gave the thumbs up that our quest for a large stillwater roach was complete.

 After our chilly but enjoyable roach session at Linch Hill, the winter remained harsh, with little in the way of sunshine to relieve the relentless cold. It was obviously tough for wildlife too, because on several days we saw flocks of lapwings and Scandinavian thrushes fleeing the icy cold in the northeast, flying to the comparative warmth of Cornwall and Ireland.

It was evidently tough for fish too, because when we tried to catch an *'Impossible'* perch they had completely lost their appetite. In two days' intense fishing we never got a bite. However, a slight lift in temperature saw us head back to the Great Ouse for the return match and this visit provided clear indication that fishing can be like that classic football cliche, 'a game of two halves'.

Nothing but the truth.

How far could we keep pushing our luck for the winter? It had given us everything we could have wished for except one final fish – a 4lb perch. Last year's search had turned into a disaster and a fish I felt confident of luring had melted away into the shadows. With the river season's end fast approaching it was time to once again return to the Ouse and search out our *'Impossible'* perch

A mid-morning rendezvous with Hugh in Buckinghamshire found the conditions to be perfect, with overcast skies and mild temperatures, completely different to last year when nature threw its very worst at us. If we could locate a big perch over the next two days I felt certain it would feed. The stretch of Great Ouse we had chosen to fish was new to me but a tip off from my good friend, Kev Newton, had pointed us in its direction. After banking a series of good fish Kev knew exactly where they were located, a knowledge which he kindly shared with us. Following the instructions given, we hurried along the river bank, the waters complexion tinged green – perfect for catching.

As the river swung left, a tree with its branches kissing the surface appeared and this, so I was told, was home

Cralusso brilliance.

to our desired perch. A worm teased under the raft would, I hoped, prove tempting but on this occasion I decided to offer it in a manner unusual for a big fish angler – with a pole. I had become convinced during this period of my angling life that standard float fishing or legering wasn't maximising a swim's potential and when compared with using 13 metres of carbon, it really wasn't in the same ball park. The control given with the pole is vastly superior.

A yellow bungee elastic was selected with 4lb Double Strength line fished straight through to a size 14 hook. The float of choice was a 3gm Hungarian flat float called a Cralusso. These are absolutely brilliant for the big fish angler, enabling you to hold the bait static in the flow. Compared with legering, the presentation and lack of resistance to a taking fish is second to none. In fact, I would go so far as to say that if the distance is within pole range, and the fish accept the shadow of carbon overhead, there is no point in legering. Even though I now felt that I was going to be fishing the swim perfectly it would come as no surprise if the hours passed and the float failed to disappear. Perch can be funny creatures, sitting motionless in the swim awaiting a trigger, namely a change in light values at dusk.

The water was a constant 8ft deep leading down to the overhanging tree. The 3gram Olivette was then positioned at three-quarter depth with 8ins of line dragging bottom and being held in place by two No. 8

How could a perch resist.

shot. To increase the rig's sensitivity I overshotted the float with two No. 1s, knowing it would be held in place by the force of the flow. How could a perch outwit such tactics?

Before commencing I needed to introduce a bait-dropper full of enticing free offerings made up of chopped worm, red maggot and casters – a concoction that few perch can resist! Swinging the lot out, I gently lowered it into place a couple of feet above the tree's branches. With these temping morsels in place, I

the top section. The initial lunges were soaked up by pulling sideways, but the angry stripey headed for the branches and all I could do was hold on. Stalemate was held for thirty seconds before the perch made a fatal error – she charged out into open water where I could now keep direct control with the pole above her until the game was over.

When she hit the surface, I was greeted by a series of black stripes and a huge blood-red tail. Panicking slightly, I stabbed down the landing net to bundle in my

Pole perfection.

nicked a lobworm tail on the hook and tipped it off with a single red maggot.

Gently, I shipped out the rig and lowered the bait smack bang on top of the chopped worm. This presentation is just impossible with a traditional specimen angler's approach. And when using the pole, I always get the feeling that I've caught everything willing to feed, not just some of them. But even if that is untrue, to have such confidence in a method is a huge advantage; waiting was easy.

Holding the Clarusso against the flow, the slim-line body remained steady, before slowly disappearing under the surface. Sharply, I lifted the 12 metres of carbon and was greeted by the sight of yellow elastic pouring from

prize. A big fish of 4lb 5oz now lay before us - the sort of monster that I will never tire of looking at until my dying day.

We had what we had come for so why did I get a feeling that all was not well at Hugh's end? The answer was poor light. In my excitement I hadn't thought about what was now plainly obvious - darkness had descended rapidly on us. Sure, the perch was filmed but those incredible tiger stripes were never going to be shown off fully in such conditions. What a bitter sweet moment and one which left us both incredibly frustrated. The decision was made to slip the perch back and find overnight accommodation in a bed and breakfast before returning in the morning and duplicating the process! Nothing like a challenge then!

I don't think either of us slept well that night, especially when the heavens opened and rain streamed down the bedroom window in torrents. Perch may love mild conditions but combine it with muddy floodwater and you may as well not bother. By dawn the stream at the bottom of the garden had turned into a raging torrent and the chance of another fish looked doomed. The only possibility was to reach the river before the colour seeped into it. If we were really lucky there would be a window of a couple of hours before all was lost.

We raced to the river and it really was heart in the mouth time - what would we find? How we continued to be so fortunate I will never know but although tinged, a foot of visibility still remained. Frantically I pulled my seat box into position and began erecting the pole and with the depth already marked I could by-pass the plumbing stage and feed the swim immediately. But would the perch play ball? If I could have let go of the pole I would have had to rub my eyes in disbelief as the float tip was immediately dragged under!

An 'Impossible' perch.

I responded by lifting the pole and a heavy weight pulled back – all I could do was try and lever the perpetrator from his home. I let out a sigh of relief when the elastic's tension began to release and by keeping directly over the perch I think I bewildered it more than out-fought it as a big deep flank hit the surface. You couldn't have made it up if you tried - another 'Impossible' was heading my way. Unbelievably a perch of exactly 4lb 5oz had now replaced the mirror image of the previous evening. I don't know who or what was looking out for us but someone certainly was!

At this moment it would have been great to wallow in the winter's success but Hugh had other plans. Before the rain water altered the river's complexion we needed to film all those little extras which make his films so special. Without further ado I nicked on another lobworm

tail and presented it under the raft. I carried on fishing while Hugh sat about capturing the different angles required – the only problem being that another big perch had taken the bait and was hanging on the end of my pole! I had by now given up trying to describe how lucky I was and simply let the elastic soak up the punishment. I think Hugh wanted me to play it hard so I could encourage a big splash for the camera, after all, we had our 'Impossible' already. But nothing in my whole angling career could have prepared me for what was about to present itself - it just couldn't be a perch because the proportions were incredible. A 4lb fish looks massive but this was enormous! All thoughts of playing it for the camera vanished – I needed to land this perch as to lose it would mean being haunted forever.

Describing the events which followed is hard as a heady cocktail of panic, excitement and joy kicked in, but somehow that perch ended up in my landing net. Struggling to keep my hands steady, a weight of 5lb 4ozs was recorded, not only an Ouse record but perhaps a national river one as well. One of the most incredible spells of good fortune in my angling career had finished with a true leviathan.

 It is difficult to describe that feeling you get when you finally overcome a challenge that has haunted you with failure for months, even years. It happens occasionally in wildlife film-making and it was certainly happening now, that feeling of exhaustion and relief, tempered by large doses of happiness. We had struggled but overcome, and walking back over the meadows from the river we were feeling good. In fact, after the extraordinary successes we had enjoyed during this past winter, we were walking on air. Martin hadn't just caught all those fish, we had filmed them all too and between us we had more or less ensured that the series would be a success. Now it was time for relaxation, and some social fishing before the season's end.

Martin was joined on the River Thames by Des Taylor, Richard Lee, John Everard and Peter Drennan. I joined Trevor, Budgie and our pals in a 'Roach Match to the Death' on the River Stour, and then Trevor and Chris Yates joined me for some last day perch fishing. It was 'fun fishing' and that's what it's all about.

An 'incredible' perch.

Echoes of Walker

 ONE problem I suffered at the end of the season was sleepless nights. The mother and cub otters had returned, and to try to stop them ravaging every fish in the garden I was up for several nights, trying to frighten them away. My antics succeeded to an extent, but we lost most of our carp and rudd, along with one of our giant golden orfe.

Once they'd more or less emptied the main pond, the 'lovely' otters moved on, but then I suffered sleepless nights for a different reason - my computer had crashed big time. We had accumulated so much good material during our monster quest that I'd had to keep buying new drives to store the material for editing. For you geeks that means 8 x 200 gig drives connected in a 'daisy chain', and my Apple G5 and Final Cut Pro system just couldn't cope. With help from a computer guru I managed to solve the immediate problems and continue editing but I could see meltdown approaching.

Sleepless nights.

Martin and I had been filming for one-and-a-half years but had only used half of the time we had allocated for the project. What's more, we still had a lot of film sequences to complete, so I'd need to upgrade my computer storage systems if I was going to avoid losing the editing that I had already done. But that headache would have to wait for another day as spring was fast approaching.

On March 19th we saw the first Brimstone butterfly in the garden and on the 28th the first chiffchaff, at least two weeks late by modern standards. The otters were back on the 30th and at 4.15 am Sue and I 'enjoyed' watching the mum and cub swimming round in the torchlight while a tawny owl called from a tree above; I could only imagine it was laughing at us. We decided we had to fence the garden off, so the last laugh might be with us.

Wildlife activity was an essential part of our film stories, but many other elements were important too, including Martin's past. Understanding how our star angler grew so passionate about angling is inspiring for us all, a reminder of our own childhood and how we 'caught the bug'. So including children in the series was highly desirable, particularly if it was Martin's son, Ryan, because he would help us to recreate the capture of Martin's first fish.

 Gameboys, iPods and computers are now what fills the minds of young lads and fish, I'm afraid, fall way down the pecking order. It seems that a world of virtual reality is more attractive than the real thing. For me this is a great shame as no Playstation could ever offer more excitement than that played out by a river or lake. If a child is given the gift of angling then he, or she, will not only have a lifetime of fun to enjoy but also gain an appreciation of how precious the natural world is. I often hear people bemoan this country but, trust me, if you take time to explore the countryside then you will see how magnificent it is and what better vehicle to experience the magic than angling?

Not for one minute though, do I think convincing a child to fish is easy. In an instant, quick-fix world, patience is no longer required and blasting monsters on the computer seems more appealing than playing a carp. I have faced the very same challenge with my son, Ryan, and while he has enjoyed our trips out together the sport has never grabbed him in the same manner it did me. I'm afraid fishermen are just not 'cool' and I would argue why should we be. But when young lads want to be footballers it's hard to compete with such glamour. For my part, I have taken Ryan fishing when he wants to go, not when I do, as I think the worse thing I could do is ram it down his throat. For the time being it will have to

A Tawny owl called from above.

An angler is born.

play second fiddle to the many other attractions on offer. Given time, and it could well take until adulthood, he may become hooked like me on this all consuming passion.

A day out with a film camera with Ryan as the star had the desired effect of making angling a priority over the mobile phone. So I bundled an excited young lad into the van and headed off to our local canal – the Kennet and Avon – and a rendezvous with Hugh. The aim was to capture a snapshot of where I first began my angling career on a canal and how magical it can be through the eyes of a child.

My friend Richard Patrick had kindly arranged with the local angling club, Bathampton AA, to allow us to fish and film at their Claverton stretch. Like so many organisations up and down the country, the club do a sterling job of trying to introduce youngsters to fishing. It's these people that are the true stars and not the so-called 'celebrities'. Without the slightest hint of money or fame, their reward is from maintaining the sport's lifeblood.

The spring sun had begun to work its magic, with the first signs of nature awakening and the canal's inhabitants now moved freely after our bait. Sitting silhouetted inside the arch of a bridge, Ryan dangled a float and worm against the canal wall. Perhaps you would expect him to have been using the latest equipment but curiously he preferred Hugh's battered cane rod and centrepin. Maybe like our bent pins and bamboo poles, it gave him a feeling of being closer to the fish. An armful of the latest gadgets can, at times, act as a barrier to such an experience.

With a broad grin, a stream of tiny perch swung into Ryan's palm, each one gently examined for its spiny dorsal fin. His description of the species was better than any I could muster – 'an army fish' he called them. It showed exactly why canals are so important. Whether in urbanised or rural locations, they offer the chance for a child to catch their first fish.

Fortunately everything went to plan and within a couple of hours Hugh's work was completed. I expected, at this point, for Ryan to be keen to leave but amazingly he asked if we could stay on. So drinking lemonade and eating cakes we sat side by side, landing a range of species including roach, bream and gudgeon, as well as perch.. It seemed

like once the modern world's spell was broken, angling could still have the power to captivate a young mind.

After the enjoyable and sunny morning with Ryan, I returned to our garden and became aware of just how quickly the spring was moving ahead. By April 1st a robin had three eggs in its nest and on the 2nd a fourth. On the 5th the first swallow arrived from Africa, and on the 30th the first swift. In early May the Avon roach and barbel were spawning, along with chub and minnows, but even filming them underwater, I couldn't be sure if the chub were eating the minnow eggs or vice versa. Whatever the truth, it was clear that spring was well advanced and the water warming up. We suspected the carp would now be moving with hungry purpose and we needed an *'Impossible'* forty-pounder - so Martin and I were on the road again...

No need for computers.

Blue heaven.

 The previous spring had seen Hugh and I introduced to the stunning Acton Burnell fishery in Shropshire. Made up of two lakes deep in the rolling hills of the county, they provide a home for some of the country's largest carp. Indeed, in difficult conditions on the last visit, a mirror of 36lb was tempted but in an era full of monster carp, only a weight in excess of 40lbs would do. While the venue chosen needed to hold such a creature it also had to convey a magical feeling via its backdrop, and Acton scores a ten out of ten on both counts.

Pulling up to the old wooden gates, I was relieved that the three hour journey was over and when I turned the handle and the gates creaked open, I felt I was prising open Pandora's Box. I was leaving the rat race behind, entering a world that felt too good to be true.

With Hugh still to arrive, I followed the bluebell-lined path to the water's edge and reacquainted myself with the lake. From my vantage point, I stared down across the unbroken surface and observed a shoal of carp heading for the shallow end. The blue overcoat of a kingfisher zoomed past while a grebe searched the margins for fry – had I died and gone to heaven I asked

myself? It seemed a shame to break the lake's spell, so for a while I sat against an old tree trunk and soaked up the atmosphere. For once, I was in no rush to fish as we had the place to ourselves for the next few days. No doubt for Hugh, the journey was also a tedious affair but eventually he too arrived to sample the therapeutic qualities Acton had to offer. It was a gorgeous May day and best of all, the forecast gave more of the same for the forthcoming week. I defy any man to pick a better time of the year. The world just looks so bright and new and I had no doubt that the fishing was going to be an utter joy.

Location of the carp was down to me but it didn't take a genius to work it out. Sun and carp go hand in hand, like strawberries and cream, so combine this with a shallow expanse of water and their daytime whereabouts was obvious. The 'day' part was vital as we did not intend to fish during the hours of darkness, with a capture after dark not fulfilling what we wanted to convey on film. So with a barrow load of tackle I made my way down the wooded bank of the lake to a swim opposite 'the conker', where I had fished the previous spring. To my left, the lake gradually got shallower until it formed into a reed-lined bay, while on my right the water began to deepen again. It was here where the carp passed backward and forwards that I hoped to intercept our quarry. To help draw attention to the swim, I laced it with chicken-flavoured boilies and halibut pellets at approximately forty yards. Here the shallows gave way to deeper water and once again a point where I hoped the carp could be intercepted. While I had been trying to discover the carp's whereabouts, Hugh had spotted something much rarer – an osprey. There, sitting on a stag's head oak over the bay was this majestic bird of prey and suddenly Hugh's attention was divided and to be honest, who could blame him? To capture both of us fishing the lake at the same time would be amazing. A little blinkered by the carp though, I placed my hookbaits over the free offerings and allowed the buzzers to keep watch while I erected the bivvy. Quite why we anglers enjoy camping outside I don't know, but when blessed with fine weather I love the feeling of solitude that living in the wilds affords us. With the work over, I could relax and watch the rest of the day unfold as a stream of carp cruised up and down the lake in front of me.

The afternoon drifted by peacefully until at precisely 4pm the silence was shattered by a screaming bite alarm and before I could reach the rod, a huge sheet of bubbles erupted onto the surface as something left my swim at a rate of knots. Striking, the rod arced over and I was forced to yield line until the carp's ferocity had been spent. I knew from quite early on that this wasn't a monster, its movements weren't heavy or laborious enough. Still, when over 28lbs of carp hit the landing net it was a pleasing start, not that I was going to get time to enjoy it as my attention was grabbed by another wailing buzzer. Incredibly, like buses, two had come along at once!

From the off, the fight was an altogether different affair, exhibiting less speed but much more power. Up and down the swim she went, boring deep into the silty bottom in an attempt to shed the hook. Fortunately, the swim was free of snags or weed, so no escape was forthcoming. As each lunge became a little more subdued, I cranked line back onto the reel until a thickset bronze torso rolled in front of me, with a beer belly any darts player would be proud of; I knew for certain an *'Impossible'* was on the brink of being achieved. Agonisingly, the fish fell just 8oz short of our target and that wasn't the only obstacle. I could tell that Hugh had, let's just say, more classic proportions in mind when he thought of carp rather than this obese

Osprey watching.

Noisy hooting.

creature I had tempted. Amazingly, a carp of 39lb 8oz wasn't quite good enough, so it was back to the drawing board once again.

As nightfall arrived, my swim failed to awaken again and I reeled in the rods for a sleep. The woods behind me though, had no intention of following suit as a range of nocturnal creatures made their presence known, with the noisiest being a pair of tawny owls hooting to each other across the tree tops. This place really did feel like a world untouched by modern society's humdrum.

Carp scarer.

Day two dawned with the promise of another splendid day's weather ahead and from the sheets of bubbles erupting in my swim, the carp looked eager for breakfast. As gently as a series of 3oz leads can ever land, I set about accommodating their hunger and it wasn't long before the rod tip pulled down and the bobbin dragged upwards. Once again I was connected to a big fish but this one, propelled by its huge rudder, was intent on smashing me to bits. The heavy gear used by the modern carper can, at times, seem a little over gunned but today I was happy to have it. Another bronze back was the first glimpse I caught of it but this time it belonged to a splendid streamlined creature, its flank interspersed by huge coppery scales – a much more appropriate carp for the series and judging by its size, quite likely an *'Impossible'*. After another couple of minutes of hard work-out for the pair of us I took possession of her in the landing net. Boy, she was heavy but how heavy? The scales read 39lb 12oz. We had come within a whisker of our target again and if sanity prevailed this would be more than adequate. The trouble was that sanity and this project didn't have a lot in common! Sure, it was a very big fish but both Hugh and I felt that such a wonderful place needed a special scene and a screaming buzzer was failing to achieve this. So what else could we do? Stalk a monster carp that's what!

The easy part was deciding on the plan, the hard part was executing it. Although the shallows were a magnet for the carp they extended a long way out, meaning a fish had no reason to venture too close to shore. The only way we could attract them within range was through a lot of patience and creating no disturbance. Can you imagine what self-discipline it takes to stop fishing a swim which is full of monster carp beyond your wildest dreams, just to implement a plan which was far from certain to work? This mindset though was vital to make the series special - I had to remember that I was here to fish for the film and not myself. While I laced a marginal swim under a canopy of trees, Hugh was now free to do what he does best and capture the lake's wildlife on film, especially the osprey. Periodically I checked the bait but alas, not a single shadow passed over it and another day slipped by.

Day three came and went without much to report on my behalf except for the appearance of one large carp which was terrified by the attentions of a swan. Had we blown it? The final morning dawned and it was judgement day, perhaps our work ethic had been a little zealous because unless a chance presented itself over the next few hours, two days of fishing would have been wasted. It felt as if our goal was slipping through our fingers faster than sand. Sure, we could cast out a lead and in all probability catch but that would undo all the hard work and time invested – for now, we were stuck between a rock and a hard place.

For the umpteenth time I made my checks but this time a large shadow swung into view directly over the baited area and announced its presence with a huge puff of silt and a shower of bubbles. Slowly, I edged out of my vantage point and ran along the path quicker than a rat up a drainpipe to fetch Hugh. I'd had loads of time to prepare but still my head whirled in panic. How was I going to catch it? Would it stay in the swim? These and many more questions flashed manically through my mind. First Hugh had to edge into position with me and do this

Within a whisker.

Living in hope.

Simplicity itself.

suck it in. Spellbound I froze, only released from its grip as the quill sunk away - I knew exactly what I had tempted and this knowledge did little to settle my nerves.

A strike was followed by a huge explosion before an uncontrollable force surged towards the reeds. In only two feet of water, diving was not an option for the carp and God, was it going to make me suffer for it! I could do no more than hold on and pray, and for a while it was definitely in control. I believe the words 'this is a carp of biblical proportions' came from my mouth. Somehow the through action rod and 15lb line handled each lunge and the carp was turned. The minutes passed by and the battle's ferocity continued - if only I could hang on, our dreams would become reality. With another heave a giant copper flank made up of huge scales hit the surface, followed by a rudder that the Titanic would have been proud of! It was a common with a back wide enough to put a saddle on.

without alerting the carp to our presence. By the time we had completed this process I had lost it, the pressure reducing me to a quivering wreck. Still the carp gorged itself though and I prepared to flick out a soft pellet hookbait supported under a length of peacock quill. With two spins of the centrepin's drum I had enough line and flicked the bait into position. I was shaking as I watched its descent only to see a huge head poke out from the gloom and

Spurred on by fear, I charged out into the lake and made a desperate lunge with the net – it was now or never. Fortunately, what was lying inside the mesh was a carp which, at last, did the lake justice and, exhausted, I pulled her ashore. At 44lb 4oz it

Moment of truth.

was, coincidentally, an iconic weight in the angling world because Dick Walker's old record had been the same. We had done it and in a manner that could only have been dreamed of. I put many captures down to luck but this one had an equally big dollop of good, old fashioned hard work. Elated, Hugh and I watched her slip back into the lake – another 'Impossible'; had been achieved and for once, we took time to enjoy our success over a bottle of red wine. Clinking glasses together, we both knew we had come a long way in the last six months.

 Remarkable as Martin's carp was and however fantastic the method of capture, the osprey's presence was almost as important for the series. These fish-eating birds are as iconic as kingfishers and due to their extinction and subsequent return to Scotland are just about the most famous bird in Britain.

The first pair of osprey's settled in the Spey valley at Loch Garten in the 50's, and when still a schoolboy, I was privileged to help the RSPB protect it from egg thieves. It was a wonderful holiday and contributed to my determination to become a wildlife film-maker. Inspired by the bird's swashbuckling fish-hunting, I eventually made a film about them when I worked for the RSPB. This film was bought by the BBC and the film's remarkable success was the launch pad for my career as a freelancer and my passport to travel the world.

I have since filmed ospreys in many countries, we featured them in 'A Passion for Angling' and it was certainly included in our plans for 'Catching the Impossible'. In fact, a trip to Scotland with Martin and Bernard was due in a few months time. Since my first encounter with ospreys, their numbers have escalated and there are now well over one hundred pairs. Our bird, at Acton, made me schizophrenic as I tried to film Martin hauling carp as well as the osprey fishing, but its presence was a remarkable slice of good fortune. I presumed it was a migrant,

Echoes of Walker.

Early arrival.

First flight.

on its way from its winter quarters in West Africa to look for a nest site in Scotland, so as it was on its travels I had to hurry if I was to get any shots. So while Martin prepared his carp swims I crept round to the other side of the lake and built a hide out of brushwood. This was tucked away opposite what appeared to be the osprey's favourite perch on an old oak tree. With my giant telephoto lens installed, I could clearly see this osprey was an adult male. And he was intent on catching a fish.

It wasn't long before he leapt off his perch, plunged into the shallows and struggled out with a victim, before returning to the perch. Exciting film for sure but when the osprey, having eaten the front half of the fish, flew off, I assumed the show was over. However, twenty minutes later it was back, without the fish, and when this behaviour was repeated an hour later my past experience indicated only one conclusion - this osprey had a nest, and it was only a mile or two away! This was extraordinary, because to my knowledge there was only one other nest in England. So this pair were true pioneers for the future. Realizing the significance of this find and knowing the risks of egg-collectors hearing about the site, I kept silent and only informed the protection department of the RSPB. And I can only tell this story now because the pair have moved to pastures new. However it was an exciting moment in my bird-watching life and provided some lovely film too, especially as I could show both Martin and the osprey fishing at the same time.

It was the icing on the cake, particularly as we were able to share our excitement of both the Osprey and the huge common with our friends, owner Rob Hales and Des Taylor. We didn't mention the nest of course, but Des came round that evening and shared a glass of wine with us. Sadly, he didn't see the osprey but we were able to lay plans for a catfish hunting expedition. Des knew a good place and we were hoping he could catch us yet another *'Impossible'*.

Catfish Capers

 LIKE a giant tadpole with its marbled, mottled skin and long whiskers, the catfish is the monster of UK angling and, trust me, when hooked, nothing else can compare. After all, three-quarters of its torso is tail and even with a fully compressed rod, line will still be stripped from the reel at an alarming rate. All the angler can do is hang on and wait for the energy to subside. You only gain control of a catfish when it decides to let you. This man versus beast encounter is what draws anglers to such a creature because its power is unsurpassed by anything else in this country.

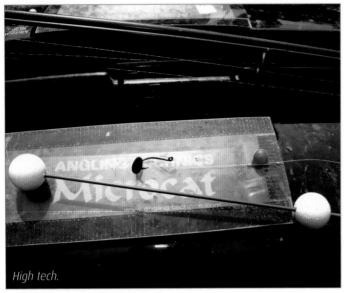

High tech.

water and hopefully it would produce a cat for the camera.

Tackle needs to be strong with these beasts, so I rigged up an outfit using a carp rod and a large fixed spool reel loaded to the gunnels with 40lb braid. This would help pull the hook home in a hard mouth, as well as be strong enough to survive the hoped for battles ahead. My first rig consisted of a dumb-bell, which is essentially two poly balls fished between a length of tubing. This is popped upon the surface, while suspended 6ins underneath is a small roach. For many years it was thought that catfish only feed on the bottom but this proved to be untrue and on warm, still, muggy nights this predator prefers to hunt in the upper layers. Its tail can often be heard smashing down on the surface as a strike results in a poor, unfortunate soul being devoured by a cavernous mouth, so I hoped my approach would help to exploit this characteristic.

The second set up was far simpler – a free-lined pellet. This was no ordinary pellet though, but a giant 40mm one and hair-rigged via a 1/0 hook ; it certainly looked the business. For even more attraction, I decided to feed a bed of marine halibut pellets soaked in oyster sauce around the hookbait, with the pungent fishy aroma hopefully providing a temptation to feed.

It had been a year since Hugh and I had targeted catfish for our film and unfortunately we had been unsuccessful. This time though, I felt sure that we would not make the same mistake. The previous trip to Linear fisheries had, without doubt, seen us on a venue capable of producing a specimen, but their numbers were comparatively low, especially when the large number of carp were factored into the equation as well. What we needed was a venue where catfish were the predominant species. In short, I needed to make a phone call. Cue the big man himself - Des Taylor. "Leave it to me son," was his answer and, true to his word, two days later we were on our way to Shatterford Lakes near Kidderminster. Shatterford is made up of six lakes staggered down a valley and fed via natural springs. Originally built in the 70s for trout fishing, it had become more famous for our target – the catfish. With moggies up to 52lb, it certainly had a big fish reputation and was more than capable of making the dream a reality. The lake we were due to target was a 'new' cat water that had recently come on line. 'The Masters' originally contained cats but had also received an additional stocking from a nearby venue, so the omens were looking good.

Bloodsucker.

Our companion for the session met us with a broad grin. Mr Controversial he might be, but Des has a passion for angling that could never be questioned. "Have you glued on those wellies?" he said. "A soft southerner like you is likely to be dragged out of them otherwise!" It was good to see Des was on form and even if the fish didn't feed it was going to be fun. The Masters' stocks were particularly impressive given that they lived in only a few acres of

Last but not least came the rod that I intended to suspend giant medicinal leeches off the bottom with a poly ball. You're probably wondering why I opted to use such a gruesome bait, with their bodies full of someone else's blood. Well, that was exactly why. While not appealing to our palate a catfish has, let's just say, an open mind on food! Being generous, I offered my host a share of these bloodsuckers but Des declined the offer, citing better baits. It certainly wasn't because he was scared of them – no, not big Des! Mind you, he nearly collapsed in hysterics when I set about hooking them on, a process that I had to do with its sucker trying to grab me. Call me a big girl's blouse but I was scared!

Desperately trying not to become its next victim, I jigged around and flapped my hands as the leech took hold of a finger! Eventually though, I had them in place and watched how they snaked and pulsed. A catfish couldn't miss these little devils. Des, meanwhile, was busy preparing his own squid offering and eventually, as dusk arrived, all our rods were in place and the witching hour fell upon us. Suddenly, the lake came alive as the slap of a large tail on the surface resounded down the valley – the cats were on the prowl, searching out their next victim.

The first take came at 11pm and my livebait rod screamed off, but unfortunately it stopped just as I went to strike. Still, it showed they were feeding. Des was next away at some ungodly hour, being pulled off balance in a sleepy daze as line was ripped off the clutch. Then it simply fell slack - the hook had pulled. Disappointed as we were, we regrouped and recast fresh baits – some you win, some you lose - but with a camera present, it wasn't something we were keen to repeat. It was not until first light that the next run came. Slowly, braid ticked off my spool as something made off with the pellet. Immediately after striking, my arms were wrenched downwards as a very angry cat struck back. For the next five minutes my tackle was tested to its limits until eventually the moggie became subdued by the landing net. At 27lb 8oz it might have only been of moderate size but it did its best to cover us both in slime. Our catfish quest had begun and by the strength of this fish I dreaded to think how its mother would fight!

Dawn didn't see a lull in the cat's movements as down at the dam end in over 30ft of water they repeatedly hit the surface. Never being one to look a gift horse in the mouth I quickly sent out a bait via my boat to the exact spot the feeding orgy was taking place. Five minutes passed before a huge head appeared, dragging down the bait in one go. Momentarily, all was calm as I tried to gain line but the instant I made contact, the peace was shattered when the monster exploded on the surface.

A night prowler.

I was about to experience my hardest fight in the UK and one which genuinely made my back ache. Every time I felt I was gaining the upper hand my opponent ripped off yards of braid in a series of savage, brutal lunges. All I could do was hang on and let the cat tire itself out. Des, of course, put it down to me being a southern softy but I cared little. Eventually I netted my prize – all 35lb 8oz of it – and looked down on a face that only a mother could love! Despite this, I found it a marvellous fish, almost prehistoric in its appearance, with those huge whiskers protruding out of its head. I couldn't wait for darkness to arrive again and, hopefully, another battle.

Unfortunately, save for a couple of dropped runs, the remainder of the night passed quietly. I did my best to console Des in the morning light but it looked like his chance had passed. At 9am the final nail in the coffin had been hammered home. It was time to pack up and in bright sunlight his chances now seemed non-existent. However somewhere, somehow, someone took pity on his predicament. With a scream of the alarm big Des was back from the dead and he was being given one final chance. The banter didn't flow like normal, the previous losses weighing heavy on his mind and I swear I heard his heart miss a beat

Southern softie.

Slowly time ticked by until eventually, as the sun set, we sensed the cats were moving again. Des was away first and by the bend in his rod this was something special. But a series of expletives told me all I needed to know – his hook had slipped again. I felt terrible as I knew how important it was for Des to catch a cat on camera and when my next fish of 22lb was beaten I felt no pleasure at all. For me, making the film had always been a shared experience with my friends and far from competing against each other we worked as a team – any success was down to a joint effort, just like the failures.

each time the cat fought back. There were no second chances now but as the saying goes 'when the going gets tough, the tough get going!' Although the fish did its very best, the Black Country boy did better. Carefully I scooped up a 39lb monster and a call rung out around the valley: "Never write off big Des," he cried in delight. We shook hands knowing another *'Impossible'* had been achieved.

 Des's 'southern softy' lines had us in stitches and once again proved that even 'serious' specimen-hunting can be a right laugh. What's more, at first glance this fishery could be described as 'ugly' due to its concrete dams and banks. But looks can be deceiving. It was actually surrounded by rolling hills, lush woodland, and meadows flushed with cowslips, and grazing these fields behind our swims was a herd of deer.

These deer had obviously grown to trust anglers, because as soon as Martin and Des had set up their bivvies the four legged friends walked down, looking for hand-outs. A loaf of bread was just the ticket but the feeding soon became competitive, not between the deer, but Martin and Des. Not satisfied by hand-feeding them, they decided they'd see who would be the first to kiss one! Placing the bread in his mouth, Martin had a taker but Des failed, claiming he'd have had more success if he'd cleaned his teeth! Martin tried again, but as soon as the deer had taken the bread from his mouth, it ran off. Des suggested he wasn't meant to use his tongue! We fell about laughing, particularly after Martin claimed he was always better at 'pulling' and Des pointed out the deer was a stag! Fishing sure can be fun.

This success with the catfish and deer gave me two problems, the first being whether I'd have the nerve to include the dodgy jokes in the film. The second was how I'd be able to fit all the material into the six programmes. For instance, I'd planned to have the catfish caught at night and our biggest fish was caught in daylight. We naturally wanted Des to be the star of the sequence but we wouldn't have time to include two captures, so Des would probably, as the saying goes, 'hit the cutting room floor'.

We were now approaching the halfway point in the time we'd allocated for the filming, namely three years, and we still had a considerable number of sequences to shoot. A one hour film requires a lot of material to make it strong enough to appeal to both anglers and non-anglers. However, we had filmed so many wonderful captures and so much wildlife, particularly underwater, that it seemed the only solution was to expand the series from six to eight one hour films. This would mean a lot more work and expense but Martin was up for it and so I put my thinking cap on and rewrote the stories to accommodate all the material.

Martin and I read through the resulting scripts and it was clear we were mad. However, because we'd come a long way already we decided we would travel the extra mile. Only time would tell if we'd regret taking on this extra burden.

Big Des delivers.

Capturing the Imagination

GIRLS can't fish! Well, all of us men know this to be a lie and Miss Ballantine's record salmon from the Tay proves it. What's more we've all heard stories of women out-fishing their husbands, along with others who beat men in matches. So the ladies are invading what has traditionally been a male preserve in increasing numbers and I, for one, believe this to be great news.

History's shadow.

After a few hours guidance, Rebecca had to leave for her final exams to become a qualified dentist, but Katie and Emma stayed on to extract rainbows and grayling from this delightful beat. Learning where to put the camera to film fly-fishing in an interesting way without handicapping their casting was a challenge, but eventually I got the hang of it. They landed the fly gently under overhanging trees and fish catching followed.

Katie and Emma were certainly skilful, having first cast a fly at a children's 'Introduction to Fishing' day at Chatsworth House some ten years previously. But what sets the Thorpe's apart is how they put a lot back into the sport they love; next day I was able to film them doing just that.

It was the annual training day at Chatsworth House once again. Rebecca had returned from Newcastle and was joined by her two sisters and several eminent local anglers to teach the basics of fly fishing to about thirty children. Most had never picked up a rod before and as I was keen to echo the Thorpe's beginnings, I followed two young lassies, Nancy and Anna through the day to chart their progress.

Keen to reflect this trend and to prove that angling is accessible to all, regardless of age or gender, we planned to include ladies in our series and were lucky to be tipped off about the Thorpe sisters. Rebecca, Katie and Emma started fishing at about nine years old and have become expert fly-fishers. What's more they are lovely both in personality and looks and we didn't think our audience would mind looking at pretty young ladies fishing!

So with their dad Simon's blessing and the help and support of Jennie Mackenzie at the Peacock Hotel at Rowsley, we all met up to fish the beautiful Derbyshire Wye. This classic chalk stream runs past the ancient castle of Haddon Hall, (as featured in the BBC version of Jane Eyre) and was a wonderful historic backdrop to put into perspective our ancient pastime.

This most natural stretch of water is managed with subtle expertise by river keeper Warren Slaney, and he helped the girls get a measure of the challenges provided by the brown trout and grayling in the crystal clear water. What also sets this river apart are the rainbow trout, one of only a few such streams in the country in which they breed successfully and are truly wild.

A guiding hand.

Within an hour, like most of the children, these nine-year-olds could cast a fly. They were then treated to an expert's introduction to the ecology of the trout's world and an analysis of the various critters which they had netted out of the river. Included among this wildlife were stone loach and bullheads and amazingly a lamprey - an ancient creature that goes back millions of years ; I was as excited as the children!

Pond dipping completed, the girls waded out into the river, over their wellies of course, and with great excitement, each landed the first fish they'd ever caught - but not without a deal of instruction from Rebecca, Katie and Emma. Admiring their chunky rainbow trout, they then proceeded to surprise us all by declaring that they wanted to kill the fish and take them home for their dinner! It seems the basic instinct of human hunter-gatherers is just below the surface, even in innocent young ladies. The day was a great success and there's no doubt that several of the children, just as Emma, Katie and Rebecca in previous years, had discovered a hobby for life.

Despite ladies being more numerous in the fly-fishing sector than the other branches of our gloriously varied sport, even carp angling, that most macho of specializations, has its female converts. Jackie is a regular at Linear Fisheries, helped initially by her boyfriend Chris Blunt. She is now Mrs Blunt, has a personal best carp of 36lb 12oz and has been known to out-fish her husband, though Chris might not want to admit it!

We filmed Jackie with Chris Yates and it was clear from her conversations with him that she just loved the peace and quiet of carping and being surrounded by wildlife while waiting for a lump to come along. During our filming she caught several good tench, plus a lovely common of about 18lb.

Meanwhile, Chris was stalking carp in the nearby shallows and it was exciting because several 20lb-plus ghosties and a 30lb mirror were clearly visible circling his bait, even twitching his float as they brushed the line. Eventually he hooked a fish and

A sport for all.

wet, I finished the filming of him landing the fish. The mirror was only 6lb but it's a sequence that would surely end up in the programme. Chris eventually landed a beautiful linear mirror of about 22lbs, though my dunking and laughter was the valuable footage.

this was only remarkable because I fell in while filming him fight it. I managed to keep the camera out of the water and running. Chris took the camera, (with bent rod in the other hand) filmed me climbing out of the lake laughing, then still dripping

As with all film-making, we were accumulating a lot more material than we could ever use, and the thorny problem of what to leave out was looming. These decisions would have to wait until the autumn's editing as we had a lot more filming to do, such as Bernard appearing at the start of each programme and hopefully catching a fish as well.

We knew the final programme would have to show the culmination of our quest for monster fish and hoped it would contain sequences that would justify our chosen title 'No Need to Lie'. Some readers will no doubt be aware of Richard Walker's famous book of the same name, and the title is based on a wonderful angler's prayer which Bernard would quote at the start of Programme Eight.

We were on a lovely pond at dawn, mist rising and tench bubbling by the lilies. I cued Bernard for the prayer and like all star actors, he ad-libbed before speaking by removing his hat, with Martin following suit:

Tea party.

"Lord, help me to catch a fish so large, that talking of it afterward, I have no need to lie."

Bernard followed this by casting a lobworm out into the mist, promptly landing a plump tench. You'll have to watch the film to find out what happened next; suffice to say, our prayers were answered.

Our 'wish list' now required a long trip to Kent to add a few details to our giant tench sequence. We were missing several shots and it's this attention to detail, as in catching fish, that can make a big difference to the effectiveness of the story. 'Continuity' is essential of course and we were fortunate to get a perfect weather match. Even luckier, we had the perfect tench fisher's dawn during which Martin caught a ten-pounder.

Nice one son.

Wake up call.

Classic crucian swim.

Some of you might notice in the films that we don't include the full weighing procedure but I can assure you that all our *'Impossible'* sized fish were indeed weighed very carefully. What's more, two of our principles for the series were rigidly enforced. Firstly, that the fish must not suffer as a result of filming and secondly that we would not cheat the size of the fish by even an ounce. So to save all our *'Impossible'* sized fish from stress, we filmed them being weighed in the landing net then rested them in water before doing the job properly in a damp weigh-sling with accurately zeroed scales. Even if romantic anglers tell you otherwise, size does matter!

The big bonus from the trip to Kent was having an extra 10lb tench 'in the can', and having a spare *'Impossible'* to edit into one of the stories might prove really useful, especially in a series featuring big fish.

Another element we needed for the editing was more underwater footage, and with the weather fine, this was our next challenge. I'd anticipated extreme difficulties with this element in our series and though it wasn't easy, it proved more achievable than I'd thought. The canal perch proved simple, just because they were 'boys' sized perch and concentrated around a sewage outfall.

Species living in still water might be more difficult but having found a crystal clear lake full of fish, filming proved really exciting. Having made nearly sixty wildlife films, it is difficult to find new subjects to explore, but this was certainly one of them, and sliding the little camera into the weedbeds on the end of four landing net poles revealed a scene of beauty.

From above, the blanket-weeded bay looked devoid of life but below, the weed had created a marvellous 'waterscape' through which numerous tench drifted lazily. They were nervous at first, but given time, I could ease the camera alongside them and move through the weed with them as if I was a tench.. Under the lilies, crucians brushed the camera and further out into the lake 30lb carp cruised by,

inquisitive when the camera was first inserted into their world, then nervous for an hour or two until eventually relaxing and giving me the privilege of close encounters.

Later in the day my friend Tim Norman joined me to steer a boat around the lake and we were able to drift through shoals of 2lb perch. Slab-sided bream of over 7lbs slid past nervously too. We also hoped for pike but they took one look at the camera and fled.

After this success, I decided a day's fishing could be allowed and joined Chris Yates and Martin for a crucian catching social, helping Martin with his Angling Times feature by photographing him in the lovely lily-decorated pool along with several 3lb crucians. I also had a stint with my pole and caught a PB crucian of 3lb 12ozs. With Chris catching crucians too, plus Kelly Kettle tea and cake and lots of laughs, it was a happy day all round. What's more, I'd left the camera behind which made it even better.

As I'm sure most readers know, film stories can't always be shot in the order they appear on the screen but are edited together to create a credible

The perfect pitch.

narrative - my wife Sue calls it 'knitting'! Anyway, on rare occasions during the making of 'Catching the Impossible' we had to succumb to these devious 'tricks' and one sequence in particular springs to mind.

We had already caught the 30lb pike from Bowood Lake when by chance we discovered in the boathouse some pictures of Alfred Jardine and glass cases full of giant pike. We felt we had to 'knit' these bonus elements into the story and devised a way to do this; enter the Marquis of Lansdowne's daughter Arabella and her son, 10-year-old Abe.

It turned out Abe likes a spot of fishing, so with Mum's blessing we collected him from their house at dawn in the hope that he could catch a tench from the steps of the boathouse. I had baited a swim by the lilies the previous evening so it wasn't long before Abe and Martin had them feeding enthusiastically. However, it was a while before Abe mastered the correct timing of the strike - but when he did the fun started.

The tench wasn't big, maybe 4lb or so, but it was determined to reach the sanctuary of the lilies and

pulled like a demon. Poor Abe had experienced nothing like it and squealed for help as his rod bent double. "Help me, help me, it's breaking my arm," he cried, and keen not to lose the fish Martin had to help pull the tench away from the lilies. Once free of the snags, Abe was flying solo again and had to win the battle himself. It was quite a fight but eventually the tench lost the war, with much delight from Abe. "I've caught a fish, I've caught a fish. Isn't he beautiful?", he kept repeating.

Peplar, to show me the ropes. He used to have a boat on the harbour and has caught numerous mullet and many will remember him as the owner of that wonderful tackle shop by the Royalty, Davis Tackle.

Graham is also a keen roach angler and on one memorable day some 20 years previously I'd invited him to join me on the famous stretch of the River Stour at Whitemill Bridge that was producing 3lb roach for Terry Lampard, Tim Norman and myself. It was a

A summer scene.

It was a lovely moment, made even better by the fact he caught three more. Then as pre-arranged, Arabella came to see how we were getting on, told us about the stuffed monsters and pictures of one of the most famous pike fishermen of all time, Alfred Jardine, and led us to the rooms in the boathouse to 'discover' its treasures. As Des Taylor would say about putting films and features together: "John Wayne didn't shoot all the Indians!"

Having completed the final sequence of our eight part series, we now had to focus on programme five and the story of the Hampshire Avon from source to sea. The estuary at Christchurch Harbour was an essential part but as neither Martin or I, or Bernard, knew much about mullet fishing, I invited an old friend, Graham

perfect, mild winter's day with the river fining down after a flood and starting at first light we had a 2lb 14oz roach and one of 2lb 3oz in the first two casts. I'd hoped we could get Graham a three-pounder but blow me, neither of us got another bite for the rest of the day. That's roach fishing for you - exasperating.

Anyway, I digress. Graham came afloat with me on Christchurch Harbour to show me how to catch mullet and he duly obliged, catching a couple of nice thin-lips and myself a little golden mullet. It was a great day of sun, beer, sandwiches and reminiscing. Next morning I was at the harbour once again, this time before sunrise, to film the Mudeford netsmen working the rising tide for incoming salmon and sea trout. Martin Keeping was

Abe's inspiration.

science, carefully taking scale samples from the fish as I filmed.

These are used so that age and growth rates can be measured, and also provides DNA samples for analysis. Some fish are tagged too and all this work by Martin is paid for by the Wessex Salmon and Rivers Trust. This group of anglers are determined to see salmon numbers return to previous historic highs, thereby proving that us fishermen can work closely with commerce, scientists and the government for the greater good of the environment and the public benefit.

one of the fishermen and it was both exciting and beautiful as the net was hauled, shimmering in the sunrise and revealing it's prize, a mullet and on a later 'shoot' of the net, a couple of sea trout. Of the salmon I'm afraid there was no sign, a sad indication of their decline on the southern rivers.

Keen to tell the salmon's story and their conservation work on film, Martin invited me back and this time the salmon were running and we caught about eight which included their best 'shoot' of the season, when five came ashore at once. With the salmon so scarce on the river, it is wonderful that an agreement has been struck that allows all the salmon to be returned. Martin receives some compensation for his contribution to the future of the hoped for recovery of the salmon on the Avon and Stour. He also does his bit for

It was great to see these lovely silver fish so carefully handled and swimming back into the running tide and as they headed upstream towards Christchurch I was thinking that it would be nice to meet one of them again soon because in the next few days I'd be filming Bernard and Martin trying to catch one.

 Catching any salmon is a far from easy task but a Hampshire Avon salmon from the Royalty Fishery, well that was something else altogether. Since the halcyon days of the 1950s when huge fish up to 50lb were captured the river has slowly declined as a salmon fishery, reaching an all time low in the 1990s. Fortunately there has, since the millennium, been a slight recovery due to far-sighted environmental practices such as a catch-and-release policy for the entire river and gravel cleaning which supplies a suitable breeding habitat. So, although difficult, my side-kick Bernard Cribbins and I approached the day with expectation not trepidation, especially as we would be falling under the guidance of river keeper Dave Burgess.

Our ace guide.

A warm summer's day greeted us when we arrived on the hallowed ground of the Royalty, famed not only for salmon but its coarse fish as well. The Avon was running clear over vast beds of wafting streamer weed so dense that it kissed the surface. There are, in my book, few more magical places to spend such a day than by a river and throw in the possibility of a salmon and, well, you're getting close to heaven. As promised, the keeper Dave was on hand to greet us but before we got down to the nitty-gritty of casting a line he decided to whet our appetites still further with a visit to the Rod Room.

For luck, Bernard and I touched the great fish before turning our attention to the task at hand with a pep talk from Dave. The approach would require locating our quarry first and only then could we wet a line. By combining a heavy spinning rod with 10lb line our outfit was hopefully strong enough and attached to this was a 1.5ins-long preserved shrimp to tempt a response. It all sounded straightforward, but alas, in practice it rarely is. The shrimp was to be fished via a running paternoster fixed in place with a size 10 treble. The secret was to get your rig set up to exactly the correct dimensions so that the shrimp sat

We could dream.

Now restored to its former glory, on its walls hang the smiles of anglers who have realised their dreams on the river's banks. Keepers, the bastions of the Avon, also have a place, from those who operated in a bygone era to those still working in the present day. But pride of place on the wall was something that made both Bernard and I gulp. There before us was the Avon's record salmon – all 49lb of it, tempted by a Mr GM Howard on the 27th February 1952. Furthermore, the inscribed plaque beneath the fish's huge frame revealed that it was a cock fish tempted on a spun natural sprat. No doubt a spinning vane would have been fitted to help induce a take and this method was the forerunner to the lure still used today – the Devon minnow.

smack bang in front of the salmon's lips. Only then, if we were really lucky, would a fish grab hold. Now all we needed was to find one.

Fortunately, working on the river does have its advantages, with the silver tourists using the same holding stations each year, day in, day out, as they make their way up river. So with Dave's guidance a salmon was located almost immediately; less fortunate was its appearance – it was dark and shabby. While worth a cast, its overcoat revealed that it had been in freshwater for a few days and therefore less likely to snatch at a shrimp. A fresh, silver-coloured fish offered us the best chance because although salmon don't feed once entering freshwater, sometimes an

Not a chance!

instinct still remains to grab at a passing meal. Whether this, or my incompetence as a game angler was to blame I'll never know, but before Bernard had a chance to tackle up the salmon had gone. I promised him that he could cast the next line.

Dave didn't seem alarmed by proceedings, instead he pointed us in the direction of a swim called 'Fiddlers West' and assured us that a salmon would be awaiting our arrival.

Peering over a bed of stinging nettles, the pair of us scanned the fast marginal water and there, as indeed he had promised, was a fish, not huge by any stretch of the imagination but beggars couldn't be choosers. Using the cover available to us we tried not to skyline the fish with our approach and then, ever so gently, Bernard poked his rod through the cover and allowed the reel's bail-arm to open. Immediately on hitting the surface the flow grabbed hold of the shrimp and dragged it downstream, landing behind the salmon. The key was to try and judge the river's power and gauge the correct spot to cast to ensure the bait landed in front of its lips. On the second try it fell almost

perfectly, the length of line spot on but it was just a little too low in the water. Both of us agreed that a lengthening of the paternoster boom was required. In the split second that it took Bernard to take hold of the reel's handle something amazing happened – his rod tip dragged downwards. Instinctively a strike was made and mayhem ensued. Quite what had occurred we'll never know but the result remained the same – a salmon had taken the shrimp and Bernard was now holding onto something intent on returning to the sea.

For a moment I feared the worst as the line cut straight through a weed bed and line screamed from the clutch. Luckily, the man playing the salmon took it all in his stride and with steady pressure the first tail slap hit the surface downstream. Now with a little give and take the fight's ferocity lifted and the rod began to sap the salmon's energy.

I waited close to the water with net in hand and despite another couple of defiant lunges a splendid enamel-flanked specimen slipped into the mesh. Quickly I lay on my stomach and took hold of a grilse made up of 5lb to 6lb of pure muscle. Slipping the treble hook out I held Bernard's prize aloft and then she was returned to continue her journey. A salmon! Bernard was quite rightly ecstatic and so were Hugh and I. The mission had been completed in hours rather than days as we had expected.

 Though we had caught a grilse we still needed film of them underwater. We felt certain such footage would be beyond us but Dave Burgess wasn't going to be beaten so easily. He showed me two lies, and one of them yielded results within a day - yes, a day, but the shot was special because it showed four grilse holding station in the flow. The problem for me was steadying the camera in the strong current but I eventually managed to hold everything together

before a 20lb common carp zoomed downstream and scared them all off.

Two days of failure followed before a grilse lay in front of the rock lie from which Bernard had caught his fish. It spooked but after a few hours it was back and now Dave was able to show his skill with a shrimp. Lowering the bait upstream of the salmon he manoeuvred it downstream so the current wafted the tempting morsel in front of its nose. Its fins twitched, its muscles became animated, and when Dave raised the shrimp to induce a take the fish rose up and nearly succumbed. But then it sank back into a sulk. Such is the fate of a salmon angler I thought, destined to fail to catch a fish that doesn't even eat in freshwater. Next year I'd be back to try again, but in the meantime we had another enigmatic freshwater traveller to get to grips with - the eel.

Nights From Hell

 THE eel is a fascinating creature and probably offers the angler in the UK his, or her, best chance to fish for the unknown. You see, an eel isn't like any other species. A big one doesn't make you aware of its presence, but spends its life hidden away in the shadows, only venturing out after dark. It's impossible to tell if a water supports a population until you actually try and catch one and even then it's far from a certainty that you will succeed.

Little is recorded of its habits but we do know it is possible for them to reach a weight of over 10lb. An eel of this size though, could take a hundred lifetimes or more to catch, as a specimen is classed as anything over 4lb, so we felt it was fair to set our benchmark at 5lb. However, I had a feeling this was going to be one of our hardest challenges yet. Given that it is the Scarlet Pimpernel of the fish world, where would the quest begin?

Waiting for someone else to be successful on a particular venue wasn't an option because once fished for and captured the eel just seems to disappear. Why? Well, that's a mystery, but the theory I like best is that on a damp night it just climbs out of the lake and heads off to a more peaceful home! The eel, you see, is able to exist out of water for short periods of time. What we needed was a a virgin water, unmolested by anglers. But what were the signs we were looking for?

The first key component is a ditch or stream nearby, which enables the eel to reach the water when it runs up from the sea as an elver. The second requirement is the water's age. Eels grow very slowly and any lake or pond less than fifteen years old would be unlikely to hold an eel of the maturity that we desired. Finally, point three is pollution. An eel is one of life's most sensitive creatures and any contamination of the water would see it either die or move on to greener pastures. We hoped that by factoring these points into the equation our search would sort out the wheat from the chaff long before a line was ever wetted.

Two friends responded to our call for help – each one supplying the name of a water which appeared at first glance to have ticked all the boxes. Taking them in order of potential we first arranged a trip with Terry Lampard to a lake in Dorset called Whitemoor Fisheries. The venue correctly answered the initial questions made of it and indeed an eel of over our 'Impossible' weight had been captured accidentally. But, alas, on our arrival not all the news was positive. The owner produced a couple of pictures of huge eels way above our target but unfortunately they no longer had any heads! Found dead on the bank, they had been the victim of a killing machine – the otter. While

I, like many people, have enjoyed this creature's revival, I'm afraid their reintroduction to the countryside has been conducted with little or no sympathy for the rest of the natural world. With fewer fish available in our rivers, the otter has been forced to roam onto still waters with devastating effect, or perhaps even worse, has removed what few fish were left in our flowing water. In many cases, what has fallen victim to Tarka is actually a rarer and more vulnerable creature. Unfortunately, in most country lovers' eyes if a creature doesn't have fur and a tail, but a set of scales instead, it is deemed expendable. I'm afraid it's a case of selective environmentalism by people who have no comprehension of how our waterways work. But enough of this, I digress. Both Terry and I still felt that it was worth fishing this spot because at least one monster might have evaded the otter and given the warm, muggy weather we would never get a better opportunity. Our mission would begin at the end of a spit which bisected the lake, with Terry taking the right side, while I concentrated on the left.

Night-time is the prime period for a bite but despite this being a couple of hours away we decided to cast our deadbaits out anyway. Half-an-hour later I was surprised to see that the bait placed under a marginal bush had been snaffled. Striking, I met with a series of savage bangs on the rod tip that only an eel could produce. It whipped its head from side to side while continually spinning and twisting up the hooklength and eventually a good fish hit the surface. Carefully, it was drawn into a huge landing net and our quest was underway. At 3lb it wasn't big enough but we were all agreed that the signs looked promising and with two nights ahead of us we wondered what else might happen?

Nothing, that's what, well certainly not on the eel front, save a small fish to Terry. The carp though, were a completely different kettle of fish. All night they continually grabbed our fish baits, making the bite alarms shriek out, denying us any sleep. After two nights of this we'd had enough. Perhaps there was an eel of our dreams still left alive but I'm afraid we wouldn't be the ones catching it.

Fingers crossed.

Snakes alive.

Next we headed to a lake near Newport with our Welsh maestro, 'Theo'. Confidence, as ever, oozed from him and he guaranteed us each a 5lb fish and most probably a six-pounder! I was a little more sceptical but on our arrival the lake owner's assessment seemed to back up Theo's prediction. In fact, he was so confident that we would catch our *'Impossible'* he placed a guarantee of £50 should we fail. Well, that was confidence for you, but years of looking for big fish has made me cynical and I would go so far as to say that in ninety-nine out of a hundred cases the fish aren't nearly as big as you've been told. Still, you have to approach each trip in the correct manner, so without further ado we pitched our camp in a spot that would be home for the next two nights and readied the tackle.

A mixture of worms and deadbaits were cast into various different spots and, as with Whitemoor, the sun was still high in the sky when everything was in place. I know when I'm in for a night from hell with eels if I receive a run before darkness from a small fish, otherwise known as a boot lace. Well, when two rods signalled a bite at the same time I suspected there were going to be problems! Quite how bad though, was unclear until the night arrived and the lake's bottom writhed with serpents. It was like match fishing for them, with the average size being no more than 1lb and this was from a lake that allegedly held only monsters! By dawn I was shattered but with the owner kindly supplying a fry up in the cafe we could, at last, catch our breath and come up with a plan.

Worms had produced a larger than average size compared to our fish baits so it seemed logical to swap every rod over to these. I still had over 200 lobbies left so I had more than enough for another night, or so I thought! During the day the weather remained warm and both Theo and I struggled to sleep until eventually dusk arrived and it was time to do battle again. By 3am I didn't have any bait left and although I had tempted three fish over 3lb there was no pleasure in it. In fact, it was perhaps the worst night of my life - I was covered in

slime and had been wrestling boot lace after boot lace continually for six hours!

Only if you have suffered the misfortune of such a night could you possibly comprehend how horrific it was. Exhausted, I collapsed on my bedchair. But where was Hugh you are probably asking? Wisely, he was tucked up in his camper van fast asleep – I guess suffering for your art didn't extend to eel fishing!

After a little 'R and R' away from our saga I once again felt ready to take up the challenge but I wasn't going to follow someone else's lead ever again! No, this time I would track down my own eel. It didn't take long before

What's the joke?

the grapevine delivered what appeared to be an ideal venue. Hidden deep in the West Country was a complex of lakes which had produced eels to over 5lbs, caught accidentally but due to a ban on night fishing, the water had never been targeted purposely for the species. I needed to make a phone call to the owner. Fortunately, like so many other kind people, he was sympathetic to our plight and not only confirmed the presence of our target but gave us permission to fish for them during the hours of darkness. All I needed now was to find a partner in crime so we could get the show on the road. Who else could it be than Des Taylor, a man with both an impressive tally of eels and a brilliant sense of humour that would get us through any dark moments. A date was set and all we could do was hope for the best.

The venue looked every inch the part. Fed by a series of streams and brooks, the fish had every opportunity to reach the lakes and with eels being caught to specimen proportions it appeared we had found our nirvana. Even Des was impressed and despite the monsoon which hit us in the afternoon of our arrival, the confidence levels remained high. The clock slowly ticked round to the moment we would surely come face to face with a monster - it was just going to be a matter of who would catch it.

"Get the bloody net, it's huge," was his only acknowledgement of the situation. So crouched down in preparation, I waited to see a boa constrictor rise out of the depths. Alas, this wasn't what presented itself. No, a carp languished on the surface before falling into the net. Suddenly the penny dropped – eels weren't the culprit, the perpetrators were carp!

Sleep didn't come easily that night but fortunately those predatory carp had struck up a connection with

Death row.

From out of the gloom Des' alarm signalled a take, followed by another one on his second rod and finally a third – blimey, it was a pit of serpents out there! In turn, each one was addressed but every time the response to a strike was identical – nothing, absolutely nothing. Before we had time for our brains to compute I was rushing down the bank as one of my alarms was screaming - I didn't intend to make a similar mistake. Unfortunately, the only thing my rod connected with was thin air! What was going on? Again I had no time to think as the big man's voice boomed out: "You don't get away from Dessie twice!" I walked back up the bank and this time his rod was hooped over.

Des and by the early hours each bite was responded to with a moan. No longer human-like, he was more akin to a wounded animal and it was hard not to chuckle at my friend's predicament.

Dawn didn't bring with it a pretty site – his swim looked like a bomb site with tackle and rods everywhere. "Any good mate?" I enquired. "Go away before I punch you," was all that Des needed to say before I decided that retreat was the sensible option. A few hours sleep brought back the big man's sense of humour and together we rallied each others spirits. Perhaps the eels weren't in this particular lake but there were others on the complex where they might be.

Headless chicken.

Locking myself in the pen, I tossed out a couple of baits while Des checked in the shed for the umpteenth time that the power had been turned off. At last he too settled down but not for long, as his baits were devoured with relish. Unfortunately, it soon became apparent that his pond held a huge population of small carp that behaved more like piranhas – he was not a happy bunny! Once again, Des had drawn the short straw, especially when a run on one of my rods did indeed result in an eel of over 3lb, showing that it doesn't take much water to support a decent eel. Unfortunately, by midnight nothing else had occurred - save about a thousand carp runs for you know who! Shattered, we trudged back up to the base camp and I set about re-baiting the rods. "What are you going to use Des?' I politely enquired. "F**k off,' was the instant reply and with that his bivvy door was zipped down. During packing up the following morning, Des had the final words.

"Next time you want to go fishing with someone Bowler, bring another mug."

A visit from the owner's son delivered some salvation. Two small ponds nearby did indeed hold eels, but there was more to his story. In a strong West Country accent he declared "There be serpents in there, there be, so big I can feel them swimming between my legs when I wade in the ponds." Immediately I conjured up the scene in Star Wars where Luke, Han and Leia are trapped in the garbage disposal with a snake-like alien brushing past them and dragging each one under. Ok, I admit I've got a vivid imagination and so might the story-teller but what if it was true? Des, I'm afraid, was less convinced and this was conveyed by a rolling of the eyes.

All I asked of Des was to take a look, so off we headed to the leviathan ponds. I'm afraid that neither of us expected what we found, with both being only marginally bigger than a large garden pond. But the best was yet to come - one was ring-fenced with an electric wire charged with enough current to bring down an elephant, while the other was actually part of a chicken pen. "Great,' said Des, "you set up in the poultry shit and I'll sit on Death Row!" I have to admit the signs didn't look good. Somehow though, I convinced him that we should give it until midnight before returning for another crack at the main lake.

Bloody hard work!

Autumn Colours

 THE summer had been long, the filming difficult, but with most of it successful, the hard graft could be put behind us. We were now entering that period of transition when the seasons change and wildlife shifts continents. On the 15th September two hobbies flew over our garden in hot pursuit of the swallows and house martins that were heading towards Africa.

Next day a more significant event for our project took place; I had my first full-on computer editing lesson with Chris Wild. Until now, I had muddled by with only the knowledge that my BBC colleague, Jill Garret, had time to pass on to me. She's the ace editor of many of my award-winning wildlife films so I was in good hands when being shown the basics. However, with eight hour-long films to complete and the best part of two years editing ahead, I needed to refine my technique and find as many short-cuts as possible. Having only just about mastered how to turn on a computer I had plenty to learn!

I needed someone who knew the Apple Final Cut Pro system and Chris is a lecturer at the film and TV dept at Salisbury College and knows it like the proverbial back of his hand. What's more, he lives in Wimborne and is a very patient teacher....he needed to be .... so there is a God (and he's it!) For the next few months Chris came for two hours each Saturday and tried to teach an old dog new tricks, and showing remarkable perseverance, he actually succeeded. So if you think the films look half decent, then you've got Chris to thank. What's more, I really enjoyed the learning process and the long haul involved in editing hundreds of video tapes into a cohesive story became a lot easier.

Despite my focus having to turn to editing whenever I had a spare moment, Martin and I still had lots of fish to catch and sequences to complete, so the midnight oil was burning brightly. When I could be out filming, migration was in full swing, with more house martins and hobbies heading south. Even better were the four ospreys that stopped off at Poole Harbour for a few days to refuel on flounders for their flight to West Africa.

The Hampshire Avon was running crystal clear and I managed some lovely underwater footage of roach and bream shoals, along with a gang of large perch and a big pike in the corner of a weir pool. Pike were something we lacked, and however carefully I placed the camera they always fled. So Martin and I were delighted to receive an invite to a crystal clear pit in the Cotswold Water Park.

brain, because we never knew when a pike might appear out of the gloom and take Martin's paternostered lamprey. So we had to concentrate intently, non-stop for twelve hours.

After two days we had some good footage of pike sniffing around, including a monster of over 20lb which hung around for the best part of the second day. It was suspicious of the camera because it could see its reflection in the glass and swept past aggressively several times in the hope of driving this imaginary rival off. The images were impressive, and what's more, it finally took the lamprey. We had also taken the front cover picture for this book at dawn, so all in all it was a thoroughly good day.

A week's holiday in Majorca followed and soon after that we had rain, the local rivers rose and encouraged the salmon upstream. My friend Stuart Wilson, reliable as ever, called me early on Sunday morning and said that there was a stack of silver tourists gathered below a weir at Britford, so I was off up the road like a shot.

When I lowered the camera into the roaring water, the scene was impressive - a dozen or so salmon lay there wedged side by side. Some were just grilse of 6lb or 7lb but a few were proper salmon of well over 10lb. Several showed signs of being in the river for a

Steve Rowley is a friend of Martin's, a very good friend as it turned out because he'd baited a spot with chopped fish for several days in the hope of attracting a pike or two for our camera. It was a technique I'd used when still a schoolboy at Ely and had caught pike to 18lbs, a result that meant this small boy was dead chuffed. Reaching the area over the marginal weed-covered shelf involved putting five landing net handles together and stretching out every inch of our cables. It was tiring on the arms ....and the

Happy boy.

while, being quite red, but others were shining silver and still had sea lice attached. They'd travelled up against the fast currents of the Hampshire Avon from Christchurch Harbour to just south of Salisbury, a journey of about thirty miles in only two days.

A salmon's drive to reproduce and the incredible journey it has to make to do so always fills me with wonder. They travel all the way from West Greenland where they fatten up, then cross the Atlantic, at risk from seals and trawlers and coastal nets to the Avon, where they have to negotiate many obstacles before reaching and cutting their redds above Salisbury. Our title for this film 'Going Against the Flow' seemed quite appropriate.

During some four hours filming, about fifteen salmon forced their way through the fierce current at the weir and past the camera. A few were driven back but tried again and finally succeeded. It sure was good to see that the Hampshire Avon still has a run of salmon, even if numbers have become dramatically reduced.

Another famous river that once had a salmon run and that we were keen to feature was Old Father Thames and now that Autumn was with us we were on our way there. We hoped to show the catching of a 6lb

chub and a 3lb perch and there's no finer exponent of Thames fishing than John Everard.

While catching big fish of a variety of species was key to our angling adventure, we also wanted to include venues which have become iconic in the world of angling. The Thames was difficult for us to ignore, a river at the very heart of England. What we needed was a guide to put us in touch with this waterway and hopefully into action with its chub and perch. It didn't take me long to come up with a name – my good friend John Everard, who is one of the finest anglers I have ever had the pleasure of wetting a line with. His approach to the river's chevins really is masterful and I'm not ashamed to admit that his techniques have greatly influenced mine.

So that's the positive about old Evy – the negative is that he's permanently miserable! No, I'm only kidding, but John is one of life's realists where a spade is a spade and smoke and mirrors have no part to play. If he doesn't agree I can assure you he will let you know, not treating fools gladly. But on the flip side, he's a man you can rely on one hundred per cent. Combined with his rich Oxford accent, I hope you are conjuring an image of quite a character, and one of the many great anglers this county has produced. With Peter Stone and Peter Drennan being his close friends for many years, he has a pedigree second to none.

"So Evy, will we catch today?" I asked as we sat at the tail of a splendid weir pool, legering a combination of his favourite baits – crust and cheese paste. "No," was the predictable reply, which I have to say made me

Cheese paste chevin.

Evy knew best.

chuckle – talk about Victor Meldrew! I knew though, that he was pulling my leg as the spot he had chosen was full of chub, a fact confirmed by the savage wrench on my rod tip. Thunderous lunges resonated down the rod as a big fish did its best to smash me on the bridge stanchions.

"Come on, get its head up and stop messing around!" were John's orders and I duly responded, while in turn a big white pair of lips hit the surface and gulped in water. There was little doubt that we had a six-pounder and once netted the scales didn't disappoint when they registered a hefty 6lbs 11ozs. In typical fashion, John told me it didn't look that big and suggested I get my scales checked!

I once again cast into the swim and allowed a large bow of line to form between me and the swan shot link leger. This slack reduces the pressure felt by a taking fish and results in a confident bite and more chub hooked. Gently tapping, the quiver tip revealed that the bait was shuffling across the bottom and into another, as yet unseen, mouth. Again I was in contact with a big fish which, like its brother, wanted anything but to be filmed. Although I was on a pre-

stretched line, the 7lb breaking strain was more than a match so before long John was netting another chub and another 6lb-plus fish. With John's expert guidance he had made our task look easy, which I can assure you wasn't the case! It was now time for Evy to take centre stage and catch a fish for the camera – a job he didn't really relish, as fame is the last thing he wants. Still, I had great fun pulling his leg, telling him he was obsessed with becoming a star! A big perch was needed and, as with the chub, John knew a few places to try.

Like many of our waterways that have produced big perch over the last decade the Thames has a rich supply of red signal crayfish, these provide a great source of protein, hence the size of the fish. A 4lb weight is definitely attainable but for our requirements a more modest two-pounder would be satisfactory. The size for once wasn't important, the experience for the viewer would be built around the Thames itself, so settling alongside John I watched as he lowered in a whole lobworm.

The swim had an underground irrigation pipe spewing into the main river, manifesting itself at our

Reluctant star.

254

The match.

feet with a broken surface and adding a slight discoloration to the river's complexion. Here, feeding on the additional food was a shoal of small silver fish and minnows but it was what was lurking in the shadows to devour these that interested us. In this 'dog eat dog' world the food chain would be played out in full with the predator at the top of the pyramid of life. It didn't take long for John's worm to catch the attention of these beady eyes and soon a flank of stripes splashed in front of us, setting the tone for the next few hours.

With perch caught to a weight substantially more than we desired it was soon declared as 'a wrap', providing us all with a sigh of relief that the task had been completed. John, I knew, hadn't really wanted to be filmed but like everyone else, gave up his precious spare time in a belief that angling could be showcased to a wider audience through the project. In his own way, he was helping to pay back his bit to a sport that had given him so much. Leaving our friend in peace, we teamed up with an altogether different personality for the second part of our Thames odyssey.

With the river running alongside Oxford's famous Port Meadow and providing a prolific fishing stretch called Medley, it's not unusual to see an angler perched on a seat box - but perhaps not a female one like Wendy Lythgoe, the former ladies England International. The pretty face shouldn't fool you because Wendy is more than capable of holding her own in the company of males, in fact I think she enjoys putting them in their place. Fortunately I wasn't going to be so gullible. Having already fished with her a couple of times during magazine features, I knew exactly what to expect. So a gentle, sedate match was on the agenda with Hugh, of course, being the unbiased referee.

This, I have to report, lasted about ten seconds when he announced that Wendy had to fish the downstream peg, quoting filming reasons. He said I needed to sit as close as possible above her, which gave me very little water to actually fish in and draw anything up from! "Funny that," I thought as I prepared the tackle, "surely Hugh wouldn't have based the decision on anything other than professional reasons?' Due to this small zone in front

of me I decided to use a pole at twelve metres in conjunction with a flat float and chopped worm tactic in a big fish approach, while Wendy would run a waggler downstream feeding maggots for a bag of fish.

As already alluded to by John Everard on our previous Thames sortie, the rich crayfish population ensured that I would never be too far away from a good old stripey, so while Wendy caught a steady stream of roach, I bided my time with a specimen game plan. Sure enough, with a little patience a bite came, followed by a solid connection and a 2lb perch headed for the net, along with the inevitable banter shared by two friends. This was then the template for the rest of the trip, matching each other weight for weight and insult for insult until I tempted a pike. This would have won the match, but much to my dismay Wendy told me that, under match rules, it didn't count! I was now convinced the match was fixed.

No further monsters came our way but that wasn't the point. There were plenty of bites and lots of laughs and most importantly, Wendy proved that angling is a sport for all, not just old men with plenty of time on their hands. So we diplomatically declared the match a draw and bid fond farewells. Now it was time to film something completely different.

Little and often.

Honours even.

Ten-year-old Abe has a back garden most children could only dream of - Bowood House and the scene of our *'Impossible'* pike triumph. With his granddad being the Marquis of Lansdowne, acre upon acre of fabulous Wiltshire countryside is at his disposal, including the lake itself, so we were surprised to learn from his mum Arabella that he had never battled with one of the resident pike. It was time to fix this and unsurprisingly, Hugh came along to capture the attempt on film. 'A Passion for Angling' had enjoyed just such a scene with Huckleberry Finn and Chris Yates – the time when an angler is born and a lifetime of enjoyment follows as the reward. So we hoped that 'Catching the Impossible' would also be able to encapsulate such a moment.

Abe was ready for our arrival and wearing a flat cap and Norfolk jacket, he certainly looked the part. I told him that the pike would test him even more than the tench we had managed to tempt together the previous summer. Armed with a rod, reel, net and an array of deadbaits, we headed to the top end of the lake where a small stream entered, spilling in via a waterfall, creating a pool which housed a shoal of roach that the pike took a fancy to on a regular basis.

Rigging up the rod, tactics would be a twitched fish under a small float which hopefully would draw some interest from a hungry eye, believing a roach was in distress. Swinging it out together, Abe was then left to his own devices, engaging the bail-arm and slowly retrieving it in a jerky manner.

'Slam!' the fishy torso was hit, sending scales cascading everywhere as the culprit sunk away with its meal. A bob on the float gave Abe his first indication as to what had occurred and I threw the bail-arm back open, allowing a little more time for the pike to gain confidence. Then came the big moment as Abe tightened up and struck, setting home the treble hooks. I had told him what to expect but the pike's response still shocked him. The clutch screamed and a head shook above the surface, intent on shattering the boy's dream. His 9ft rod cranked over as the pike tried its best to break it and turn this story into nothing more than 'the one that got away'. The tackle though, was stout and it was more a case of who would win the tug o' war.

Vivid memories.

 By November, the Autumn frosts were biting into the trees and their leaves were glowing gloriously. Looking into the golden reflections as the Avon flowed past we were reminded of that lovely writing by Patrick Chalmers: "A river is water in its loveliest form," and who could deny it as a roach rolled at the tail of our swim. Martin landed a couple of plump chub before the roach responded, just as it was almost too dark to see the float. Three roach to around 1lb was his reward and it was yet another little vignette to slip into the portrait of the river.

I'd been suffering sleepless nights quite frequently during the last two months, not because of all the editing I was doing but because of numerous otter visits to the garden once again. They had to be chased off to protect our fish and running round the garden in the dark is not conducive to a restful night, particularly when my prize rudd and golden orfe became victims. No doubt anglers on the nearby River Stour were losing some of their specimen chub and barbel too but they wouldn't be seeing the evidence as the river was in flood for the first time since last winter. With England awash and the weather mild, it was time for some lake fishing and an attempt at that enigmatic species, the zander.

A polka dot flank hit the surface and Abe's eyes bulged out on stalks. I waded into the lake to take hold of his pike; this could then be ticked off the list of 'what a boy must do before he grows up'. He was not to be denied and with a 'Yes!' and a punch of the air we had his prize. Gently, she was laid in his arms, giving Abe his first chance to admire her and stare at an inhabitant of a world he had been unable to see. Angling allows this environment to be appreciated and therefore protected, so not only is an angler born but at the same time a conservationist as well.

Over the course of the day, a few more pike fell to Abe's rod up to mid-double figures but I guess as one muddy, tired lad was dropped off with his mum, it was the first that was still the most vivid.

Otter food.

Over the last couple of years we had tempted and filmed a wide variety of species, with only a few exclusions - and one of these was the zander. A double-figure specimen took on the *'Impossible'* tag and it was then my job to find a suitable venue for the Count Dracula of fish, their fang-toothed appearance and nocturnal habits giving them this rather sinister nickname. But where would we find one lurking in the shadows? The Fens, of course, are their spiritual home but this adventure would be for another day; a less obvious lair was chosen instead.

Bury Hill Fisheries sits in a secluded valley among rolling hills and woodland in otherwise suburban Surrey, giving travelling and local anglers alike a chance to be close to nature and, importantly, in contact with fish. The outer complexion, therefore, is serene but under the surface the predator we so desired had a habit of making life for the silver fish a little tricky. I knew it had produced zander to 16lbs so its credentials were without doubt, but what I didn't know was the inside track on tips and tactics to fool such a specimen. A good asset to have in such a case is a man who knows the ropes, so cue a top carp angler, Ben Hamilton, who I had met previously on my various jaunts around the country. Not only was he an excellent fisherman but he also knew Bury Hill well and, most importantly, its zander population.

So after a series of phone calls I felt equipped enough to take up the challenge and as an added bonus Ben had also agreed to come along and lend a hand. This would not be the only companion to accompany Hugh and I, as a mission to tempt his first zander saw Mr Cribbins also signing up for the trip. So it was on an overcast, late November day our gang rendezvoused at the venue and were greeted with a warm handshake by owner David De Vere.

Resistance-free outfits combined with a fresh deadbait were the keys to success I had been told, so obediently we obeyed and set about the task. Daytime needed to give way to darkness for our best chance and it proved to be the case with little to report as the twilight period arrived. We had all agreed to give it to ten o'clock on the first evening, so we hoped the next few hours would prove rewarding. Lighting up the Tilley lamp, a warm glow surrounded us while Bernard did what he does best, recounting tales and telling jokes. Alas, though it didn't seem as if the zander wanted to listen and our bite alarms remained silent.

Ben decided something was wrong and like all good anglers do, set about fixing it. He suggested a move to the opposite bank and although we would have loved to have made the change, filming, I'm afraid, doesn't make life simple. With logistics and the tale already being set in our initial area, we decided that Ben should go off and investigate and only if he was successful would we contemplate the move.

Only half-an-hour had passed when Ben rang and his excited tone was soon explained when he told us he had caught a twelve pounder. It was enough to see us all on our way to the opposite bank to join him. We arrived a little out of breath and Ben showed us what we needed to tempt. The zander's eye glowed under the torch light and its impressive flank shone out as Ben held it up for us all to see. It wasn't surprising that the captor grinned broadly as I took a couple of trophy pictures. Could we mimic his success? I'm afraid to say we couldn't and the other zander melted away into the shadows, showing no interest in our offerings.

Beautiful Bury Hill.

Ben's beast.

It was time to get some sleep. Bernard headed home, while Hugh and I kipped in the vans. Ben also had to leave us but, unlike Bernard, he wasn't able to return the following day due to work. He had though, showed us the way, so with a handshake and a thankyou Ben left us to our own devices.

That night's sleep couldn't have been easy for Bernard because when he returned he divulged the plan that he had formulated in bed. A two hook paternoster rig was baited with the bizarre cocktail of a fish head and a prawn on each one. The coloured water had convinced him that the scent trail had to be increased if success was to come his way. Personally, I was less sure and told him that I would eat my hat should a zander fall for such an offering. I know I don't need to end this story for you to guess the outcome but just in case I will...

Five minutes later the indicator slammed against the butt and after frantically untangling it from his line, Bernard hooked and landed his first zander. It wasn't

very big but it didn't matter and I had to eat my words – together with a large slice of humble pie. Bernard, of course, enjoyed serving up every slice of it!

That was it then, and with the weather closing in a halt was called to filming and we all headed for home. Personally, I felt that I had unfinished business with the lake and a double still to catch. We would return, but for now we had another first and another set of teeth in the can.

Showing all aspects of our sport was essential if we were to do justice to the glorious variety that angling has to offer, so match fishing was also on the agenda. I was keen to show a match on a canal in an industrial setting and was lucky to get an invite to a big contest on the Beeston Canal near Nottingham. It was an Angling Times Winter League between some of the finest teams in the country, so it was a serious contest. What's more, it gave us an opportunity to once again show that angling is accessible to all, regardless of age or gender, because one of the stars of the crack Daiwa Trentman team was 17-year-old Sam Perkins.

I'll eat my hat.

As Sam explained while preparing for the 'all in', her dad and uncle fished competitively too and helped her to become a winner. She had already fished for England as a junior with notable success and by talking to her fellow competitors, it became clear to me that she was much admired for her skill and dedication.

When the match started I was amazed at the speed and accuracy she showed with the pole - shipping in and out and rebaiting in a blur, and she soon had several roach in the net. I had grown up roach fishing on the Grand Union Canal in Paddington (and loved it) but this was in a different league. However, she was fishing bread-punch, something I like to do when roach fishing on my local River Stour, so while filming her I learnt a few tricks to take back home!

Keen not to completely ruin Sam's chances of winning her section by sticking a camera up her ear for the full five hours, I left before the end, but I gathered afterwards that the guy on the end peg next to her had won the section on his chopped worm line by snaring a large perch. However, it gave me a chance of filming some lovely images of lines of anglers concentrating intently in the sunshine, even if overnight frost had made the fishing hard. It sure was a contrast to the image of a lone angler on a misty summer pool. The other obvious difference was the enjoyable camaraderie everybody showed, despite the competitive nature of the event. They all made me welcome too - so thanks guys.

Travelling back home on a busy motorway was another dramatic contrast to the peace we enjoy when out fishing but little did I realise that in two days time I would be driving back the other way, and this time in thick fog. It was madly dangerous and I questioned my sanity. Surely this wasn't worth the risks and expense just for a fishing film, because as I often say 'it's only television'.

However, we were now well into our third winter's filming and one element that was sadly lacking was any images that showed it was actually winter! Global warming or whatever, it seems the days of snow and frost are a thing of the past. The films would certainly be poorer without beautiful winter scenes, so I was risking

my neck on the motorway on the off chance of overcoming this missing element.

The forecast was for frost in East Anglia but when I arrived in the marshes created by the flooded Ouse Washes, there was only thick fog and Icelandic Whooper Swans calling as if lost in the gloom. What is more, the water was so high that a BMW had been abandoned with water lapping its doors. I took a risk, (mainly because my B&B and a warm bed were the other side of the floods!) gingerly edging my Volvo through the rising water and made it to the other side.

As darkness fell, the fog intensified and Whooper Swans called anxiously above the pub in the moonlight, unable to find their way to their roosts. The scene had an ominous quality and I slept fitfully and when I woke just before dawn, there was an eerie silence. The fog had lifted, the frost had descended and the world outside had been transformed into a winter wonderland. Every twig, branch, reed and blade of grass had become encrusted with a thick layer of hoarfrost, as if a fairy Godmother had scattered diamonds across the landscape with her wand. It was absolute magic and I was soon wading into the floods to try to do justice to this beautiful landscape.

It was just what we needed for the start of our winter programme and with the help of old friends from the RSPB and Wildfowl Trust, I was able to drift over the water in a boat to film the flooded trees. I then filmed the massed wildfowl from the trusts hides. I grew up just across the Fens at Ely and would regularly cycle the sixteen miles from the school to watch birds on the floods, but never had I seen it so magical. It was a huge slice of good fortune because by sunset, the fog had descended again and stayed down. So next day I returned home through traffic chaos, thanking my lucky stars I'd taken the risk.

Christmas followed soon after and so did yet more sleepless nights as the otters continued their nocturnal fishing trips. At least I was able to do lots of editing while waiting for their visits! Progress was slow, but our series was certainly taking shape.

Floods and Frost

 AS soon as the New Year celebrations were complete Martin and I had to try for roach on the Hampshire Avon again, but after the customary lack of success we turned our attention to helping Bernard catch a 20lb pike. We needed this for the end of Programme Two so on the 15th January the three of us met at Wellington Country Park.

Head Ranger Andy Pye had kindly arranged with the Duke of Wellington for us to try this beautiful crystal clear lake for a big Esox. It was famous for large carp and tench but had also produced pike to well over 20lbs so we were in with a chance. What's more, we understood that the lake had hardly been fished for pike and there's nothing they like more than neglect. So it was puzzling that our legered lampreys and assorted dead-baits garnered no response, especially when the weather was ideal - dark and drizzly with a gentle breeze. When we did finally get a run at dusk it was only from a jack.

Puzzled by this lack of action, we debated what had gone wrong with the fishing and our worst fears were realized. Talking to another pike angler, it turned out that there'd been a pike match between thirty anglers the day before our visit. This amount of activity is not conducive to locating a monster so we had to seek Bernard's big pike elsewhere.

Before we even had time to re-group we were hit by the worst storms for seventeen years. January 18th dawned with winds of ninety-nine mph and torrential rain. Flood warnings were widespread but with the weather mild this signalled only one thing - barbel!

We'd been waiting two winters for the ideal conditions to catch a winter barbel because seeing Martin walking on water and fishing waist deep in the middle of a field would surely prove amusing. What's more, it

is one of Martin's favourite forms of fishing, so it wasn't long before my phone rang.

 I love all forms of fishing, but one of my favourites is floodwater barbeling. When the rivers can take no more and spill their now very dirty contents all over adjacent fields, it's more than likely that you will find me wading into likely looking spots in an attempt to get a bite. Perhaps it's the awesome power of nature all around me that is such a thrill, or the fact that providing the rain is warm and the temperature is rising barbel will feed in earnest. Whatever it is I simply adore it.

Our plan was to film such an episode, so all we could do was wait for the winter rain to arrive. However, Hugh also threw another spanner in the works, namely that the sun should also be out to ensure it looked lovely too! Now it doesn't take a genius to work out that a flood and sun don't often come together so we just had to hope that the river would rise by night and the sky clear during the day.

The obvious river to target was my local Bristol Avon as not only was it a prolific barbel river but also being on my doorstep I could easily monitor conditions before Hugh and I made the call to film. Early winter provided a perfect river a couple of times but alas, the sky remained leaden grey and the months ticked by. At last though, our vigil was over and on the 18th January 2007 I phoned Hugh to report the highest river levels of the season. What's more the sun was beaming down, illuminating the inland sea that had previously been fields.

Hugh would be with me in two hours so I returned home to collect the tackle; this has to be strong and stout for such

Country park piking.

Walking on water.

conditions. Light carp rods, 15lb line and 6oz leads may seem a little over gunned to the uninitiated but, believe me, in such conditions not only the barbel but the river will test it out fully and leave you smashed up should they find any weakness. Two baits were also packed, a potent smelling paste laced with essential oils and some halibut pellets; all that was then left to do was meet up with Hugh.

Our vehicles could go no further such was the extent of the flood blocking the bridge that spanned a once sedate river. Safely, we parked by the old church and donned our waders as walking was the only option. It seemed though that not everyone shared our view as a boy racer in his BMW tore into the water intent on getting to the other side. For the first fifty yards all seemed to be going well and then the engine died and the seals on his doors gave way, allowing water to fill his car. I have to say, sympathy was not on my mind and Hugh and I began laughing as a drowned rat emerged and dragged himself to dry land! Amazingly, as if this wasn't enough of a warning, another lemming like driver made exactly the same mistake.

Anyway, it was time for us to leave the sideshow and get on with the main event. While I waded about Hugh captured the images he wanted. They were certainly spectacular and a reward for our patience. Poking and prodding each and every likely looking haunt, I made my offering to the prince of the river. However, not a single opportunity came my way. For some reason the barbel just didn't want to play ball, proving once again that angling is a never ending challenge. Normally the lack of activity would indicate a poor trip but for once nothing could be further from the truth. Images for the film were as important as any *'Impossible'* so with a good chunk of the Wiltshire countryside looking like a giant mirror, showing a reflection of puffy white clouds tracking across the sky and one mad angler trying to find the river, Hugh eagerly devoured every moment with his camera. A chance of a barbel would come again another day.

No wrong notes.

snow covered banks but we couldn't wait forever, having failed to get snow on the two previous winters. So on January 29th we decided we had to give it a try, even without wintry weather.

 We might not have caught a barbel but had captured some lovely images of winter fishing, so good progress had been made. What's more there was progress next day too, for I had a long meeting with the music composer for the series, David Poore. David is an old friend, for we'd collaborated on several films together, most notably, one on the South American camel, the guanaco, called 'Spitting Mad', a film on crocodiles for National Geographic and a film on the Arctic Inuit's culture for the BBC. David creates lovely music and has done so for many of the BBC's major series so I was pleased to have him adding dulcet tones to our pictures. If my previous angling series, 'A Passion for Angling' had taught me anything, it was the value of Jennie Muskett's music that, when combined with our lovely images created so much enjoyment for so many. I felt sure that David could help capture the same magic. Each film would take several weeks to compose and record with musicians so there was a lot of work to do - but David left Dorset with numerous ideas and eager anticipation of a rewarding journey ahead.

On January 21st a pair of mallards visited our ponds for the first time, so spring was on its way, confirmed on the 25th when we heard the hesitant song of a Blackbird. We had hoped for a proper winter, particularly in the Welsh hills where we planned to catch pike from the River Wye. I had reckoned it would look wonderful with

 Is there a more magnificent location in Great Britain than the Wye valley? How could we miss out of our series the river that carves its way through this beautiful landscape, thus creating a natural border between England and Wales. The river Wye is home to specimen chub and barbel but it's the pike that really captivate me. Wandering down to the river through it's limestone gorge full of trees coated with frost resembling an icing sugar dusting on a winter's day, followed by dropping a dead bait into countless slacks for a few minutes at a time to check if Esox is at home has always been a trip I look forward to. At times the fishing isn't easy and every bite is a hard one to attract but when the float does eventually sail away I allow myself to dream about a pike that resembles a railway sleeper, big enough for the tale of its capture to last a lifetime. I cannot think of a more perfect place to land a monster pike. So our mission ahead was sure to be an enjoyable one.

'Spitting mad'.

We headed over the Severn Bridge, through Chepsow and on past Tintern Abbey where the road starts to wind itself alongside the river, proving a distraction to any angler who passes this way. Hugh and I weren't alone on this journey though as good old Theo, Wales' 'most optimistic angler' was accompanying us. It was Theo who had originally introduced me to this slice of heaven when I first moved west, so it was nice to have him on board for our pike hunt.

The river looked in perfect condition as I grabbed glimpses while trying to keep us on the road, but as per normal with the trials and tribulations of filming, the weather wasn't so obliging. Grey and dull was the best way to describe it, preventing the countryside from sparkling and instead giving it a lifeless complexion. We all wanted snow really and had this grey weather been forecast then this trip would have been postponed. But with time now pressing, compromises had to be made, given that there were eight one hour films to make. Theo, of course, was still enthusing about how many 20lb pike we were going to catch so it was hard to remain glum and who knows, if he was proved only half right then we wouldn't need the sun at all.

Over the last few years the Wye has opened its doors to the coarse angler, partly because of the declining salmon stocks but in main due to the efforts of the Wye and Usk Foundation which has dozens of day ticket sections on its books. It would be a selection of these stretches situated south of Hereford that were to receive our attention, with the key to success being mobility. In my experience, if you drop a bait into a slack that contains a pike willing to feed, then you will know about it within five minutes - sitting and waiting is just not the name of the game with these fish. So with a single rod each, a landing net and a small rucksack, Theo and I made our way along the boulder-strewn bank. The surrounding fields were testimony to the river's strength with tree trunks tossed onto them during a recent spell of high water. The landscape afforded us a novelty for modern Britain - splendid isolation.

A series of salmon groins provided a refuge against the flow for any fish and it was here that we first lowered in our dead baits, supported by large buoyant floats. Each and every slack was investigated while Hugh waited patiently behind us, but nothing stirred and the water remained calm. As is common with us anglers, the grass always looks greener on the other

Wye fun.

The big girl.

side or in this case the far bank. Maybe the pike were lurking over there in another series of slacks, for cover was provided by a row of trees and bushes. A quick conference led to us jumping in to the van and crossing the river. Mobility as I've already explained is the key to success and so it proved when Theo opened our account with the Wye. It wasn't a big fish but it still gave his tackle a workout and saw him scrabbling down the bank to reach his prize.

Meanwhile, I had positioned myself in a shallow natural slack a little way upstream where the river pushed into a row of bushes, providing an ideal ambush point for any predator. For once the pike agreed with me and a run of them into double figures took a fancy to my baits, each one intent on crashing into the vegetation with head shaking ferocity. A big pike would have been nice but capturing the Wye's beauty was what was more important to us. As we headed to our Bed and Breakfast accommodation for the night we reflected on what an enjoyable day it had been. It also left us eagerly anticipating the following morning and a date with an even larger slack, almost an ox bow lake, that I knew just had to hold pike.

A hearty breakfast is always a great way to start a day and with full stomachs we headed off to the hotspot. Normally, calm water on the Wye is at a premium but it wasn't here, as an area plenty large enough for two anglers sat beside the main flow. With no more than three feet of water at its deepest it could to the uninitiated give a poor first impression, but I just knew it would contain pike, especially as it was opposite the most prolific chub swim on the whole stretch, providing a larder close at hand.

That morning, six more pike fell to our rods, each one launching itself into the air before smashing back down against the surface, and despite the overcast sky, this magnificent place did its best to shine for us. Theo continued to tell us that a twenty would be next but when Hugh called time I'm afraid it hadn't materialised. Despite this we had achieved what we had come to do and it was time to head home. The ox bow though remained in my thoughts and I agreed with Theo that a big fish wasn't far away.

With only a couple of days left of the season I found myself once again in a position to visit the Wye but this time I was alone. A bite soon followed in the ox bow and my hunch proved correct with 22lbs of pike making me a very happy captor indeed! This wasn't to be the last time she crossed my path as a year later I took Tim Norman and Terry Lampard to the bay and watched as Tim battled 26lbs 10oz of pike - and yes, you've guessed it, it was the same fish. I suppose for the filming it was a case of right place, wrong time.

 Martin and Theo had caught plenty of pike and I'd captured plenty of action, but we were still disappointed by the lack of a wintry 'look' to the sequence. I guess we could go back if winter arrived but with global warming being a constant issue it didn't seem likely. On February 1st our blackbird was now in full voice, a glorious sound but a date so early it seemed difficult to believe.

In such mild conditions I fancied some roach fishing but this wasn't an option as I felt sure the carp would be stirring in a nearby lake and with the water clear, I might get some good underwater footage.

Right place, wrong time.

Sliding the camera through the overhanging branches of a willow tree, the scene was wonderful. Lying together, densely packed, were dozens of big carp, but if we had the impression spring had arrived, no-one had told them. They lay torpid, hardly moving, even too sleepy to avoid the camera in their midst. When fishery owner Wayne Little came to look through my video screen he too was excited because he recognised some of the commons and mirrors as known thirty pounders. They sure did look impressive as they drifted gently past the camera, rubbing their scales on the lens.

Two of our friends, Tim Norman and Terry Lampard fished this lake for carp and had also mentioned that it held pike. In fact, Terry had only recently landed a couple of twenty pounders so we felt sure it might resolve Bernard's pike problems. Wayne kindly gave us permission to try, even offering us the use of his punt. So on the 5th February, filled with eager

anticipation, we stood on the banks of this lovely lake and offered a little prayer to Isaac.

 The battle that lay ahead was not signalled by a bite with matching ferocity; instead the bung gave a single 'bob' before sliding away sideways. Bernard Cribbins may well have come into contact with monsters in Doctor Who but now he needed to face one with fins, for this pike wasn't prepared to give up without the fight of its life. A sedate day was about to be turned on its head and only in fishing can this happen so quickly.

The day had dawned with a splendid blue backdrop and while the winter sun failed to radiate warmth, it shone as brightly as it could. Under our boots the frost crunched and crackled, its foothold still possible on such a day due to the wooded canopy surrounding the lake. Passing by a series of fallen trees, their tangled branches had now provided shelter for a group of carp. In the gin clear lake every scale could be admired, but my companion would not allow our mission to be derailed. We had come for pike and nothing else would be an adequate substitute. Walking along, talk changed to esox and hope for the day ahead. Hugh had arranged for us to make use of an old green punt, enabling the lake to be searched thoroughly in our quest.

Loading a boat correctly is vital, not only for a successful day but an enjoyable one as well. The first rule is to ensure that the minimum amount of tackle is taken on board as clutter has a way of turning into a disaster when afloat. Each of us did the housekeeping at our end of the boat while a large soft unhooking mat lay on the deck between us. The net was also propped up in this zone but instead of being of the unwieldy carp variety we chose a solid framed salmon model.

At last the day began as Bernard slipped anchor and I pushed an oar against the bank, the wake breaking the spell of a mill pond surface. As we drifted out, the lakes secrets were revealed as every spot on the

bottom could be seen clearly. Clumps of weed still held on, interspersed with clear gravel patches, no doubt formed by the summer's feeding orgies. The question was though, where were the pike ? It would appear at first glance that none existed but a pike, with its mottled green overcoat blending in perfectly with the surroundings, has an incredible ability to become invisible.

An anchor dropped either end fixed the boat in the first likely looking area, a spot where an old gnarly branch protruded from the water. Both Bernard and I chose to offer a similar menu with a smelt and lamprey selection. Each one is a pungent bait full of attraction, the smelt with its cucumber aroma while the lamprey's bloody trail is hard for any pike to miss. To maximise this I always prefer to use the head end as this is where the majority of the blood is to be found. On hooking up the dead baits, they were duly cast out into the lake, positioned to maximise the area covered.

Bite indication would be via a float supporting a paternoster rig. In such weedy conditions a straightforward bottom rig would become snagged up in the blanket weed; instead we hoped they would be suspended above it. When fishing paternosters though, it's vital to use an up trace to prevent being bitten off; this I make out of 40lb wire. Why, you probably ask do I

Two men in a boat.

use such a high breaking strain? Well, thicker wire doesn't kink so easily, thus preventing me from constantly having to change it; in fact they last me several months.

With preparations complete Bernard reached into his rucksack and produced Fred Buller's book called Monster Pike. He then recounted the stories of the leviathans held within its pages and the words 'it frightened me' drew them to a conclusion. Bernard was adamant that we would come face to face with a monster but only time would tell.

An unproductive hour saw us heading up to the far end of the lake where once again the baits were splayed out around the boat. This time Bernard kept me entertained not with someone else's tales but his own encounters with huge fish. A nine foot tiger shark off the Australian coast was hooked on mere 15lb line, giving a glimpse of its frame on the surface before a young Cribbins lost control as the beast realised it had been hooked, leaving him with smashed tackle.

The bite recounted at the beginning of the tale was now only moments away - would it end like the tiger shark? Well it was time to find out. As the float

disappeared, Bernard engaged the bail arm and swept back the old spinning rod to set the trebles. I swear I heard a groan as the strain built and it's arc intensified. At first, neither of us was sure of the pike's size and Bernard's voice questioned its credentials 'are you the lump?' In response, more line was stripped from the spool. Bernard was losing ground fast and with each surge the Mitchell reel squealed in fright. Would it stand up to such ferocity?

I had never seen a longer pike fight, the shallow water meant surges replaced dives and all Bernard could do was hang on, for it was difficult at times to know who was playing whom. I guess a good five minutes passed before he began to gain the upper hand and at last a polka dot flank of a pike resembling the proportions described by Mr. Buller headed towards my gloved hand. Quickly, I slipped it under the gills and his prize was lifted skywards. "You've got a twenty pounder" I pronounced. It was Bernard's biggest ever pike and the scales confirmed this at 22lb 9oz, made up of the most splendid esox I've ever seen. Bernard was right, we did indeed come face to face with a monster.

"Are you the lump?"

Tying Loose Ends

 LUCK is an essential part of any major undertaking and we were certainly getting more than our fair share during the making of the series.

Boyhood hero.

When I was still at film-college, my first freelance job involved Peter in a programme called 'Tackle and Tactics'. I had to film several famous anglers, fishing on venues around the country and Peter 'did the business' on cue, catching bream from the Thames and barbel from the River Kennet. The success we had during the making of the series with several well known anglers encouraged me to ask Dick Walker if I could make a series of six half hour films with him. He agreed and we discussed how we'd go about it while he and Pete Thomas fished for trout on Grafham water. All was set for starting when I graduated from college but then I immediately got a job with the BBC Film Unit in London. I was soon travelling the world and that left no time for filming Dick's series. I'm still sad

It is said that it's better to be a lucky angler than a good one and though that doesn't necessarily apply to Bernard it was certainly more than we could have hoped for when he caught a twenty pound pike on camera. That dear friend to many, including myself I'm happy to say, Peter Stone had a lovely saying if accused of being lucky "...no, it's blinding skill and superior knowledge...." spoken with a stammer of course - and in Peter's case the claim was probably true!

about that, for what an interesting snapshot of angling history it would have been. However, maybe one day 'Catching the Impossible' will be a part of our heritage - but if so we'd have to finish it first, and time was cracking on.

Bernard's big pike would make a great ending to the second programme of the series but our third spring was approaching fast. On February 1st the rooks

Ambush.

were nest building, so too a pair of long-tailed tits. What's more, the frogs were already spawning in our ponds and a heron had latched onto this bounty, visiting every morning to feast on frog's legs. Meanwhile we had lots to do, including the filming of some build up material to finish off the big roach sequence of Terry Lampard catching his 3lb monster.

Mid February saw us on the Avon, with Martin being joined by friend Tim Norman. The river was in good nick and this time they actually caught roach, not two pounders unfortunately but both had good fish approaching that magical mark.

We hadn't yet finished the floodwater barbel sequence and when our prayers for rain were answered again, we were much relieved. The weather was really mild too, with the first Brimstone butterflies on the wing, so it was time to head to the river armed with chest waders and some powerful tackle.

 Praying for a week of heavy rain isn't what most people do, but then again most people haven't hooked a barbel with a river bearing down in full spate intent on smashing your fishing tackle to pieces. The weather might be dull but winter angling is at its exhilarating best when a barbel is set on ripping your arm off! So that is why I did a rain dance every week hoping for a flood - the time for the biggest of the species to feed and a chance for us to complete our winter scene. We knew a swim on the Hampshire Avon that would be perfect; what we needed was the right conditions.

Of course, the river stains regularly during the colder months but this wasn't what we required, we wanted much more - banks bursting, fields flooding and the river full of debris. This is not only a time when a feeding rampage can occur, it also gives me, the angler, a huge thrill, knee deep in water my rod fully compressed while an unseen force moves slowly across the flow, occasionally holding station, convincing me I'm snagged until it

again moves ponderously upstream. The 15lb line strains and stretches to its limit and still I make little headway. It's for this experience that I pray each year for the heavens to open and for this winter a suitably eccentric scene to match the madness of the Bristol Avon we had filmed.

It had taken a good few days but at last the river had admitted defeat with fields saturated and sluices open; the rain could no longer be managed. Spilling over into every ditch, stream and low lying land the scenery, once shades of green, now blended into a single fluid brown canvas. It was time to get out the extreme tackle and meet Hugh.

A 2lb test curve rod would cope with the sea leads that I intended to use. Terminal tackle of course was going to be strong enough to pull a bus so all that was needed was a bait - pungent and potent - allowing it to stand out in such demanding surroundings. A selection of paste and pellets was slipped into the rucksack.

As I headed along the country lanes I had to weave my van from side to side to avoid a series of huge puddles and the farmland I passed resembled that of Flanders in the First World War. I was expecting an angry river and that's exactly what I got. It no longer slipped through the countryside unnoticed, now it rumbled along with a weir nearby making it difficult to hear yourself think.

Both the barbel and I love a warm flooded environment but this was too much even for us. So we headed downstream where the flow smoothed out and we could relax a little. All I needed to do now was to pinpoint their location and present my offerings. Easier said than done when Mother Nature wanted everything to be tossed around and dragged off. Hugh quite wisely deemed the camera equipment more important than my desire to wade, so for once he took up station on the opposite side of the river rather than alongside me.

A series of near bank bushes, which during summer offered cover were now half submerged and presented the best chance of respite for my target.

So pitching myself five yards upstream I prepared to make a cast. With a sideways motion the heavy lead and PVA mesh bag full of broken boilies and pellets was lobbed alongside the snag and by holding back hard on touchdown I allowed the whole lot to sweep in towards the bank and deep under the roots. I guessed years of flow may well have carved out a cave, giving the barbel a home for riding out the worst of conditions and it was here that I hoped my hookbait sat.

My rod didn't take too kindly to what was being asked of it, folding over to the spigot under intense pressure from the river. I could not place it on rests for it would have been dragged in instantly so instead I stood

response that I couldn't fail to notice. A strike wasn't required as the rod was already bent; now it was time to see who was going to win the bout. I couldn't yield for fear of snagging while my opponent not only had its own brute strength but also that of the river to aid it. Quickly a critical condition was reached and for a moment it seemed like neither of us was prepared to blink. Fortunately the stalemate ceased and the barbel changed tactics by heading upstream. Given the strength of my tackle all I needed to do was hang on and enjoy the ride. 12lb 8oz of bronze torpedo was the reward and although great fun, I was desperate for another heart pounding 'do or die' encounter to keep my addiction fed.

Knee deep.

heron-like, holding the handle until a bite came. Not that this was a chore as I adore the sensation of a barbel bite, stabbing my index finger forward while the rod tip whips round.

For a while, as I always do, I questioned my swim selection but it didn't take long to realise that I was in the right place at the right time. However, when the moment I wanted came I still failed to acknowledge it on the first indication. Momentarily I froze until the barbel got bored with me and gave a 'wake up, stupid!'

Today though was going to be the day to satisfy my desire as another of 12lb 13oz followed, giving me a further workout and Hugh all the images he needed. Such had been the speed of our success that Hugh decided he could, for once, take the afternoon off and wet a line himself, fishing for his beloved roach. I however had no intentions of calling it a wrap. If the barbel wanted to play it would be rude of me to ignore their invitation. Up next was a brute of a fish with a battle to match. Long, lean and mean was the best way to describe it, having never been given the chance to become obese in the fast flows and natural environment. This was how a barbel should really look without a constant supply of pellets. Was it time to stop? Not on your life - I was enjoying it too much.

Once again the rod top sprung round and both the barbel and I drew a line in the sand. Neither of us intended to budge but which one would? Grimacing, it was more like a tug of war than a fight on rod and line - my feet slipped in the mud and I had to dig my heels in to prevent ending up in the river. "Come on", I screamed to the sky, pushing the rod even further towards its limit.

The end of the season was nigh, so it was a relief to have tied up some more loose ends, even if there was another sequence that required some work too, the Bowood pike. We needed some shots of Martin out on the lake in the boat - simple enough you'd think. However, our problem was continuity, for our *'Impossible'* monster was caught in very calm and overcast conditions and we had been waiting all winter to get a match for the weather. (I would have filmed the shots immediately after catching the pike, but the rain had started

Biggest of the bunch.

At first this desperate manoeuvre made no impact but then I gained an inch, then a foot, followed by a yard. I had pushed my luck on each occasion and somehow it had held. Rolling in front of me was the biggest of the bunch and at 14lb 3oz it looked more like a bull terrier than a barbel ! What a roller coaster ride! Being a venue record the river keeper, Pete Orchard, came to witness it and informed me that this particular character was called the 'silver fish' due to its complexion. I now felt that it was time to call it a day, but what a day! I challenge anyone to beat the thrill of a big floodwater barbel.

during the capture and the light had gone.) Luckily, on March 12th the conditions were just right and another sequence was put to bed. Martin had to have a cast or two of course, but as if to prove how lucky we had been the previous winter, all he caught were tiddlers.

Next day, I skived off work on the series to have a last cast. It was a lovely day, with chiffchaffs celebrating their recent arrival from Africa by singing happily in the riverside willows. And as if to prove that spring had finally arrived, I caught a tench. I'd actually caught a carp too, even before I'd set up my tackle. The river had receded so fast after the floods

that a fifteen pound mirror had become stranded in the reeds, so I waded out with a landing net and rescued it from its prison. On release, the carp swam off strongly, despite it's two days of detention during which it was only partially covered with water - tough critters carp.

After my 'good Samaritan' act I'd hoped the river gods would smile on me, but I never did catch a roach. Worse still, my traditional last day of the season roach fishing was scuppered by having too much work to do. Going fishing wasn't an option.

With the river clearing after the floods, I could tidy up several more sequences by filming some underwater scenes. I knew a spot on the Avon where perch hung out, and carefully sliding the camera across the river, there they were under the bushes, two and three pounders drifting gently around the cover, before frightening the shoals of minnows when they pushed on upstream.

The fourth film of our series planned to feature the four seasons and what the freshwater wildlife gets up to at certain times of the year. I needed more film of wintering carp so I returned to the lake where Bernard had caught his big pike.

Sliding the camera through the branches of some dense willows where I'd found the carp on a previous visit, I discovered they were still there, literally dozens of carp, wedged so tight that it was difficult to push my camera amongst them without it being barged out of the way. This time I attempted to get them to feed, emptying some pellet through the branches with the aid of a pole cup. They woke up slowly, responding to the feeding stimulus by drifting back and forth before dipping down for a snack. The scene was a carp anglers dream, or maybe a nightmare, because there was no way you could get a bait within ten yards of them. Full marks to the carp for finding such a safe winter haven.

Immediately above their heads, the dense willow branches provided a secure place for a pair of Great Crested Grebes. They had draped their floating nest

of waterweeds over the stems and on the 24th
March they laid their first egg. I planned to return in
three weeks to film them hatching and swimming
with their delightful stripy young on their backs.

Spring was certainly in full swing, for on the 30th
nuthatches were adding mud to their nest hole to
make it a tightly secure entrance and chiffchaffs came
to blows as they argued over a territory in the garden.
So intense was their fight that they fell into the pond !

A pair of jays were prospecting for a nest-site too,
and the male was showing off to his mate by
imitating a crow, a buzzard and a black headed gull
all in the same 'song'. They are the most wonderful
mimics and we have one individual who does the
perfect tawny owl call. If we hear a tawny owl
during daylight hours, it isn't !

One aspect of angling that couldn't be ignored,
despite the attitudes of a few less enlightened souls,
is the importance of lady anglers to our sport. I was
convinced that showing angling to be accessible to
all, boy or girl, young or old was an essential part of
the message and our next guest would illustrate this
point perfectly.

Lisa Isles is a classic example of a child who, when
encouraged by her family, becomes hooked on the
sport. For her, though much more was in store and
she blossomed into an England star. As I write, she
has just grown too old for the England Fly Fishing
Youth Team, but during her time with them she
enjoyed remarkable success.

Lisa started fishing with her Dad and Grandad when
nine years old, and with such experienced teachers
she soon became proficient, so they entered her into
the England Youth Fly Fishing National Final. She was
the only girl competing against forty boys and on her
arrival the lads and Dads just thought "that's a girl -
girls can't fish!" Well, she came 4th and got a place
in the England team - aged just thirteen!

In her early days the team won two golds and a
silver, then in the more recent world championships

Nest building.

she competed in Czechoslovakia and Portugal and for her final year, in the USA, she was made Captain. They fished in Pennsylvania and won a bronze medal, beating the Americans into 4th place - they weren't happy!

Some of Lisa's quotes from our filming capture a snapshot of her enthusiasm for the sport: "Ever since I was a kid I loved being by a river - with a little bit of adventure inside of it. I don't really know why I have to go fishing - there's something inside me which always draws me to a river. I just love fishing now - absolutely love it, and for me fishing is my freedom".

Keen to capture her story on camera, we arranged to meet on the Welsh Dee at Llangollen so she could natter away while catching trout and grayling. She did both to good effect and we found some beautiful places to fish too. What's more the sun shone from a cloudless sky, remarkable only because it was the fourth time we had tried to film this sequence. The previous three times we had been rained off, so in the end, perseverance won the day .....again!

As with most things in life, problems disappear if you keep trying ....well - sometimes. Enough of the homespun philosophy - I had a book to finish and a series to complete and we could never afford to lose sight of the quest for the *'Impossibles'*. A ten pound trout was one of them, so we called up Lisa once again and so she had some expert guidance, our old friend Des Taylor. He's caught over two hundred double-figure trout, many of which have come from a favourite water of his, the Lechlade Trout Fishery. Surely he could help Lisa catch just one more - and with the blessing of owner Tim Small, we picked a sunny day in April to try.

Box of tricks.

My wife Sue and I arrived the day before so we could film some underwater footage of the trout in its crystal clear waters. While trying, we noticed anglers leaving the fishery with their catches of big trout, not carried on strings or in a bag but in wheelbarrows! The signs looked promising.

We've all heard the saying "You should have been here yesterday ....", and as soon as Lisa started fishing it became apparent that this sentiment might be appropriate. We'd been given the privilege of fishing the private section of lake from Tim's lawn, a spot where numerous trout cruised in full view due to the freshly oxygenated water flowing into the lake. We were certainly in the right place but despite Lisa casting like a dream, as you'd expect from someone who represents England, the trout wouldn't play ball.

Des helped Lisa work all the different permutations of fly patterns, little green tinheads, green and black montanas, even a fritz lure, but after a couple of hours, all they'd raised was a half hearted pluck or two. However, Lisa doesn't give up easily and much to our delight, she finally induced a lovely brownie to take her thin-bodied pheasant tail nymph. It was a cast that I had followed with the camera and zoomed in on the fly and saw the brownie approach and turn away. Lisa quickly recast short with a deft flick of the wrist, raised the fly up towards the surface, and the brownie just couldn't resist.

As Des said, it was top class fishing and though the brownie didn't quite make our ten pound target it put up a spirited fight. What's more it was such a beautiful specimen that we chose to return it to fight another day. Lisa and Des tried all day for a bigger one but alas, it was just one of those dour days when the weather was better than the fishing. Still, we had a lovely sequence in the can and one that certainly proved once again that girls certainly can fish.

The gentle touch.

North of the Border

 THERE were two major aspects of angling that I felt sure we had to include in our series, apart from those we'd covered already of course. One was to catch a Scottish salmon .... and it was likely that landing any salmon would more than fulfil our *'Impossible'* category. The other was to film a sequence with one of the 'big hitters' of the carp world and for this we were lucky enough to receive the help of Frank Warwick.

Frank is as good a bloke as you could wish to meet and is also an ace carp catcher, as well known in Europe as he is in the UK. All we needed him to do was catch a carp of twenty to thirty pounds, and we'd been fortunate to get permission to film at one of his favourite venues, Wellington Country Park. Once Head Ranger, Andy Pye had seen us settle into our chosen swims the catching of a large fish was surely a formality - but the best laid plans......

Firstly, the swims Frank fancied were already occupied and the carp just didn't seem to be in residence in our alternative swims. Luckily, the guys in our preferred swims were packing up, so next morning we hauled all our gear half way round the lake and set up with renewed confidence. The lake was beautiful, the weather warm and all was well with the world .... until the carp decided to spawn ! Luckily I had my underwater kit with me so even if we couldn't catch them, at least I could film the carps' nuptuals in the clear water. The camera then decided to malfunction, so that was Plan B scuppered.

However, Martin had found a pod of fish that hadn't yet started to spawn and they were feeding. When he finally hooked one, out came my normally reliable camera only to find that it too had developed a fault. All I could do was watch helplessly as Martin landed carp after carp up to thirty pounds. Frank then latched onto some big fish too, and I couldn't film those either. Sometimes things aren't meant to be.

When the camera had been repaired it was too late to return to Wellington as Frank was abroad and I had a holiday booked with Sue, walking the Thames path. The previous year we had completed the section from the source to Oxford, and loved it. Mid April is a wonderful time of year with migrant birds arriving in droves and we'd seen eighty species in just six days walking. I'd also seen enough delectable swims to keep my casting arm twitching for a month; the Thames sure is a lovely river.

This year we planned to walk from Oxford to Marlow, doing about twelve miles a day. The sun had been

Fishing for the family.

Luckily I was back in time to film a big shoal of chub spawning on the Hampshire Avon above Downton. I'd hoped for barbel as well because they had already started, only to lose heart in the cooling water temperatures. Our pair of Great Crested Grebes were due to hatch at the end of April but a disaster had struck and they'd lost their eggs, to crows or moorhens probably. We badly needed shots of young grebes for our seasonal film of the series and fortunately my good friend John Levell came up trumps.

A pair had just hatched their three eggs on one of the lakes on Somerley estate and John told me where to find them. Getting good film of the family took me a week. Grebes with young are

shining for weeks, but you've guessed it. After the first day the rain started, and trudging through mud carrying rucksacks in the dripping wet for two days began to lose some of its appeal! When Sue started to fantasize about beaches on Crete I knew our walk was over. We just cancelled our B & B's and caught the train home.

notoriously shy but by using my camper-van as a hide I could edge close enough to film the charming, stripy young being fed fish and riding on Mum and Dad's back. It took me a week because the birds kept on getting disturbed by walkers, work parties, or salmon anglers. I'd spend two hours or so edging close enough to film and just as I'd done so someone would arrive

Across the Boggach.

Scotch mist.

I'm often asked about 'ratios' - how much film you shoot compared to what is used - but a much more pertinent question is how much time for each second on the screen. In the 70's I was working for the RSPB, making a film about Ospreys and this required a shot of the male bringing a fish to a perch before taking it to the nest to feed the young. I filmed this shot at the famous Loch Garten Osprey site, so was clocked in and out of my hide by the wardens. I'm told the ten

and inadvertently frighten the birds to the other side of the lake. It happened so often I nearly went mad ....the van filled with 'effings and blindings'! Contrary to popular belief, the wildlife film-maker doesn't have any patience, only perseverance. It took a week to get the forty seconds that we needed for the film - no wonder wildlife cameramen need certifying!

second shot took me one hundred and forty hours to get on film, a ratio of 1,400:1. That's probably my PB and no doubt a Drennan Cup winner. It was a good shot though!

Ospreys just have to be a feature of any serious fishing show, and it was one of my ambitions to get

Martin and Bernard watching a nest ... from a safe distance of course. So in mid May we all headed north of the border to try to catch a salmon and some trout, while enjoying the delights of the Scottish wildlife.

The place I chose was familiar ground, for I'd filmed there for 'A Passion for Angling' and before that it had been my northern home for three years while making two films for ITV's 'Survival' series. I had a caravan and landrover hidden in birchwoods overlooking the wonderful Boggach, a marshy area lying between Loch Alvie and the River Spey, the haunt of otters and pike. Overlooking it is an Osprey's nest and the local forest provides a home for roe deer, crested tits and red squirrels. It's a heavenly place and Bernard and Martin thought so too.

I was able to show them the Osprey's nest and the male flew over our heads as it fished for pike in the Boggach. Roe deer wandered nearby and we even found fresh otter spraint by the river, just a few hours old, along with a dipper family that performed for the camera. Sadly the otters eluded us, but not the red squirrels. A friend of mine, Neil McIntyre, lives nearby and he keeps a spot baited with a steady supply of hazel nuts to ensure regular visits from photogenic squirrels.

Neil is a wonderful wildlife photographer (he supplied the lovely pictures shown overleaf) and I'm happy to say that I gave him encouragement when just a youngster and introduced him to the basic principles of using hides and the best use of light etc. It was only fair to do so because his Mum and Dad, gamekeeper Torquil and Jean, had helped me when making an Osprey film for the RSPB when I too was a youngster in the 70's.

Nearly forty years on, (scary how time flies) I was back in their living room sharing a cuppa and a wee dram. Then it was time for some filming and a meeting with Neil's red squirrels.

Red Squrrel.

Crested Tit.

Dipper.

Roe Deer.

Going to Scotland in late May for filming was a bind I thought, as I boarded the plane at Bristol Airport. Carp, tench and bream would be feeding like mad on my local venues and I had no chance of catching these where I was going. Instead small, wild brown trout were on the agenda – how inspiring could they be?

Hugh and his wife, Sue, along with Bernard, had already arrived in Scotland a few days earlier in an attempt to lure a salmon, so on touch down I hired a

definitely needed an extra layer of clothing. I still wasn't sure why I was there though, and to say I was wishing I'd said 'no' to this trip was an understatement.

After an evening's rest and a good sleep we made the five minute journey into an estate that Hugh had arranged for us to visit. Heading down a track, round a corner and over a bridge, everything changed. Bright yellow gorse and broom flowers filled my vision and then the horizon fell away into a valley with the bottom made up of a sparkling, dancing sheet of river outlined by yet

That looks good.

car and set off to rendezvous with them. Then we planned to head off in convoy down to Aviemore and the location of our river, Scotland's finest, The River Spey. Alas, on meeting my companions it transpired that the salmon hadn't been obliging so we hoped that the trout would play ball.

Aviemore sits in the shadow of the Cairngorms which fill the skyline with their snow-capped peaks and we found them surrounded by dark, menacing clouds. This was certainly as far away from the south's tench-rich gravel pits as you could possibly get and I

more broom and a gravel trim. From here the bank began to rise again with a forest wall, continuing upwards until it appeared to touch the snowy peaks away in the distance. As if that wasn't enough to convince me of Scotland's beauty, an osprey circled overhead before returning to its nest and tending to its eggs. Sure, it was May and the fishing I had left was good but this view was worth a hundred carp. It didn't matter that the trout were tiny, all I wanted to do was make contact with the environment. My outlook had altered in seconds.

Over the next couple of days Bernard and I acted out a true adventure, watching ospreys and tracking otters (he also insisted that I smelt some of their poo while muttering about it smelling of violets!). Then came a close encounter with red squirrels, which still hold out against their grey cousins, and by dropping a handful of hazelnuts at the base of a tree trunk their natural shyness was forgotten. A meeting with a rather posh gentleman provided me with a laugh when he asked me if I was a 'bounder'. A quick reply that I was with the Miles' party saw him placated. But I could understand his concerns - a long haired stranger in a camouflage coat with a rucksack and a rod on a private estate could, I guess, look suspicious.

All of this was enough to keep us entertained and we caught trout as well. They were no bigger than the palm of my hand but each one gave me the same joy as a fish ten times the size. I had never caught a wild brown trout on the fly and what a place to do it. I enjoyed myself so much I was sorry to leave but all too quickly the trip drew to a close and with my

Touching heaven.

Offering advice.

prejudices firmly put in their place, I headed for home. No sooner had I got back than I was off again back up north, such was our hectic schedule. This time, however, it was by van to the equally stunning scenery of Shropshire's Acton Burnell.

Hugh, too, was making his way to the same location but as a stop off on the long journey home from Scotland. The *'Impossible'* carp had been caught the previous spring but, as always, attention to detail was important and some extra shots were required. This in turn meant that I had to relocate in the same swim, despite it being solid with weed and fishless! The only way I could wet a line was by donning chest waders and taking the bait past it all. Of course, a capture would have been nice but as long as we got the work done it would be a success.

Des Taylor joined us the following evening and over a bottle of red wine we spoke of the lake's monsters and how popular carp fishing had become. We planned to leave Acton the following day for the last time and I hoped a fish would send me on my way. I'm afraid to say things were now about to go very wrong. During the previous evening I had begun to feel a cold coming on and by 3am it was much worse. Lying on the bed chair, sweat rolled down my forehead and

despite this I shivered, feeling chilled to the bone. What felt like a throat full of razor blades and a blinding headache didn't help either and all I wanted to do was to go home. Hugh, I discovered, had already gone, so slowly I began to break camp, making seemingly endless journeys to the van before I too could leave. By now I really did feel ill and how I got home I will never know. But by 7.30am I sat in a bath full of hot water, shivering like an Arctic explorer, before crawling into bed.

Strike action.

Red alert.

The next few weeks were truly terrible. The antibiotics did nothing to temper my symptoms and I knew it wasn't any normal cold or flu. At first I suspected Weils Disease but a discovery at the top of my leg was to solve the mystery. A tick, and a dead one at that, was imbedded into my skin and this find understandably got me searching my body. Normally I remove my watch every day but being so ill I had failed to do so and it was here, hiding under the strap, that I found a blood sack the size of a blackcurrant with its owner still feeding on me! A pair of tweezers put an end to his fun and then it dawned on me – this was the reason for my illness. Searching the internet I read the words 'Lyme Disease' and decided it was time to call the doctor, who in turn told me to go straight to the hospital.

Blindness and heart failure were two of the possible results I had noted during my research, so as I waited for the tests to be completed I was, well, just a little concerned! "I am ninety-five per cent certain that you have Lyme Disease" was not what I wanted to hear but that was the doctor's verdict and he gave me a prescription for anti-viral drugs with a whole host of side effects for good measure! On a

brighter note, the doc told me that I was lucky to have found out that I had the disease early, as the worse cases don't get diagnosed until severe damage is done.

I could only surmise that I had picked up the ticks in Scotland where they feast on deer. I just hoped that the scene where I crawled along the forest floor to feed squirrels would be appreciated!

How and where it happened could be debated but the end result was the same – three years of full-time filming on top of another job that meant I had to write up to seven articles a month had left me shattered. My love of angling remained but something needed to give. Unfortunately, I knew that nothing could until the project was completed so it was a case of head down and carry on the best I could. Understandably, my wife Jo wasn't happy about the situation so I made her a promise that once it was over I would never over-commit myself again – which she quite wisely didn't believe!

 Poor Martin was well and truly grounded for a spell, but that didn't mean I had time to go fishing. We had plenty of bits to do that could be completed in his absence and, for a change, one involved me being in front of the camera.

One consequence of showing sections of the edited films to friends and the public was the reaction to the underwater images. These varied from amazement to disbelief, all very positive except in many sequences the water was so clear that some folk thought we must have used an aquarium.

Throughout my life as a wildlife film-maker I had always attempted to film all the critters actually 'in the wild'. Any captive simulations smacked of cheating, and even if the audience didn't notice, I would be cheating myself. So as a matter of principle I avoided captive filming and I certainly wasn't going to start while making 'Catching the Impossible', however difficult wild fish might prove to be.

Convincing the audience we hadn't cheated might be tricky, so I devised a sequence for the first programme in which I would be seen operating the underwater camera. An old friend who helped me with my snow leopard film, Ralph Bower, met me at dawn by one of our favourite locations. The sun shone and the sequence was in the can. What's more, on lowering the camera into the lilies, a carp swam past and tench rooted around in the lily stems. We hoped that by showing how the underwater scenes were filmed the audience would believe that the incredible world they saw beneath the surface was indeed true.

Once this little sequence was completed, I then tried and yet again failed to film barbel spawning on the Hampshire Avon. The fish were on the shallows but a drop in water temperature had cooled their ardour. Friend John Levell had tipped me off about their activity but sadly, despite three days trying, I wasn't able to do justice to his kindness. However, by the time these bits had been put to one side, Martin had recovered sufficiently

from his illness to attempt some more filming. The weather was warm, the forecast good, so another attempt at Frank Warwick's carp sequence became the priority.

 The look on Jo's face said it all when I was preparing to leave the house still suffering from the symptoms of Lyme Disease for a two-day film shoot at Linear Fisheries with carp ace Frank Warwick. I knew I shouldn't be going but our busy schedule didn't allow for illness and after the disaster at Wellington Country Park I felt duty bound to attend.

Fortunately, the weatherman gave a prediction for two days of sun, so with a bright blue backdrop I shook hands with Frank and discussed our options for the session ahead. Hardwick & Smith's lake felt as subdued as my mood - the surface unruffled, the air close and heavy. At first glance it seemed that no life existed but as we wandered out onto the peninsula which bisected the two lakes, pin prick bubbles popped on the surface – a sure sign of either a hungry tench or carp rooting through the bottom debris. The sultry conditions also saw large shadows rising in the water, waiting for the sun to break through and warm the uppers layers where they could bask. There didn't seem to be much of a decision to make - here was the spot we needed to fish.

Frank took the first couple of swims where the bottom had actually been coloured by feeding fish while I positioned myself on the end of the peninsula which gave the advantage of countless, very shallow areas to cast into. Given my condition, it seemed a sensible place to be. I had decided even before I left home to keep my species option open, as I knew Frank would concentrate solely on carp, so a bucketful of maggots seemed the sensible choice for my bait.

For a while I weighed up the spots available and indeed crashed the marker float down before I came to my senses. Why, when I could clearly see carp and tench passing close by, did I want to cast out into the lake? From my vantage point I could also see three feeding spots. By fishing under the rod tips I would avoid lines cutting through the swim, an issue which can cost an angler bites. With the minimum amount of monofilament out, the better it is for shy fish.

Surrounded by weed, the areas I had chosen only needed lacing with maggots to provide the perfect dinner table.

Difficult conditions.

Marginal spots not only give you an advantage with accuracy but also an ability to feed little and often, depending on action. This is a vastly superior method to the standard bait and wait technique and ideal when fishing with maggots.

The heavy weed and the possibility of a very big fish got me reaching for a rig which has taken the carp world by storm – a mag aligner. It's basically an artificial

lead on the mainline would keep the tubing snug to the bottom but by also sliding one on from the top of the rod it would act as belt and braces for any spooky fish which may have passed by.

Quietly, I settled into position and watched the water, waiting for the grubs to draw a fish's attention. In fairly shallow water it is very rare not to see a few tell-tale signs before getting a bite but on this

Come to Frank.

maggot threaded onto the hooklength and then pushed up onto the eye of the hook to create an acute angle - a clever idea maximising the pulling power of maggots with the hooking properties of a modern rig.

By using separate rod rests I could cover each spot but also at the same time keep the rod well back from the edge. A shadow cast on the water by the carbon blank is enough to spook fish, especially in clear water. Likewise I had ensured that the bivvy was not silhouetted against the skyline but tucked against a large bush instead. It's this attention to detail which will catch you those extra fish.

My fluorocarbon mainline hung limp off the tip eye but still I felt this could be improved. A flying back

occasion even a blind man would have known something was going to happen. Within an hour bubbles fizzed, tails slapped and the fish sent up plumes of silt. The end result was hardly surprising, as the alarm squealed in delight and a bow-wave headed out of the swim. A 20lb-plus common was seriously angry but after five minutes of gentle persuasion he began to see my side of the argument.

Its muscular bronze frame glistened in the sunlight as I proudly lifted her for the camera. Two more carp, including one of Oxfordshire's finest, a scaly mirror, plus a cricket score of tench to 10lb were then to follow, keeping me busy and my mind off the illness. Frank, meanwhile, hadn't fared so well and despite his best efforts was still to trouble the scoreboard.

However, given another warm day was forecast, the chances of a carp off the surface looked highly probable and he began to arrange his tackle accordingly. This, I'm afraid, is where things began to go wrong for me. As I dipped my hands into the margins I became acutely aware of a stinging sensation which felt as if I had placed them in acid!

Worse still, on examination I noticed a swelling of my palms which didn't look good to say the least. I had promised Jo that if anything changed I would go immediately to the doctors, so that was it – I left Frank with carp sucking down dog biscuits. We hadn't enjoyed the best of luck together but I was grateful for his efforts, which I hope gave a glimpse of the modern carper and one of the modern day greats.

The diagnosis? Well, I had been taking the course of anti-viral tick drugs and they had, like the doctor warned, 'side effects', and one was turning my skin photo sensitive. The advice from the doctor was to remain inside for the duration of the medicine – another two weeks in total. I bet you can guess whether or not I followed his advice!

Mid June is a special time, not just because it is the 'busy' season for wildlife, including spawning fish of course, but because it is the opening of the coarse fishing season. Whatever your arguments for or against closing waters on scientific grounds, there is no doubt that stopping fishing for a while enhances angling's reputation for being a sporting pastime by giving our quarry a break.

What's equally true is that having a period when we can't go fishing means that June 16th becomes a magical day. Chris Yates and I tend to stick to traditions, so for us that first day starts at dawn on a mist shrouded pool with a float by some lily pads, and if we're lucky, a tench and a crucian or three. 2007 was perfect, only spoilt by catching too many fish! From first cast to last a succession of lovely fish pulled our floats under - tench to 3lbs, small fiesty carp, and joy of joys, lots of crucians, several over 2lbs, the largest close to 3 lbs. So by midday it was time to pack up for fear of spoiling the magic.

Linear's finest.

Long Journeys

"A river is water in its loveliest form," wrote Roderick Haig-Brown and who could argue when standing by the Hampshire Avon .... trotting a float for roach of course.

Houdini.

It was obviously vital that rivers should feature strongly in our series and Martin and I decided early on that the fifth programme should follow just one river from source to sea. The choice of river was easy, the Hampshire Avon, and not just due to its close proximity to our homes or our familiarity with its lovely waters.

Chalk streams are a vital part of our national heritage and need all the protection we can give them. Their waters are clear and rich in minerals, having percolated upwards through a bed of chalk. As it comes up from the ground the water stays at an even temperature all year round, providing the perfect conditions for plants and animals. They are wonderful places for wildlife, including trout and grayling and the insects that provide their food. However, they are very vulnerable to droughts and abstraction and with reduced levels and flows, life is very tough for the inhabitants.

The Hampshire Avon is one of the most famous chalk streams in southern England, (the River Test is another of course) and provides some of the widest variety of freshwater habitats in Britain and therefore the greatest variety of fish. Firstly there is a dwindling but still regular run of Atlantic salmon. The upper reaches provide a home for trout and grayling, the middle reaches roach, chub, dace and barbel while the estuary is a summer home for mullet, even bass. If you add the increasingly widespread carp, plus bream, and predators such as perch and pike along with migratory eels, then its waters support a veritable encyclopaedia

of fish life. Add to this the clarity of the water and abundant wildlife above the surface and the choice was a 'no brainer'.

Rising from underground aquifers in the Marlborough Downs, the chalk- filtered water is fast flowing, so any fish living here has to work hard to hold station in the current. So it seemed appropriate that we'd call the film 'Going Against the Flow', particularly as we hoped to follow the salmon from the sea to their spawning redds in the upper reaches.

By July 2007 we had filmed most of the fish-catching on the river, from Bernard's grilse on the Royalty to Pete Reading's barbel in the middle reaches, and Martin's grayling up in the shallows above Salisbury. However, we still wanted to catch a mullet in Christchurch Harbour. It's in this estuary where that mysterious alchemy takes place when the freshwater meets seawater and the salty species push up into the river. Bernard had fished for mullet in Ireland but they would provide a new challenge for Martin. What's more, I had wanted to fish for these enigmatic creatures ever since moving to the area nearly thirty years ago, so we were all excited when launching the boat into the rising tide.

 The mullet was one species which I didn't have much experience of before filming commenced, in fact I had never caught one. So when I boarded Hugh's boat in Christchurch Harbour with Bernard it was a case of the blind leading the blind! Through a little research we had come to the conclusion that trotted bread flake under an Avon float was the way forward and fortunately the previous summer had seen Hugh out on a reconnaissance mission with a friend of his, Graham Peplar, so at least we had a starting point to try at the Clay Pool, directly downstream of where the Hampshire Avon and Stour merge.

By soaking a white loaf and squeezing it hard, we produced the perfect groundbait. This could be dripped into the river over the side of the boat and then pushed slowly downstream by the ebbing tide. Hopefully, somewhere along its path a mullet would begin to feed and our lumps of breadflake hookbait would prove irresistible....or so we hoped.

For what seemed like hours Bernard and I trotted our baits dutifully at various depths and speeds then, quite suddenly for no apparent reason, I hooked a mullet. At first it failed to exhibit the promised power I had read about and with ease I began to gain line onto my centrepin. Bernard warned me of

was ready for any charge but as it weighed certainly no more than a couple of pounds it didn't have enough power to smash me in a similar manner. Soon I was the proud owner of my first-ever mullet. With its grey marbled flank and white stomach it was an attractive creature and I certainly wanted to catch a bigger one.

Heading back to the slipway as the tide began to turn we all agreed that it had been a great day and started to plan another trip afloat, even before we had docked. Alas, the date was never to take place

Trotting flake.

the impending danger and told me to 'be careful of the anchor rope'. I dismissed his concerns with a confident air. "Don't worry, I know what I'm doing," I said. Seconds later a whizz of the pin and a bang on the rod as it hit the water was followed by a loud cracking of line. Its brute strength had taken me completely by surprise and left me looking a little silly. Why did I have a funny feeling that this clip wouldn't be left on the cutting room floor?

Licking my wounds, I retackled and after another long period of trotting I once again hooked a mullet, more by luck than judgement. This time, however, I

as wet weather scuppered our plans, but not to be beaten we eventually did make it out into the estuary again at the end of August and were confident of making contact with a monster mullet.

For the first part of the trip we returned to our previous swim but after a couple of hours with no joy, we headed upstream and into the Hampshire Avon itself, just below the famous Bridge Pool. Tactics were once again a piece of flake trotted under floats in a haze of mashed bread. Now, for the first time we could see the mullet heading upstream, seemingly oblivious to our offerings.

Undeterred, we continued until at last the float sunk away and a fish shook its head in defiance. Sadly the battle was over in seconds and all I was left with was snapped line – I even had the indignity of watching my float disappear, towed away by the unseen mullet. Convinced that I must have damaged the line accidentally, I cursed but soon retackled and was back fishing. A chance to redeem myself presented itself almost immediately... but then the bent rod sprung back poker straight and another float trailed off into the distance! Something was seriously wrong and a quick tug on the mainline showed exactly what it was – rotten! Luckily I was prepared with a spare spool so while trying to be positive I set about the task of rectifying the problem.

'Surely nothing else could go wrong,' I thought as a third mullet was hooked and sure enough this time the line did hold; just a shame the hook didn't! I couldn't believe it - what was going on? I tried to laugh it off however, as I had a camera pointing straight at me!

A bite is meant to be something to enjoy but instead, now I was terrified when the float went under and could not see how I was going to actually land the latest mullet that I had just hooked. As the minutes ticked by and she drew closer to the boat, I allowed hope to once again rise above the self-doubt, especially when the first roll of exhaustion on the surface took place. Then I turned the air blue with every swear word I knew. Forget the camera - I couldn't keep it in any longer - another hook hold had slipped!

Turning away in disgust, I realised to my horror that a couple were sitting on the boat opposite, watching the whole sorry episode. Apologising, I slumped to the floor and took a few moments time out to re-compose myself.

Alas, this was to be my last duel but we did have an enjoyable final hour tempting pristine roach from among the boats where they had, no doubt, sought sanctuary from the dreaded cormorants. The curse of the mullet had blighted us and I left with my tail between my legs. I had been well and truly defeated.

Mullet madness.

The mullet had certainly enhanced their well-deserved reputation for being difficult to catch. They had also proved that their extraordinary fighting qualities are no myth. As a result I couldn't wait to get back out there in my boat, though that would have to wait until I'd finished making the series. As Sue kept reminding me, "Going fishing isn't an option!"

However, I was allowed one day out for my birthday, and as a treat I'd booked a sea fishing trip with Bob Watton, an old friend from the days when I made a film about Newfoundland with Patrick Morris for the BBC. The programme won many international awards for conservation because it charted the sad story of the decline and closure of the world famous cod fishery and the life story of the capelin, one of the cod's major food sources. As with herring in Alaska (also the subject of one of my films), if you catch too many capelin their population collapses and so does the ecosystem. No cod = no livelihood = no fish and chips.

The film was called 'People of the Sea' and was so well received by the Premier of Newfoundland that he asked the BBC to supply a copy to every school in the land. He reasoned that if the country's children understood a bit more about the interdependence of species then they might not make the same mistakes when they were adults. It would be nice to think that we might all learn these lessons before it's too late.

Anyway, my birthday skipper Bob appeared in the Newfoundland film, masquerading with three other fishermen as down and out would-be cod catchers. To help them act the part I suggested that they should pretend they would never catch another fish again, to which Bob quipped 'that should be easy!' And just to prove I do 'cheat' at times, I then grafted in Poole, Dorset for a harbour in Newfoundland. Luckily Bob and his colleagues were brilliant and as a result I don't think anyone noticed.

My birthday trip out of Poole with Bob was marred by foul weather and rough seas, so much so that most of my friends ended up queasy, including poor Mr Yates who duly fed the gulls! He was so white I didn't have the heart to pursue bass under the cliffs, but we did achieve some of our aims - to see the last puffin of the summer, the peregrines scything around above our rigging and a bucketful of mackerel which Bob cooked back in the harbour. They were absolutely delicious, and when he'd recovered, even Chris enjoyed them.

As most of you will remember, the summer of 2007 was dreadful, with so much rain that all our filming was flooded out, though that was of little consequence compared to the poor folk who had the rivers flowing through their living rooms.

Those who benefit from flooded rivers are the migratory fish, the salmon and particularly eels. Lots of coloured water means the eels can ascend rivers easily and penetrate up little streams and drains, exploring the possibility of new homes in lakes and ponds.

A tiny stream flows into our garden and through three ponds, then on leaving the garden, flows through a wood and over the fields to the River Stour, a mile away. Apart from the otters that follow this stream and raid our garden, eels also ascend this tiny watercourse and even manage to wriggle up sluices and across our

Birthday treat.

Eel feast.

finds home in the tourist attraction of Wookey Hole and while holiday makers marvel at rock formation, the real miracle goes unnoticed.

It's these epic tales that draw me to this much maligned species - untamed, unknown and unloved, angling can offer no bigger mystery. After all, you've never heard of one called Fred, Charlie or Bill! Therefore our series would be incomplete if this story wasn't told, but catching an *'Impossible'* sized fish of 5lbs or more had proved difficult, with a number of failures already chalked up. Some of the worst nights of my life had been spent in pursuit of this challenge as it seems tall tales and eels go hand in hand – pythons turn to bootlaces all too quickly and believe me, if you've never faced such adversaries at night you don't want to! Dead ends and sleepless nights are all part and parcel but the unknown was enough to draw us back again and again.

lawn to colonise the ponds. It's a bit of a miracle really, all the way from the Caribbean to Corfe Mullen, and the eels grew quite big too, at least two feet long before the otters got them.

Unfortunately, eels have declined dramatically in the last few years, but we still wanted to catch a big one for our series. As Martin described previously, we'd tried several places which produced 'nights from hell' but we hadn't given up as a result and with warm nights forecast, we were on the road again.

Standing on Brean Down, overlooking the Severn Estuary, it was difficult to comprehend how far an elver had travelled to reach this point. From the Sargasso Sea to Weston-Super-Mare is one hell of a journey and, even then, it was far from over. Here the River Axe pours into the estuary and attracts the eel's attention, fulfilling the urge to transfer from salt to freshwater. The river cuts over the flatlands of Somerset, with numerous ditches and drains offering sanctuary to our weary traveller. Amazingly though, some continue into the Mendips, indeed the source itself. Two hundred feet under the ground, in rock pools hundreds of feet deep, this remarkable creature

Somewhere out there was a tall tale that might just become a reality and it was the River Axe catchment area that gave us our latest lead. Our friend Theo had located a small lake which he swore held our goal. Now Theo is a man who sees life as a glass half full not half empty so I had experienced his guarantees before; two nights and two hundred bootlace eels later

An Elvers journey.

Could it be here?

even he had to admit defeat. Enthusiasm is infectious though, so we were once again on the trail of an *'Impossible'*.

First impressions and eels are very difficult to call, for we had caught everywhere from a puddle in a chicken pen to vast windswept pits. However, this didn't look good – caravans everywhere and tone deaf Pontin's singers squealing in the background. Theo appeared to have surpassed himself this time! Judging a book by its cover though, is dangerous and as I took a walk around the pool my mood began to change. Its owner and anglers obviously cared about their venue – it was rubbish free, had good swims and a series of bays breaking up the skyline, giving each fisherman their own little world. More importantly, however, it was stuffed with fish, perfect eel fodder. Whole families sat

Fishy offering.

side by side enjoying what's great about angling. Their enthusiasm was plain to see and their hospitality was warm; they were all willing us to catch an eel. I have to say I felt a little ashamed of my initial impression – angling can mean so many things to so many people and that's why I love it.

Could we catch an eel here? First and most importantly, did they inhabit the lake? Well, the locals certainly felt so, telling us tales of smashed tackle and landing nets too small. Perhaps the owner, David Scott's testimony was most conclusive, for when the pool was created some fifteen years ago the ditches which navigated the field were dredged and eels turned up. These were then re-housed in the new waterway in among a bonanza of fry. Factor in trout pellets, and the larder was certainly full. In such environments I now believe science is on shaky ground because fifty years is no longer necessary for an eel to reach specimen size – the high oil content of pellets has thrown all of this science out of the window.

So with a new found optimism the tackle was erected for a night in pursuit of 'anguilla anguilla'. I tend to take no prisoners when eeling so a set of 3lb carp rods were loaded with large fixed spool reels and 30lb braid. At the business end sat a 2oz lead on a large ceramic run ring, with a bead and swivel connected to 18 inches of soft 15lb wire. My hook choice was a long shanked size 2 which I find prevents the deep hooking of eels. Now I needed the bait. Lobworms were instantly ruled out, because in such prolific waters they are just not viable. Instead a small fresh deadbait, like a roach or a gudgeon formed the basis of my attack.

Fish baits can be ripped off the hook if just lip-hooked so I prefer to thread them on. A baiting needle can be used but it does mean removing your hooklength continuously, therefore I sew the fish on. By passing the hook in and out of the flesh from the tail downwards I come to the gills – and now the hook is threaded through here and out of the mouth. The hook is then pushed back into the skull, setting it in place. Finally if the bait is to be cast any distance the tail is fixed to the shank with braid.

My plan of attack was to position two deadbaits either side of the island some twenty yards out, while the last fish was lowered under the rod tip and laced with four pints of dead red maggots. All I could do now was wait for the sun to drop behind the trees and a shadow to form across the surface. It was then that the eels would leave their lair and search out prey.

We had one good fish at dusk but disappointingly, the night passed without incident. Then in the half light of dawn I watched the braid on the margin rod continually twitch as the remaining maggots were devoured. Surely this commotion would attract a predator's attention? Lifting steadily, the braid once again rose but this time levelled out at the tip eye and began coiling off the spool. My bite alarm told me what I already knew and I lifted the rod from its rest. Between thumb and finger braid jagged out so I flicked over the bail arm and a swift strike met with an equal measure of power in return. Thrashing from side to side my rod bucked with the eel's head movement, a snake-like body then hit the surface, spinning like a crocodile with its victim. In the face of such sheer

Monty the Python.

brute strength I was glad of such stout equipment and a net especially designed for eels. With an almighty heave the head touched the spreader block before the body was wrapped in mesh.

A magnificent fish now lay before me, painted in shades of browns and bluey greys – its life the most interesting of any creature, with an amazing tale to tell. Long but lean, the scales fell tantalisingly short of our goal at 4lb 14oz, but how could I judge an eel by a number? We may not have had an *'Impossible'* but its life had certainly been an impossible story!

 Having returned home from our eel expedition, I was clearing one of the small ponds of silt and what should I find in the net but an eel the size and thickness of a pencil. We were delighted that the cycle was continuing, even in a garden on the top of a hill in Dorset. Mind you, that isn't as remarkable as the one we found in a pipe on Ramsey Island off the Welsh coast.

When working there with my best mate, RSPB warden Robin, we wondered why our water supply had been cut off. Lifting the manhole cover, there was an eighteen inch eel stuck up our water-supply pipe. Unbelievable really, because the only way it could have reached this spot was by following a trickle of water that dribbled down a precipitous cliff to the sea. So this eel had climbed and slithered one hundred feet to look for a new home - remarkable creatures eels !

Back in our garden, I was busy filming the visiting kingfishers trying to catch our minnows when I received a call from friend Pete Reading. The River Frome had cleared after recent flooding and he'd found a shoal of big grayling within range of my underwater camera. So next day we gave it a try.

The grayling were exactly where Pete had predicted and one was close to 3lb. Trouble was, these old grayling were shy and living in the strongest currents.....and with the Dorset Frome being a salmon river that meant the flow was fierce. However, with patience we overcame the odds. Pete trickled red maggots into the flow from well upstream and when the grayling had gained some confidence, I carefully slid the camera through head high stinging nettles and onto the gravel bed of the river. It was great to see them feeding enthusiastically and with colourful dorsal fins raised, aggressively driving off competitors.

With that sequence complete and the sun continuing to shine, we could consider tackling our next challenge - a tricky one too. We fancied trying to catch a carp on a floater - straightforward you'd think, but this was going to be attempted using a fly rod, with Bernard doing the fishing. Martin agonized over where to try this, but in the end a call to Uncle John solved the problem and we were off up the road to his lovely lakes.

The long journey to Norfolk was, as always, made even more tiresome by the dreaded A11, but eventually I pulled down the lane and my childhood memories came flooding back. Holidays to 'Uncle' John's with my elder brother Richard meant a week filled with fishing and a chance to catch carp that we could only dream of on our local canal. That was when we had learnt to tie our hooks on properly and open the reel's bail arm to stop having our rods dragged in!

bravado we set off feeling success was assured; after all, how could we fail? I could simply sit back and wait for my scene because a carp on a floating pellet and a fly rod was as good as in the can. John's lakes are what everyone dreamed of as a kid. Shrouded by trees, the water gives off an intimate feel, broken up by islands, bays and beds of lilies with every nook and cranny seemingly an ideal spot from which to catch a carp. Spoilt for choice, John and Bernard settled down next to a huge bed of lilies and began to introduce some dog biscuits. All that we wanted

Intense concentration.

Despite the naivety, it was the best time in my angling career – I was constantly wide-eyed and continually excited. So why was I back at John Wilson's house with Hugh and Bernard? Well, for the next couple of days John had been tasked with helping Mr Cribbins catch a carp on the fly rod. Why we had to make it difficult on ourselves I was unsure but I knew we were in safe hands with two old pros. After all, the camera wouldn't faze them and for once the onus wasn't on me to catch.

An evening in the local pub and a good night's sleep saw us rendezvousing back at John's the following morning, fighting fit and raring to go. Filled with

now was the 'glooping' sound of a hungry carp sucking down food.

If you have days where everything goes wrong then you should find solace in this tale because as the hands on my watch slowly spun round we lurched from one disaster to another. Fish melted away into the shadows, bites were missed and lost carp were followed by more lost carp. In desperation, they put on a bottom bait and a bite duly came - the only problem being that the hook fell out five seconds after making contact! Had the pair become poor anglers? Of course not, but combine bad luck with a film camera and you do have a recipe for disaster.

Hang on Bernard.

Frustration turned in the end to laughter because everything that could go wrong did! To rub salt into the wound still further, after the pair had finally given up, I took the fly rod and crept down to the waterside. Instead of casting I simply gathered up the line and threw it in to avoid any disturbance. Yes, you've guessed it – thirty seconds later I was playing a carp! Its capture wasn't down to anything I did better than John and Bernard, it was just that I had no pressure on me to catch. If you've never tried to catch to order, especially on film, then it might be hard to realise how difficult it is. An evening back in the pub was needed to drown our sorrows and regroup.

Day two dawned and the promised sunshine was replaced with heavy cloud. Still, it was difficult for the lakes not to radiate beauty especially as they had been designed to be the perfect venues. Having taken decades of painstaking work to sculpt, they were a credit to John and a fine example of how anglers can add to nature, and not detract.

When in the first swim the carp once again did an impression of Houdini, and we all looked to the sky – failure was not an option but reality was beginning to

At last!

dawn. For the umpteenth time John and Bernard crept into position. With a flick of the wrist Bernard's pellet hit the surface and a shape rose in the water. "Come on baby," he muttered, as a pair of lips gulped at the bait. With an explosion at one end and a spinning spool at the other, Bernard uttered the words, "and they said rock and roll was dead!" At last Hugh could capture the moment he wanted – two grown men whooping with delight! It certainly wasn't the biggest carp we had caught but it was definitely one of the hardest!

Rock and roll.

Keeping Bernard Busy

 IT certainly was a relief to film Bernard and John finally succeeding in catching a carp, if only because we'd filmed so many near misses I was running out of tape! What's more we had so many tense but entertaining moments of failure in the can that editing the best bits down so the sequence didn't consume a whole programme would no doubt prove challenging.

Editing our films was now a major concern; we'd been filming for over three years and had a huge pile of tapes. Past experience indicated that each programme would take at least two months to put together, plus a further month to edit the sound tracks, record Bernard's narration, compose and perform the music and blend all the ingredients together to produce a completed film.

Simple mathematics proved that I had already run out of time .... 8 x 3 months = 2 years, and I hoped to finish in one and a half so I could spend the last two weeks of the fishing season trotting the Avon and Stour for roach! If we were going to meet our March 2009 deadline I needed to cancel any plans to actually sleep at night! We still had lots of Bernard's sequences to shoot, the kingfisher needed to be filmed in the garden, this book had to be completed and the Rugby World Cup required attention too; I needed to crack on.

Our plans for the journey down the Hampshire Avon from source to sea included Bernard casting for trout in the upper reaches, and due to the kindness of Mike Locke and the Salisbury and District Angling Club we found ourselves on the river's verdant banks at West Amesbury one evening. Sue and I had recce'd this stretch earlier in the summer and seen how beautiful it was. We also saw lots of trout and grayling, so catching one would be simple - wouldn't it ?

Well, the best laid plans ... we had lovely light, a big hatch of sedges and several fish moving to these, along with a few olives but could Bernard catch one? The trout had other ideas, plucking half heartedly at his offerings in several pools until a beautiful golden sunset put an end to proceedings. The evening rise had failed to materialize and Bernard's parting words were "Trout 33: Cribbins 0 !".

This result was grossly unfair, for it was the first time during the past two years that Bernard had failed to catch the required fish. However, we had to move on downstream and a landmark we couldn't ignore was the wonderfully restored water meadows overlooked by Salisbury Cathedral.

The Harnham water-meadows are run by a Charitable Trust, with their scientific advisor Hadrian Cook and the warden, an old roach fishing friend of mine, John Beckett. The Trust and it's volunteers have done amazing work to restore these historic meadows and their irrigation systems, digging out silted and overgrown channels and rebuilding the sluices. These are vital in order to control the flooding of the fields - intentional in this case.

'Floating ' the meadows with warm chalk water and it's nutrients was an ancient agricultural practice that encouraged the growth of grass and provided rich early grazing for the flocks of Wiltshire Horn sheep, thereby getting the local farmers off to a competitive flyer in the markets.

More important to us anglers is the shelter carriers create for the fish in times of heavy flooding. Even more vital are the spawning and refuge they provide for small fish. In fact, I'm not alone in believing that the abandonment of these ancient meadows and consequent loss of these 'fishy facilities' has been a major contributor to Avon fish stocks declining, particularly roach.

Casting to the spots.

These declines have had a serious impact on this heavily protected ecosystem that is famous for its biodiversity. However, there are encouraging signs throughout the valley. Many estates are now dredging out these carriers and ancient oxbows and I filmed friend John Levell and

his dredging team clearing out two of these on the Somerley Estate. It was only a matter of days before they were colonized by fish, with kingfishers following, and even an otter, where only the previous week there had been dry land. The estates are clearing even more oxbows and carriers now and the Governments Environment Agency are contributing to the future of the Avon by allowing angling clubs to install refuge areas, much needed too because It can be an unforgiving river for fish survival when in flood.

I filmed Bernard walking past the meadows at Harnham, 'the best view in England', as well as friend John Beckett operating the sluices to demonstrate how well the meadows have been restored. Bernard walked on downstream to Britford, the majestic cathedral reflected in the carriers that harbour larger shoals of roach than anywhere else on the Avon. We all hope that one day roach will re-colonise those stretches of river where they once thrived, all the way down to Christchurch, benefiting in turn the herons, kingfishers, otters and grebes.

Our story for programme two required Bernard to catch a trout while fly fishing with Martin and we were privileged to be granted permission to film on one of the loveliest stretches of chalk steam in England, the River Kennet on the Hungerford Fishery. Long time friend Rob Starr is the keeper on this exclusive stretch of river and he led us to a delectable weirpool, suggesting to Bernard that he fish the 'crease' between the white water and the back eddy.

Bernard duly lured a beautiful near 3lb brownie into taking his fly and once it was landed and released, the rain began falling. This put a bit of a dampener on proceedings, the fish sulked and we headed for home.

Next on the schedule was a return trip to Old Bury Hill Lake in the hope of catching our *'Impossible'* zander, so a few days later we met Bernard on its wooded banks to consider our options.

Zeds on the move.

 Once referred to as a pike-perch, the zander is a curious creature that has not always found favour with the British angler. Accused of crimes against silver fish stocks, this predator has faced random culls in the past with the intent of banishing its presence. This over zealous procedure, I'm glad to say, has abated, for in comparison, the cormorant's arrival showed the zander's appetite to be positively small. So now, in enclaves up and down the country, this toothy predator has found a foot-hold and to some anglers their pursuit is now for sport, not extermination.

Laying my cards on the table, I cannot claim for one minute that I am an expert in this field because somehow our paths have very rarely crossed. I knew the species demanded resistance-free rigs and had a fondness for low light levels but that was about as far as my knowledge went. The odd trip I had made in their pursuit had ended in failure. So with the autumnal season upon us and a backdrop of browns, bronzes and yellows, our minds once again turned to this creature and perhaps, at last, a chance to fool a specimen.

The Fens, the River Severn and Warwickshire Avon all seemed good candidates but each, we felt, would present us with a baptism of fire such was their sheer size. No, a return to Bury Hill with Bernard seemed the sensible option if we were to get a double-figure fish.

After what seemed an eternity I pulled off the main road at last and down a lane whose surface was awash with fallen leaves. I had left the hustle and bustle of the real world behind, and this feeling was reinforced at the turn of a corner when the lake splayed out in front of me. It was easy to surmise that this was without doubt one of the prettiest day-ticket venues in the country. In the car park my two companions were there to greet me and as we chatted I stared out across the lake. Somewhere lurking in the shadows was what we had come for and although on the surface everything looked peaceful, I hoped to find the world below far more dramatic. To aid the search I was pleased to find that the lake had yet to experience a drop in temperature and with a good level of cloud cover predicted it seemed like there were few excuses for failure.

The first day's swim choice had been made for us due to a two-day match taking place. A complete bank of the fishery next to the house had been taken up but it mattered little to me, as I didn't know where my

A fistful of dollars.

A tasty morsel.

Due to the zander's finicky feeding habits I opted to use a very soft 10lb wire and two tiny size 12 trebles, which nicked into the flank of the bait. The choice of what would be used for this though, was less straightforward. Perceived wisdom is that zander do not eat sea deadbaits, preferring coarse fish. Bury Hill zander though, by all accounts, had not read the text books and local opinion found favour with the complete opposite. Then Bernard's prawn success last year was added into the decision making process. It was all very confusing for a novice like me, but just to be on the safe side I had brought along both sea and coarse baits.

target was in the first place and instead of remaining in one swim we intended to keep on the move until we stumbled across fish.

Tackle was a pair of soft 2lbtc rods combined with a set of fixed spool reels. To these I had loaded on 12lb mono, which then housed a simple free-running leger rig.

When the crunch came and the first two casts were made, I have to admit that the sea baits remained firmly in the freezer bag as, I'm afraid, an open mind in theory and practice are two different things. Nevertheless, I stuck to the game plan and worked up and down the bank, alas, to no avail. Twilight, we hoped, would be our saviour and when in the gloom the bobbin began to dance I felt at last that I had

The final 'Impossible'.

found the answer. The result was indeed a zander, but unfortunately it wasn't much bigger than the deadbait! Its arrival also failed to herald the start of action, and when time came to head back to the van for some much needed sleep, neither Bernard nor I had failed to trouble the scoreboard any further. Still, I would be ready for dawn – another hot time in a predator's day.

Refreshed, we wandered up to the very top of the fishery and a bay filled with lilies. As the sun began rising above the horizon, carp and tench rooted deep into the silt, sending up continuous frothy streams of bubbles. Alas, the zander failed to share a similar appetite and after two hours I figured that perhaps I was in the wrong place. Time, we felt, for our breakfast in the café and a review of the game plan.

Over a full English we pondered our next move, unsure of what to do. But luckily help was at hand in the form of a match angler who had fished the previous day's event. He recounted tales of catching small zander and of fry scattering at the sight of unseen predators – all music to our ears, especially as the area was now free. It wasn't going to be hard to guess where we were going to fish!

With two baits positioned out over the groundbait line of the previous day, I hoped that the match men had done the job of attracting zander for me. A jig of the bobbin twenty minutes later confirmed this, but my strike found just thin air. The first time it happened I didn't think it was anything to worry about but by the fourth missed take I decided a wholesale change of tackle was required. The bobbins were reversed to make very light drop arm indicators, the trebles replaced with a large single hook and, finally, the coarse bait swapped for a sprat head; hopefully now the tactics would overcome this timid creature.

Whatever I did was obviously to the zander's liking because the misses ceased and the action began with a string of fish to 7lb. Having never banked many of the species before I was having a whale of a time and if I continued to catch at such a rate I knew our target may be possible.

The day drifted by all too quickly and as dusk arrived so did a bank of cloud and, with it, rain. Our time was drawing to a close but for now, another bite kept me from packing up and cursing the conditions.

Unfortunately a pike had grabbed the bait and with each run I moaned at it for interrupting the evening. Heaving it to the surface I expected to come face to face with a polka dot flank but instead was greeted by a bloody great zander! How my mindset changed. I loosened the clutch and grabbed the net. Fortunately it had little energy left and with its spiny dorsal erect my mesh swallowed it up.

11lb 4oz was more than enough to make me a happy man and as I held her up for a picture the rough flank and beady eye illuminated in the flashlight. It was mission accomplished and time to go home, but as she was slipped back the remaining bait was picked up and you know what – that was a double as well! The last of the *'Impossibles'* had been banked and although there was still lots to do, my main part in this incredible journey was drawing to a close.

Specimens may not have been on the agenda any more but the rich tapestry of angling is made up of much more than the capture of super-sized fish and

A royal reward.

we still had to add to the adventures Bernard and I had taken part in. Working with him had been a real pleasure, for he had the enthusiasm of a man half his age, and combines this with a marvellous sense of humour. So when Hugh told me that we were all off to the Royalty Fishery on the Hampshire Avon for a spot of pike fishing I was happy to clear a space in the diary.

Walking back onto this famous river, Bernard and I reminisced about his success with the salmon the previous summer and for good luck patted the cast of the Avon's record situated in the venue's rod room. Today though it was old esox that we needed to tempt but from the start the high pressure and bright blue sky, combined with clear water, made our chances look decidedly iffy. Ideal conditions for filming unfortunately very rarely go hand in hand with those for fishing.

The turbulent water supplied by the main weir seemed a logical place to be and we peppered the river with a range of deadbaits and lures. Alas, none provoked a response and by lunchtime we were frustrated and fishless – it was time for a move. The other smaller weir on the fishery situated at the Parlour was also a known pike hot-spot so we decided to up sticks and move to this swim, made famous over the decades with captures of huge fish by legendary anglers. If there was a swim to come up trumps for us, this was it.

With both our floats bobbing about in the white foam we spoke of leviathans and wished one would grab hold in the optimistic mindset that all anglers possess. Maybe someone was listening to our plight as my float smacked under and a pike, albeit a modest one, headed into the net, closely followed by Bernard's bait being devoured. His wasn't a monster either but it gave Hugh exactly what he needed. My adventures with Mr Cribbins were over and an honour it had been too. For many, he's the voice of the Wombles and an actor of stage and screen, but for me he will always be the only man whose narration has captured the very essence of angling. I couldn't imagine our series ever being made without him.

Light in the Tunnel

 OUR last Autumn's fishing had arrived and with the colours of the beech trees along the River Avon looking glorious there was no time to lose. We needed some scenes of Martin searching for roach among the colourful trees and departing swallows. With the sun shining it didn't take long to finish the filming and when completed, Martin went fishing and I reluctantly returned to the computer to press on with the editing.

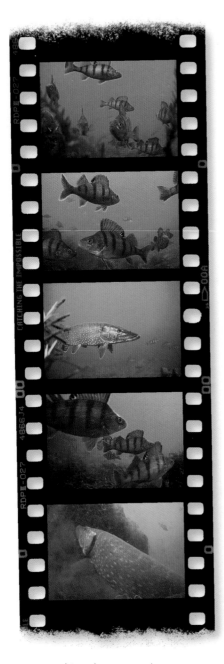

trout and now my major 'filter' for errors and omissions, along with incorrect scientific facts. Ace BBC editors Mark Fletcher and Jill Garrett cast a knowledgeable eye and my mate Chris Yates gave each film an 'emotional response indicator'. Wife Sue and daughter Katie weren't afraid to criticize and their observations were certainly 'penetrating' and invaluable. So having gathered all these opinions I then had the tricky decision on which ones I'd respond to and which I'd ignore. Of course, Martin and Bernard had their say, and I'd never ignore their wishes !

Editing apart, I had to film an opening sequence for the second programme, so once we'd gained permission, we met on the banks of the graceful lake at Fonthill for a spot of perch fishing. The dialogue was carefully written but it soon became clear that the fish hadn't read the script because Martin kept on hooking pike on his lobworm perch tackle and landing each one wasted a good fifteen minutes. As it was the shortest day of the year I was growing anxious about losing the filming light, but in the end the pike backed off and the required perch were swung into shot for the dialogue. We also needed underwater shots and the scene was amazing - perch as far as the eye could see - there must have been thousands of them. No wonder the pike were hanging around - and I even managed to film a pike grabbing a perch. However, its strike was so quick I could hardly see it; from stationery to 'perch into mouth' took just one eighth of a second !

A couple of weeks before that filming I'd received a call from our keeper friend at Longford, Pete Orchard, informing me that some trout were cutting spawning redds in his garden. The River Ebble flows around his house before entering the Avon below Longford Castle and as the Ebble is nearly always crystal clear and the forecast good, I was there like a shot. I'd been waiting three years for this opportunity so I didn't want to screw up.

We were now reaching the stage where I was torn between completing programmes and shooting more sequences and was caught in the dilemma of how best to invest my time. When it was raining the decision was easy, but if the sun shone I wanted to be outside. However, programme one of the series was virtually complete and had been sent out to my 'critics' for their observations on its successes and failures. Praise is encouraging but far more valuable is criticism, so my panel of 'judges' were important contributors to the outcome of each programme.

Firstly there was Dr. Nick Giles, expert fishery biologist, keen angler, author of excellent books on barbel and

Sliding the underwater camera ever so slowly into the fast current didn't prevent the trout spooking, but given time they returned and over the next two days I was able to catch some lovely moments on film. The females are very tenacious when it comes to their

Autumn glory.

chosen patches of gravel, so it was easy to position the camera within inches of where they wanted to be. One particular 2lb female was the most 'attractive' so I focussed on her and she was soon clearing silt and stones alongside the lens. Trout do this by tipping over onto their sides and energetically flapping their tails to dislodge unwanted stones. It looked exhausting but she carried on for hours, blasting out a depression in the gravel. This hollow ensures that her eggs receive a constant flow of well oxygenated water when they are finally laid and hidden under the stones. Suffocating silt is the curse of many species of fish, especially trout and salmon, so she worked tirelessly, 'cutting' her redd, her chosen egg-laying spot, every five to ten minutes.

Her commitment to successful pro-creation didn't go unnoticed among the males. They were constantly jostling each other to ensure they were alongside to fertilize the eggs when she finally released them. There was a 'pretty boy' of about 3-4 lbs and a bruiser of more than six pounds, bright red and beaten up, showing evidence of many previous prize fights. I think my lady preferred the 'pretty boy' and so did I; he was a gorgeous golden yellow, with great big spots.

Periodically, the whole circus would move on up to the weirpool and during one of these interludes I went exploring and found the freshest possible otter spraint, still with bubbles on it. The otter had passed less than twenty minutes previously, at midday on a sunny morning ...... and who claimed that otters are only nocturnal in fresh water!

Searching among the trout stews just behind the weir, there were lots of fresh otter tracks - no surprise perhaps but they had also raided the trout redds on the previous night, for there was a fresh spraint on the weir and flattened reeds where the otter had slept off a meal. No wonder the trout were nervous and no wonder I waited in vain for my lady to lay her eggs. Undaunted, I left the camera in place alongside her for the night and phoned my scientific advisor, Nick Giles, to find out what time of day they tend to lay their eggs. He is a trout expert, having recently written a great book about them, and he said they tend to lay at night because of their vulnerability to predation when spawning. He was right

of course, because when I returned early next morning and turned on the camera, she had filled in her depression with stones to cover the eggs and had departed. It was a big disappointment but at least on the previous day she had performed like a star.

It was clear that the trout's spawning season was over, so yet another sequence would have to wait a further year to be completed. Trouble is, the 'next years' had run out ! It's just amazing how fast time flies when you are trying to film wildlife.

Thanks to Pete I'd been lucky with the trout, but I also wanted to film salmon on their redds and this proved a little tricky. Recent heavy rain had swelled the rivers and

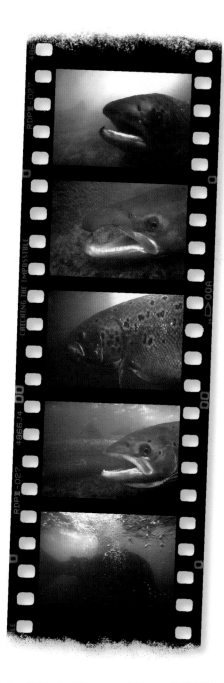

enabled the salmon to reach their redds two weeks earlier than predicted. There's nothing worse in wildlife film-making than suffering that 'should have been here yesterday' syndrome. And when you miss something in the wildlife calendar, it usually means you have to wait a whole year to have another crack at it.

Missing the salmon was frustrating because it wasn't due to my error or idleness. My VW camper engine had blown up and Sue was in London with the car, so I was grounded for the crucial week. Sometimes things aren't meant to be, but I'll be trying again this next Christmas in the hope I can insert the sequence before the film has to be completed. All very frustrating but wildlife film-making is like that ..... still, it sure beats working for a living !

The summer before, Bernard and I had travelled north to Scotland's glorious River Spey in the hope of an *'Impossible'* salmon. Any salmon was likely to be impossible and so it proved, with three days intense fly casting failing to produce so much as a pull. What is more, we had been kindly invited to join the Chairman of the Salmon and Trout Association, James Carr and his party and despite James working tirelessly to try to land us a salmon, it just didn't happen because the only one he hooked had got off.

Undeterred, he invited us to join him again this last summer. We had yet more lovely weather, the river was in fine fettle and each pool looked like a banker. Their

Gaelic names are lovely too and working downriver James covered the water inch by inch: Dalbreck, Pool-o-Brock, Delene (where he lost the fish the previous year), Pol-ma-Cree, Delagyle (in front of the fishing hut where we enjoyed delicious lunches), the delectable looking Little Turn, Rhynd, Pool Shuan, and finally the Boat Pool, (where an Osprey dived in the previous year and caught a trout). All were fished time and time again but no salmon fulfilled our dreams. I suspected the 'curse of the camera' was operating and I even hid behind a tree so the salmon didn't know we were filming - but that didn't work out either!

James felt that he had let us down but I tried to assure him this certainly wasn't the case. Thanks to him we had some lovely film of salmon angling on one of Britain's most beautiful rivers and even more importantly, he spoke eloquently to Bernard about the problems salmon face during their extraordinary life cycle.

They start their lives as an egg in the gravel high up in the hills, then spend two to three years in the river, avoiding goosanders, cormorants and otters. Gathering into groups, these salmon parr have grown to become smolts and head downstream to the sea where they face one of their greatest challenges, the remarkable transition from breathing in freshwater to the alien world of saltwater. James

Always a chance.

suspects that numbers of these smolts fail to adapt quickly enough and the stress kills them. There are other challenges too.

Estuaries are more dangerous now because global warming and increased water temperatures have enabled sea bass to move further north and fatten up on salmon smolts. One bass was found with seven in its stomach. If they make it out to sea, the young salmon search out the Gulf Stream, drift up the Norwegian coast and past its many predators to their feeding grounds off Greenland. Here they depend on a narrow band of water temperature in which to find enough food, and with global warming a threat, that area for effective feeding might be contracting. What's more, there's no certainty that the Gulf Stream will continue.

Leap of faith

The feeding grounds off Greenland are home for one winter, maybe two, then the salmon head back to Britain, across the Atlantic, and past the Irish drift nets, which hopefully won't be used anymore! Returning to our coasts, they face predation from dolphins and increased numbers of seals and due to the impact of changing weather patterns such as droughts, the salmon may have to wait longer in the estuaries and so are more exposed to this predation. If they survive this dangerous coastal phase of their lives they head back to the very river where they started, even into the exact pool where they themselves hatched. As James said, "A 15lb salmon that you might be lucky enough to catch has had a hell of an adventure and that is why you want to put it back"

Internationally, salmon stocks are low and there are many reasons why that might be, but at least there are lots of anglers trying to ensure rivers are healthy and pollution free, that there is sufficient water, that enough invertebrates survive to feed the parr and smolts, and that the spawning gravels are clear of egg suffocating silt.

However there is no room for complacency because it's estimated that Scottish nets still take about 100,000 salmon every year. James summarised by saying, "There's a lot of work to do if we're to ensure a future for these magnificent creatures and we're very lucky to have them in our rivers. Fishing for them is a privilege and a wonderful escape from the cares of the world because I find it requires intense concentration. And when you catch a salmon, you are looking at a little miracle". For James, Bernard and I the miracle didn't happen and we could only put it down to pure bad luck. However, we weren't surprised to hear that as soon as we'd left, James caught a salmon. The 'law of sod" had certainly played its trump card.

Having enjoyed so much success during our four year long journey, it's easy to forget just how difficult it can be to catch a fish to order, 'any' fish, let alone big fish. The salmon attempt had highlighted this and then a return trip to the Fens reinforced it. I needed more wildlife film out in the flooded fields and that was easy - catching a zander was not. Martin and Mick Rouse had come to join me to photograph a feature for the Angling Times, and despite shooting some beautiful film at dusk, the zander failed to show. As they say "You can't win them all", and we certainly didn't, despite trying hard.

With filming almost complete, editing the material would become a full time occupation and this can be the most rewarding stage of any programme-making because it means becoming part of a team. It's a time of fascinating collaboration because after months of isolation on the computer I have to integrate my ideas with fellow professionals.

Each film's completion is a thoroughly enjoyable occasion, for not only is it the moment when all those four year-old ideas come together and create some magic - or not ?! It is also a moment of relief, for it means that one more of the eight films is finished !

The process takes about two months, for after all the pictures are edited ..... which can take up to ten weeks, I then write the narration and visit Trevor Barber's studio in London, where Bernard breathes magic into my words.

The recordings are then edited with the pictures so they fit like a glove before I transfer all the memory from my computer onto a hard drive. Then I take this to Bristol where ace colourist Tim Bolt grades the pictures and Fred Tay finishes the titles and credits.

Meanwhile, the sound tracks I have laid are transferred to Kate Hopkins, who re-lays them properly, adds lots of stereo atmosphere and bird song and ensures that, when all mixed together, the viewer doesn't notice she's done anything at all! That's up to three weeks work to create over forty tracks.

The next stage is great fun because Chris Domaille and Graham Wild go into a studio and pretend to be fish. With the best will in the world, even when Martin and I are filming and the radio mics are always on, some sounds are missing or 'off mic', so Graham gets very wet as he fakes the splashes and swirls of fighting fish, along with missing footsteps etc. while Chris tweaks the levels so they don't sound phoney. The studio sounds create another six tracks, so we're up to fifty now.

Trevor recording Bernard.

Bernard narrating.

Tim grading pictures.

David working with the orchestra.

Lots of sound tracks.

Graham's final mix.

Meanwhile, during all these processes, David Poore has been composing the music. This takes about three to four weeks to write, perform and mix, creating a further ten tracks. David and I are both ex-Cathedral choristers, so music is in our blood, the difference being that David went on to make it a successful profession whereas I gave it up to chase wildlife in the mountains. David's music has been heard in many of the Attenborough films so he's very good at it, and as I mentioned earlier, we have enjoyed creating music together in the past.

How the combination of pictures and music can create moments of magic is a bit of a mystery, and what works for one person's ear might not sound right for another's. However, how David and I work is firstly to decide what instruments will create the right 'pastoral romance' for a British countryside series. For 'Catching the Impossible' we chose a string quartet and clarinet, the same with 'A Passion for Angling' (for those that enjoyed that music), along with a harp and piano, plus lots of computer generated music and sound effects.

Having provided David with a carefully plotted guide to within the nearest half second as to where the music should start and end, plus indicating when moments like sunrises or trout rises should be 'enhanced', David then creates beautiful tunes and orchestration to help capture the essence of the moment. Then comes the difficult bit, because when I have listened to each music cue I have to tell him where I think there are 'wrong notes'! David claims that "there is no such thing as a wrong note in composition - only in performance", but after much tooth grinding and midnight-oil burning, the music is complete and performed and judging by what I've mixed onto the films so far, I think you'll agree that it is not just appropriate, but lovely too.

The ten tracks of music are then added to the other fifty and the final stage with Graham Wild in Bristol is blending all this together with Bernard's words to create a beautiful soundtrack in which all the key elements can be clearly heard. I mention all these technicians by name because I consider them my 'A' team. They are simply the best in the business and if and when my films are a success, it is largely down to

A spectacular backdrop.

commissioned from that most famous of sporting artists, Rodger McPhail, were almost complete as well. It was Rodger who created the beautiful illustrations for the 'Passion for Angling' book, though we were all exasperated by the 'cheapscape' publishers when they reproduced his colour illustrations in black and white - such a waste!

This time our publishers MPress are doing a much more generous job. I'd worked with Rodger on the 'Passion' book of

their patience and skill. Having worked with them for thirty years or more, the collaboration is one of the most enjoyable bits of my life.

Finishing the films wasn't the only creative pursuit occupying my time; finishing this book had plenty of 'deadline doom' surrounding it too. I was almost on the last chapter and the lovely illustrations Martin and I had

course and then he kindly agreed to illustrate the book I was writing about Pumas in the Andes mountains. He came out to Patagonia and shared our camp for a couple of weeks, enjoyed the wonderful fishing and our tame fox, and even saw a puma or two, one of the most elusive critters in the world. It was even more fun because Rodger is one of the best story tellers anywhere, even if the ladies might have to withdraw after a dram or two! It's an indication of his love of life .... something I hope all of us anglers share.

Feeding the fox.

One mistake I made in those final stages of writing and producing this book was to suggest to Martin and our designer, Paul Moulder, that it might be nice to add film clips of the actual images from the programmes to the text. It was only a mistake because extracting the pictures was a very time consuming business, but I think you'll agree (as Paul did unfortunately!), that they enhance the stories and help the book and films to harmoniously converge. It was just a shame that time was running out so fast.

However, the book was almost finished and four of the eight films virtually complete, so we had nearly reached the final stages of our long journey. There was light at the end the tunnel.

Last Casts

I have to admit that the overwhelming feeling I have as I write these final words is one of relief, for I never comprehended at the beginning how much work was involved in making this series of films. But I would also argue that if I hadn't reached this mindset I wouldn't have been trying hard enough during its inception. I love angling. It has been an all-consuming passion of mine since childhood and it's my sincere hope that I've done the sport justice, helping to go some way towards settling the debt I owe. So I remain nervous of how the films will be viewed by the angling and general public alike. I can only hope that I haven't let anyone down, especially all those who contributed so much to its production.

Cold comfort.

While I pray this book has helped to convey the amount of effort which has been put in, it could never cover the endless preparations and countless hours of waiting that have been necessary .... and mine pale into insignificance compared with Hugh's. How many times did I get everything ready only to have it cancelled by poor weather? A lot I can assure you and this was just one of many factors involved in making the films. For the best part of four years I've been unable to change my appearance or clothes in a bid to sustain continuity during filming, as revisits to add the essential details that Hugh is famous for have been a common occurrence - I've even visited a voice coach to improve my presentation skills (it didn't work very well,) which involved reading from Shakespeare! So as you might imagine, there was a lot more to the 'Catching the Impossible' project than just fishing.

It's also ironic that I will not initially gain the same enjoyment from the series as, hopefully, the audience will, despite it being a culmination of Hugh's and mine's efforts. I'm sure though, given time and when the dust has settled, I will be able to look back on this epic journey proudly. So why did I do it? Well, I thought at the beginning, and still do today, that angling may never get a better opportunity to portray itself through the lens of a world-renowned cameraman, one who produced the peerless 'A Passion for Angling'. Who could refuse a chance to try and make another spectacular? I wasn't the only one who thought this either, with a string of anglers and fisheries supplying a huge amount of help and assistance on the long journey. Hopefully you will all be aware of how grateful I am and "thank you" will never be enough. All I can hope is that you will always

An Avon reward.

be proud to be an integral part of this series which, with luck, will get the message across to the widest possible audience and help to protect our sport for future generations.

For me, nothing would have been possible without the understanding of my best friend and wife, Jo. She has put up with me working ridiculously long hours while filming because I still had to supply up to seven articles a month to meet the needs of my 'day job' as a professional angler. Yes, I do have the best job in the world but the work still has to be completed, with never enough hours in the day. So thank you Jo from the bottom of my heart and I promise not to over commit again. (She doesn't believe me!).

Not only was it a chance to capture the field sport I love on film but the years have allowed me to learn from Hugh how best to portray the world we both cherish. In the beginning I didn't have a clue how a film was created but now I have even invested in my own camera equipment. This wouldn't have been possible without Hugh and it's hard to think of how I could have a better mentor. I've never seen a more dedicated professional, bordering on the obsessive - or even madness! He is the epitome of the 'harder you try the luckier you get' and I have to thank him for his friendship and dedication to the cause – angling owes him one and hopefully it will settle its debt when he catches another monster roach from the Hampshire Avon.

On the journey itself, we kicked it off in the best possible style with a giant barbel from the Great Ouse, giving us an immediate *'Impossible'*. However, this capture only serves to show how fragile big fish hunting can be as today such a fish would not be possible. The stretch has been ravaged by otters, and the leviathans of yesterday, flashing their golden bronze overcoats under the drooping willow are just a memory. Then came the first winter and a change of fortune. This was my lowest point as I not only struggled to catch but I was also coping with having a partner in crime! I am by nature a loner who is never happier than when in my own company on the bankside and I found coping with another individual's

Brewing up.

needs difficult. I also felt uncomfortable in front of the camera (a feeling which still remains today). We got through it by hard work and determination and maybe Hugh was correct when he told me in the early days that to make a worthwhile series we would need to suffer! Let's hope that the blood, sweat and tears haven't been wasted. Fortunately I can revert back to my old habits in the future and if life allows this, then I will be a happy man as I can't think of a better way to waste my time!

While the Impossible targets we set felt, in the beginning, like a noose around my neck their achievement gave me a huge high each and every time. I can hardly believe what we managed to catch on film, with, I guess, the 5lb perch and the 3lb river roach being the best specimens banked. The memory of that huge stripey coming up on the end of my line will live with me forever. It's size was so incredible it was hard to comprehend that perch do indeed grow that big. Every time I gaze at its picture I am blown away and I doubt if I will ever witness such a monster again. Maybe it was predictable, but living legend Terry Lampard was the man responsible for the 3lbs 5oz Stour Roach, caught on the simplest of baits, breadflake, proving that skill is the most important ingredient for success.

Friendships forever.

Out of those fishing trips with Terry it wasn't just a string of big fish that were the highlights but a friendship built with both him and Tim Norman. Now I regularly speak to the pair and enjoy more adventures off camera.

This has included specimens of most species, putting the icing on the cake to time well spent with a couple of mates. Personally, on the film front, it was the 32 lb pike that supplied the greatest exhilaration, convincing me that the journey could be completed. So this was without doubt my highlight, a time when the tide truly turned in our favour. I can still remember walking back to the van with the biggest smile on my face I've ever had. Amazingly, it seemed that all our failures had led us to the perfect day, culminating in a never to be forgotten moment when a pike beyond comprehension hit the surface next to the boat and I frantically scooped up her immense frame.

Curiously, my favourite sequence on film is not the pike but the capture of a 20lb river carp off the Hampshire Avon. As the quill began twitching I was a nervous wreck and this wasn't helped by the incredibly savage bite which followed. Hugh zoomed out at the exact moment this occurred, showing events were exactly as they seemed and not manufactured out of a series of takes and fake bites. The centre-pin went into melt down as the carp bore upstream with uncontrollable ferocity, testing the tackle and the strength of my arm! The end result certainly wasn't an *'Impossible'* and nowhere near our biggest fish, but the excitement I felt was captured on film brilliantly, proving that there is more to angling than just huge fish.

Guests too did their best to make the series special and I still laugh when I remember our time with John Wilson and his massive Broad's pike. I doubt that had you scripted the tale you could have come up with a better story. My commentary on film calls him a "jammy old bugger" but this is unfair because if my life depended on it, John is the man I would call upon to catch a fish. He's certainly got the T-shirt when it comes to producing the goods for the camera.

Another legend, Des Taylor may not have been as successful in a fish catching sense but to me he was in many ways the best character, larger than life and with a love of the sport few can match. It is a surprise that the big fella has never had his own TV show, such is his talent for off the cuff remarks and one liners. I could go on but with these and all the other unforgettable moments created by a string of willing

Still smiling.

A hobby for life.

stars, I feel justified that the title Catching the Impossible is now a suitable one.

I also believe that I improved as an angler during the tales told within the pages of this book, gaining knowledge and advice from the anglers around me to add to the years of similar experiences of my own. I feel I can now class myself as a genuine coarse fishing all rounder, something that has taken since childhood to achieve. Of course, I still make mistakes and fail, but today I understand why a lot better. So in many ways, two journeys have been completed, even if I have no intention of ending this apprenticeship. No matter how proficient we think we are, the fish have an uncanny knack of putting us in our place and that is why I love angling so much.

A child who has his dreams captured by this underwater world is blessed and I count myself very lucky indeed that I have been able to learn my trade by gaining glimpses of this environment. I never thought as a kid, dipping my net into every nook and cranny, straining to unlock its secrets, that I would be in such a fortunate position. Hopefully, the underwater element to our series will give everyone a chance to marvel at this hidden world as I know how much effort Hugh has put in to capture the images, managing to open Pandora's Box for everyone.

Maybe too, I've reached the pinnacle of my professional career as it's going to be hard to improve on this series and I hope that I'm not mad enough to even contemplate trying! The very thought of it gives me a headache. However, once again, if one non angler understands and appreciates why we go fishing, even if they choose not to go themselves, then it has been worth all the effort. To become an angler is to become a very lucky person indeed, blessed with endless adventures played out in the greatest theatre of them all, Mother Nature. Let's hope that the films inspire a child to pick up a rod and line and unlock a lifetime of adventures.

Its time now to close this chapter, not only in the book but in my life, knowing that I have tried my hardest throughout and no matter how successful Catching the

Impossible becomes, that will be good enough for me to end it fulfilled and happy. Thank you to everyone involved for the memories - and I hope your next fish is an *'Impossible'* one.

 For Martin, the long journey is complete but for me there is still about eight months editing to go. Four of the eight programmes are now complete, number one, two, three and eight to be exact, and if you think it's odd that I'm completing them out of order you'd be right. My excuse is logistics and deadlines and it's these elements that constantly prey on my mind, - the three D's - 'dreaded deadline doom'.

Time to reflect.

The next few months are going to be tight and intense but also exciting for I just love the creative process of making films and it's always fascinating to see how each programme turns out. I'm editing programme four of the series now, called "A Sport for All Seasons", during which we hope to prove that on every day of the year there is always somewhere you can go fishing and have fun. The contrasts between the seasons are just magical, from a mist shrouded pool in summer to a frost encrusted river in winter. There is so much beauty out there, and a fishing challenge as well and the great thing about angling is that it is accessible to all, regardless of age, gender or race.

Angling takes us closer to nature, gives us direct contact with the living world and that is good for our well-being, good for the soul. And regardless of whether going fishing is described as a sport, a hobby, a pastime or a passion, it is certainly a privilege, and because it brings so many people closer to the natural world, it is a privilege that all of us anglers must respect.

One of the surprises I enjoyed while filming the series was the sheer beauty of the underwater world and the glorious variety of the species and their behaviour in that 'other world' that I was briefly allowed to share with them. But what saddened me was to see several fish that were damaged by anglers' carelessness and that is simply unacceptable. Fish are a vital part of our wildlife heritage, an essential element in ecosystems and all the species that depend on them for their survival, so they deserve our utmost care and respect. The series of films is intended to be a celebration of angling and the freshwater world and it is important that the wider public are able to share our interest and understand the incurable passion.

Angling is such a big subject. There are so many great fish to admire, beautiful places to visit and lovely characters to meet, so doing justice to all this was always going to be a challenge. We needed more time really, but in the end you have to call a halt, and when the filming is finished, try to balance all the elements when editing. I was on a tight schedule here too, but being short of time just concentrates the mind. It is this 'living on the edge' that I find exciting and it was Tim Smit, the restorer of the famous 'Lost Gardens of Heligan' who said "If you're not living near the edge you are taking up too much space!".

This 'extreme living' philosophy is a principle I've tried to follow in my wildlife film-making, tackling the 'impossible, never been done before', subjects such as mountain lions and snow leopards. I'd suggest that 'Catching the Impossible' has certainly fulfilled the principle of 'living near the edge' because catching such large fish of so many different species constitutes one of the great challenges in fishing .... and to do it on camera .... well, the fact that Martin, Bernard and friends were able to pull it off is a testament to their determination, perseverance and skill.

As for Martin, he and I have spent over four years living in each other's pockets and under pressure for much of the time and we've hardly had a cross word, despite the many trials and tribulations. He is the ultimate professional, learning quickly about film-making and what is required to make a story flow. He was always on time, thoroughly prepared and totally

committed to making a success of whatever challenge we faced. In short, he is one of the most professional colleagues I have ever had the pleasure to work with and I include in my list the likes of David Attenborough. What is more, he has become a family friend and you can't wish for more than that. And what I need to add to this accolade is that you simply cannot overestimate the patience required when being filmed, or the pressure created by having a camera pointed at you while trying to catch.

We've almost finished the filming we have to do at last, apart from a sequence of Bernard on the top of Marlborough Downs talking about the importance of freshwater while he stands above the source of the Hampshire Avon. We are also hoping that Bob Church can pull a rabbit out of the hat by finally catching us a Scottish salmon and who knows, we might even get lucky with salmon spawning on the redds at Christmas and just have time to edit that into the programme before it's too late.

What we have to do is one thing, what we'd like to do is a wish list as long as your arm. The underwater world is fascinating and with more time I'd love to film

Heavenly dawn.

fish communication in greater detail. We did film them signalling to each other by flicking their fins, but they also use sound. Did you know that a grunting fish helped scientists date the origins of vocal sounds to about four hundred million years ago!? No, neither did I but there's obviously a lot to explore there, though that will have to wait for the next series.

One thing's for sure in any wildlife venture. You never get everything you need, let alone desire, so there are bound to be disappointments along the way, even if, as in our case, despair sometimes turns to delight. We really struggled with our *'Impossible'* perch but ended up with a dream fish that was a river record. Then the pike hunt was long and hard but as it turned out all the failures were a blessing in disguise as we ended up with our *'Impossible'* thirty pounder from one of the most beautiful lakes in Britain.

As for the finished films, it's impossible to tell if we've fulfilled our aims of trying to raise awareness of the importance of clean freshwater and its fish populations.

Have we provided entertainment for a wide audience, inspired people to go fishing, created a series that will stand the test of time? Only time will tell and if we didn't succeed it wasn't for the lack of trying.

Martin and I have given our time free to this project so that the limited funding we had available could be used to show how beautiful freshwater fish are and how exciting angling can be, purely in the hope that the films might benefit angling as a whole. We need to raise the public's awareness of the challenges facing our wetlands and it's wildlife and making these films is our contribution to the cause.

Clean freshwater is a big issue. All life depends on it and the signs of global shortages and serious conflict over supply and demand are already alarming. Add in the issue of global warming and the climatic extremes this is causing and the future looks worrying. On the one hand you have the catastrophic flooding in 2007, on the other there are serious droughts. Then there is fish disease to consider. For instance, when salmon

The magic hour.

contracted a particulary virulent desease in Norway, whole river systems had to be wiped out to stop it spreading. With all these problems to contend with, the future for aquatic life seems bleak.

However, due to two initiatives these are exciting times for angling. Firstly, the 'Blueprint for Water', a booklet that highlights the issues and threats to water resources. This document was compiled by all the major conservation organisations in Britain, including strong representation from anglers and this was highly significant. All conservationists are on the same side, and the more we work together the more likely we are to be able to successfully overcome the challenges ahead. This document was passed onto our government in the hope that it would contribute to positive changes in our attitude to freshwater.

Secondly, angling unity is now a priority and deserves all our support because when it happens our combined voices will be heard more clearly. Such an organisation will also be able to commission scientific case studies on issues of concern and there is no doubt that only by having the facts will we achieve protection for fish life and the invertebrates they feed on. There are many people doing fine work for wetlands and fish, including

the government, but if we all join up and work together with other conservationists then we can achieve so much more.

As for Martin, Bernard and I, there is still one *'Impossible'* challenge outstanding, perhaps the most difficult of the lot - and that is to carry our message to the widest possible audience via television. Getting a showing on TV would help us to fulfil our original ambition and though unlikely, terrestrial TV with its access to wide audiences is our dream. And if we fail? Well, I couldn't imagine a better way to spend these last five years of my life. It's been extremely rewarding, we've received generous help and kindness throughout the country and met some of the nicest people you could ever wish to meet.

Finishing the journey might be a relief but it will also be tinged with sadness, for I will miss the creative challenges, the failures and successes, the laughter and above all our friends. And when it's all over and the dust has settled, I hope we'll remember that it is only fishing, and just a bit of fun.

Midwinter rarity.

A summer idyll.

With Special Thanks

To our Angling Guests
John Beckett, Jackie Blunt, Ryan Bowler, James Carr, Bob Church, John Everard, Jerry Hammond, Lisa Isles, Nancy John, Terry Lampard, Wendy Lythgoe, Anna Mayer, Tim Norman, Pete Orchard, Sam Perkins, Pete Reading, Peter Rolphe, Rob Starr, Des Taylor, Terry Theobald, Rebecca, Katie and Emma Thorpe, Abe Unwin, Arabella Unwin, Frank Warwick, Ray Walton, Nige Williams, John Wilson, Chris Yates.

Photo Credits
All photographs by the authors apart from:

1.	Mick Rouse	page: 04, 09, 29, 30, 31, 40, 45, 46, 79, 80, 81, 83,110, 141, 186, 237, 238, 256, 257, 258, 349, 352.	
2.	Laurie Campbell	page: 36, 48, 71, 90, 167, 184, 282, 316, 343, 347.	www.lauriecampbell.com
3.	Mike Read	page: 203, 208, 282, 289, 295.	www.mikeread.co.uk
4.	Neil McIntyre	page: 298, 299.	www.neilmcintyre.com
5.	Richard Bowler	page: 10, 12, 16, 25.	
6.	Michael W. Richards/JDP	page: 89, 145.	
7.	Jerry Hammond	page: 41.	
8.	Bob Hornegold	page: 43.	
9.	Ray Walton	page: 37, 38.	
10.	John Wilson	page: 11.	
11.	Chip Houseman	page: 61, 90, 166.	
12.	Terry Lampard	page: 275.	
13.	Rodney Jackson	page: 62.	

Jacket design: Matt Donovan   www.matrixdesign.info

Authors websites:
Martin Bowler   www.martinbowler.co.uk
Hugh Miles   www.passionforangling.info
          www.catchingtheimpossible.info
          www.wildwiseltd.com